Advance Praise for

"Tired of people who've never worn a badge telling you what cops do, how they feel, and what they think? Read Steve Pomper's book for a real cop's perspective on the anti-police madness infecting America today. Want to know why cops do what they do? Then stop guessing and get the info from somebody with the guts to wear the badge."

—Kevin Jackson, author, political commentator, FOX News contributor, and talk radio host. Website: theblacksphere.net/about/about-kevin-jackson

"Steve Pomper is a recently retired cop who's undeniably tired of the Left's social justice indoctrination, especially as it concerns police officers. De-policing is only one intended consequence of the Left's propaganda, and it puts all Americans at risk. Fostering an anti-police state is another deliberate ploy of the Left, which has seemingly become a reality. Therefore, I implore you to take time to listen to Steve's poignant perspective. Even in retirement, he's still upholding his oath to protect and serve. However, his service weapon is a pen and the aim is sharper than ever. Targets, you've been warned."

—Taleeb Starkes, author of the Amazon #1 bestseller, *Black Lies Matter*. Website: blksvsnggrs.com

"If you want to understand how Chicago can go from solving 67 out of every 100 murders through arrests in 1991 to just 20 per 100 in 2016, Steve Pomper's book *De-Policing America* provides one answer, especially for recent years. How does teaching police, even black police officers, that they are racist against blacks affect their ability to do their job? What has been the impact of political correctness in many urban areas and under former-President Obama? Pomper, a Seattle Police Department veteran, gives the reader a police-eye view as to why many police believe that they have been discouraged or prevented from doing their job. He justifiably worries that the real innocent victims of these policies have been the most vulnerable people in our country, poor blacks who live in high crime urban areas. Making life easier for the criminals comes at the expense of making it much more difficult and less pleasant for the innocent."

—John Lott, president of the
Crime Prevention Research Center and
the author of *More Guns, Less Crime*.
Website: johnrlott.blogspot.com

A STREET COP'S VIEW OF
THE ANTI-POLICE STATE

DE-POLICING
AMERICA

STEVE POMPER

Post Hill
PRESS

A POST HILL PRESS BOOK

ISBN: 978-1-68261-669-7
ISBN (eBook): 978-1-68261-670-3

De-Policing America:
A Street Cop's View of the Anti-Police State
© 2018 by Steve Pomper
All Rights Reserved

Cover art by Christian Bentulan

Post Hill Press
New York • Nashville
posthillpress.com

Published in the United States of America

CONTENTS

De-Policing, Political Indoctrination, and Community Education

If you want to understand the police officer's world, start by asking yourself this question: when was the last time someone looked you right in the eyes and with a straight face said, "These aren't my pants?"

* * *

Will a police officer respond when you are having the worst day of your life—what could be the last day of your life if they don't? Will police officers in your town hesitate to act out of fear of being fired—or worse, going to prison? You hear from "experts" but rarely from those directly affected by destructive political policies—cops. This book gives one street cop's perspective on *de-policing*.

I was compelled to write this book because many American cities are forcing their cops to undergo leftist political indoctrination and squelching the free speech rights of officers who speak against it. Seattle has implemented its radical left agenda through the insidious Race and Social Justice Initiative (RSJI). In Seattle, and through similar efforts in other law enforcement agencies, this is a leading cause of what has led to what has become known as de-policing. Leftist anti-police sentiment from groups such as Black Lives Matter (BLM) has resulted in a growing phenomenon where American law enforcement officers are forced to avoid certain types of police work. De-policing is the provocative term used to describe that caustic, anti-police environment where cops shun proactive patrol. Proactive patrol includes self-initiated police work separate from answering 911 calls. Things such as traffic enforcement, pedestrian violations, and checking on suspicious people.

Liberal policies force cops into this diluted policing approach because the left shows little respect or appreciation for law enforcement. Often, they demonstrate outright animus toward police. Police officers get scant support from many city administrations. Even worse, some leaders within the police department take the anti-police side. What do you expect? Police chiefs are appointed by liberal politicians. Cops have to adopt a career-survival approach to avoid discipline, termination, even incarceration.

It's no surprise that this leftist disease would infect police departments as it has already infected America's education system. Consider The Evergreen State College, an über-progressive institution of higher indoctrination in Olympia, Washington. In 2017, amidst other radical leftist turmoil, flamed on in part by BLM, one liberal college professor, Bret Weinstein, had the audacity to describe a call by student groups for white people to stay off campus on a particular day a violation of American civil rights. Which, of course, it is. Well, the professor did stay off campus but on a different day for a different reason. The Evergreen State College police chief told Weinstein it would be better to hold his class off campus due to safety concerns. Because of his principled stance, and for daring to appear on the Fox News program *Tucker Carlson Tonight*, these students called for Weinstein's firing.

Thank you, Professor Weinstein, for reminding liberals of their former commitment to civil rights, including free speech. The professor and his wife, who is also an Evergreen professor, initiated a court action against the college. They agreed to a settle with Evergreen for half a million dollars. *The Wall Street Journal's* Jillian Kay Melchior wrote an excellent piece, describing the situation in detail via college emails she obtained through Washington State's Public Records Act.

I don't speak for all police officers. In fact, I don't speak for any other officer. I speak for one officer: *me.* However, after speaking, emailing, and texting for years with officers from all over America, I believe my viewpoint reflects that of many if not most American patrol officers. Remember, it's cops who are directly affected by the left's destructive social justice policies and laws that officers are expected to implement and enforce.

Still, people, both cops and civilians, will not agree with me on every issue. That's as it should be. That's America. We can learn from our disagreements. But we need to have this discussion from a perspective different from that of the left-wing politics, academia, and media that demonize anyone who disagrees with them. We can disagree, but let's do it respectfully. And if what I say bothers you enough, write your own book.

Now, as great as pro-police books written by conservative academics are (some from which I quote), I'm sure the authors would agree that police officers' voices are essential in the conversation. This brings up a point: why should you care what an ordinary patrol officer thinks? Good question. Well, I hope I'm well-read, educated, and articulate enough on law enforcement issues and the politics affecting them to present a rational argument. Most police officers strive to stay objective on the job. If they're doing their jobs well, people will have little or no idea of an officer's political slant. So, my having been a conservative street cop with a libertarian bent (perhaps what radio talk show host Larry Elder refers to as Republitarians) should interest the average person who might not have considered that cops can and do hold strong political views.

Too many liberal academics are eager to turn police officers into social experiments, testing new policies to advance their own preconceptions based upon partisan political ideology. It's similar to how they make their case with so-called, manmade global warming. If you don't agree with the supposed scientific consensus, you're called a climate denier. This derision includes dissenting scientists. It's not much of a consensus, or even scientific, when you attempt to malign scientists who refuse to join it. Well, in a similar vein, if you don't agree with the anti-police faction, you're labeled a police brutality-denier. It's a standard leftist tactic.

When something goes wrong during a use-of-force situation, it's *always* the cop's fault. In fact, it's the cop's fault anytime an officer uses force. *Come on, people.* I know it's weird, but some folks just don't want to go to jail no matter how much you think you can sweet-talk them into a cell. Regrettably, most people don't understand the nature of law enforcement. I can help.

The public cannot be held totally responsible for the massive public ignorance about what police do. Political entities, cities, and towns are notoriously poor at educating the public about law enforcement. Instead of teaching the public about the complexities of a police officer's job after a controversial incident, political leaders are prone to "teach" police officers what they did "wrong" even if it was right when it was taught. I don't know another profession where more people think they know how to do a job better than those trained to do it.

If anything will stress a cop, it will not be the blood, guts, and vomit they see on the job, or the injuries, verbal abuse, or absence of appreciation. It will be the lack of support and outright antagonism from an officer's own city and department leadership.

This book provides a recently retired street cop's perspective on some of the causes of de-policing and their devastating effects on American law enforcement. I also try to convey some of the nuts and bolts of policing and why looking at law enforcement from a street cop's viewpoint is crucial to understanding and evaluating police actions. You need to hear from street cops, the people directly affected by the liberal political decisions so damaging to police work in America. Street cops are the ones who show up at your door when you call 911. I might have stayed on the job ten years longer if not for the circumstances that lead to de-policing. Cops know the job better than anyone; our leaders need to let them do it.

Many police critics are people for whom progress toward an integrated, equal justice-based, and race-blind society amounts to their own demise. Appallingly, anti-cop agitators have fabricated a mythological rift between the "minority community" (*leftist* minorities) and their police officers. "Hands up, don't shoot" never happened!

How can we blame young black men for feeling they are "under attack" by police and society when so-called black leaders such as former president Barack Obama, Jesse Jackson, Al Sharpton, and those in what *Black Lives Lies Matter* author Taleeb Starkes refers to as the Race Grievance Industry (RGI), teach them this every day? That they are victims of a *currently* institutionally racist society?

You know the old saying "perception is reality"? Well, these racialist crisis entrepreneurs make sure that when black people are denied loans or jobs, get Cs instead of As in school, or receive poor service at a restaurant, it's *every time* and *always* because of their race. When respected people constantly teach this, some will believe it. And since the perspectives of black conservative intellectuals such as Thomas Sowell, Shelby Steele, and Condoleezza Rice aren't widely disseminated in black liberal circles (in fact, they're often denigrated), alternate points of view remain scarce.

Street cops tend to be conservative even in liberal cities such as Seattle, which explains an inherent conflict. Society has to confront this. Continual unwarranted criticism of the police will not be effective in improving police-community relations—especially when it's as hysterical as it's been. For example, take the police shooting of an armed black man, Keith Lamont Scott, in South Carolina. Anti-police leftists felt the officer should have been charged with criminal homicide. Why? Incredibly, because Mr. Scott didn't actually point his gun at the officer. This view is head-spinning-around-360-degrees-stupid to every police officer who hears such nonsense.

I use scenarios, anecdotes, and vignettes to convey ideas and possible solutions. I tell some stories the way they actually happened, while others are composites to illustrate a point. Some of the allegories and anecdotes come from the Seattle Police Department (SPD), some from other local departments, and others from agencies across the nation. Mine is just another voice in the conversation—an unabashedly pro-police voice. But all accounts are based on the anti-cop reality in which police officers have to function today. As they say, some of the names have been changed to protect the innocent—and to honor my heroes.

It seems the liberals will always have it their way, and there is never room for dissent. If they're for it, it's right, and if they're against it, it's wrong. According to liberals, dissent is patriotic except when it comes from a conservative. Then it's Hitlerian. After I wrote an article, the one that helped precipitate the idea for this book, people at every level of Seattle city government publicly attacked me for daring to question the city's radical leftist, social justice agenda and the liberal political indoctrination of its police officers.

Before that article, I was an ordinary patrol officer with very few Internal Investigation Section (IIS) complaints, several commendations, and a solid reputation. I'd never had a sustained complaint in nineteen years. But that didn't stop the mayor, police chief, city attorney, members of the city council, and even—*get this*—the director of the Office of Professional Accountability (OPA) from coming after me publicly. Why "*get this*"? Because the OPA director was the person responsible for objectively investigating my "wrongdoing." And, not one of them spoke with me before either libeling or slandering me. *Hang on a sec. Deep breath...okay.*

I was surprised at just how smarmy this got. Like in a movie, an officer I know well called me during this investigation. He said some "higher-ups" had asked him to contact me. They wanted him to ask if I would be willing to stop talking and writing about my opposition to city social justice policies if I were offered an officer or detective assignment of my choosing equal to my rank. Think about this: this "offer" was posed in such a way that it could never be tied to whomever initiated the idea. He or she could easily deny making it, since they hadn't made it to me personally. It was simply a "casual" question from a fellow officer. I said I wouldn't accept such an offer, and the officer said, "I knew you wouldn't, but I said I'd ask."

Now, let's look at how government-sponsored social justice, liberal political indoctrination camouflaged as law enforcement training, and the lack of public education about police work, have cops constantly looking over their shoulders. Let's find out how leftist political laws, policies, and procedures create an environment where cops have to adopt not only a physical and mental survival approach to police work but also a career survival mode, which increasingly includes de-policing.

CHAPTER 1

DE-POLICING

De-policing is not about police apathy toward their jobs. De-policing is about liberal antipathy toward the police.

Officer Michelle Malken leans back in the seat of her patrol car. Michelle has worked a dozen years all on the streets. This cop knows what she's doing. She observes a young man step into the crosswalk against the Don't Walk sign. The jaywalker locks his cold eyes on hers, maybe a challenge or a dare, and strolls past. Is he looking for a confrontation? Is he fingering the cellphone camera in his pocket ready to record the event?

Michelle should confront him, but will she? Just last week two fellow officers got jammed up over a simple littering incident. A man waiting in line for a nightclub show threw a food wrapper into the street in front of two passing officers. What should have been a simple, "Please pick up your litter, sir," turned into a melee when the man became combative after refusing police orders to pick up his trash.

Officers eventually subdued and arrested the man. Of course, news media reported that the police used excessive force and arrested a man for "*only* littering." No. Police arrested the man for refusing to follow lawful commands and then resisting arrest.

Should Michelle enforce the law? Yes, she should—in a perfect world. But cops do not work in a perfect world. Still, many people believe cops should be perfect. Well, they're not. They're what anthropologists call human beings.

The question *should she* becomes, *will she*? The answer has become, *why would she*? She doubts her superiors will support her if things go sideways. The officer subdues her instinct to enforce the law, chooses the better part of valor, and drives to Starbucks. After all, why should she chance having to use force or arresting the man for *only* jaywalking? De-policing.

* * *

De-policing is, again, that provocative term used to describe a phenomenon where cops reduce or avoid proactive patrol. Though it's become a hot topic, it's been around awhile. In 2010, I wrote about a fellow Seattle police officer (a black officer) describing a "training" he attended as "de-policing classes." Today, everyone knows de-policing.

In August 2015, Colin Flaherty, writing on *American Thinker. com*, titled an article "De-Policing: The Scariest Word of the Year." The title hits the mark dead center. If only the political left knew just how scary, they might rethink their pogrom against the cops. Flaherty quotes a Chicago cop as saying "suspects are refusing to comply with lawful orders…or answer simple questions…they know we can't or won't do anything about it. Defiance is now the rule." Yeah, scary!

Are police officers in Seattle and across America de-policing? Yes. In this hostile, anti-police climate, who can blame them? But is de-policing an *intent to* or a *result of* equation? Does an officer form the intent to avoid proactivity, or is the officer refraining from proactive police work as a necessary response to external pressures?

One of the external pressures causing de-policing is the left's campaign for government-sponsored social justice. This is not a matter of persuasion. This is a matter of coercion. Liberal governments across America (until recently, including the Obama administration) have been engaged in an effort to indoctrinate the nation's police officers with leftist political ideology. The seemingly innocuous term *social justice* is playing the part of the Trojan horse, sneaking liberal dogma into the police station.

Some people said they supported Hillary Clinton over Donald Trump in the 2016 presidential election because she supported "more training" for police officers. Well, what kind of "training"? Masquerading as law enforcement training, liberal governments "teach" police officers about white privilege, minority victimhood, and so-called level playing fields—social justice. They seek not equal opportunity but equal outcomes, which is impossible. The left's version of police training is not law enforcement training. It is political indoctrination.

What on earth is Seattle's leftist government teaching its cops? Several years back, under former mayor Greg Nickels, Seattle adopted the Race and Social Justice Initiative (RSJI). This initiative's socialistic tentacles have slithered into every crack and crevice of city government, including the police department. Seattle is forcing its officers to attend social justice day camps where it purports to teach its cops about America's racial history. Unfortunately, it's not objective history, presenting a balanced perspective.

For example, it doesn't have liberal scholars such as Cornel West and Tavis Smiley on one side versus conservative intellectuals such as Thomas Sowell and Benjamin Carson on the other, debating the issues. Instead, through a thoroughly leftist PBS presentation (*RACE: The Power of an Illusion*), cops hear about minority victimhood, white privilege, and how unconsciously (and consciously) racist and bigoted cops are—especially white cops. Don't even try to argue; to argue also means you are even more racist. The left isn't interested in your point of view.

Consider what conservatives are up against in liberal areas. In Seattle, following Donald Trump's election, I read about some public high school teachers leading *mourning* sessions in their classrooms. In other schools, students walked out of class—with teachers. This, after witnessing a democratic election process envied by the world. But this time they didn't get their way. At Hampshire College in Amherst, Massachusetts, the American flag was lowered to half-staff (and someone burned it). What about students who genuinely supported the Republican candidate? Americans still have that right, *don't they?*

Matt Maloney, CEO of Grubhub, a food delivery service, issued an email encouraging employees who supported Trump to find work elsewhere. As Dennis Miller remarked on *The O'Reilly Factor* on November 10, 2016, "There are a lot of people with love in their hearts who wish you dead if you don't have as much love as they do."

The RSJI has been popular with subsequent administrations. After Mayor Nickels, Mayor Mike "McSchwinn" McGinn snatched up the liberal baton and giddily biked away with it. After the inept McGinn left office, following his defeat in 2013, the relatively few fiscally conservative Seattleites hoped that Seattle's next mayor, Ed Murray, would be more practical, as he seemed to be, and would leave social justice to the private sector where it belongs. Unfortunately, under Murray, the RSJI continued to slaughter common sense, and the political indoctrination of the city's cops continued, as did de-policing.

I don't know if it was karma, but on September 12, 2017, within the tumult of allegations of sexual abuse of teenaged boys in the 1980s, Ed Murray announced his resignation. Coming full circle, former U.S. attorney for the Western District of Washington under President Obama, Jenny Durkan, is running to replace him. She is one of the feds responsible for inflicting a bogus consent decree on the SPD. Think she'll have Seattle's cops' backs? Not a chance.

At its root, the RSJI has the ostensible goal of "leveling the playing field" for minorities the liberals label *victims*. Doesn't it seem that leftist politicians promise to *fix* people—in exchange for their votes—but only *after* they convince them they are *broken?* To further this illusion, local, state, and federal government policy is now seasoned with a sprinkle of social justice before it's poured down its cops' throats. To see how insidious this effort is, just go to Seattle's city website and peruse its RSJI page.

Seattle's liberal propaganda efforts branched out even further into the community with a race and social justice exhibit. The exhibit ran at the Seattle Science Center during the busy holiday season, from September 28, 2013, through January 5, 2014. Progressive proselytizing does not take a sabbatical.

The DOJ arrived in Seattle a few years back toting a prejudiced conclusion of police wrongdoing. The feds then coerced the city into a lucrative consent decree—lucrative not for the city but for the enforcers—worth millions of dollars.

The DOJ issued a ludicrous finding that 20 percent of Seattle police officers' uses of force were unconstitutional. The DOJ then persuaded Seattle's mayor to subject the city's cops and residents to an invasive, unnecessary, and extortive consent decree. The DOJ transformed the SPD, virtually overnight, from one of the most respected and emulated police departments in the nation to an enfeebled version of its former self.

As a result of their fake investigation, the DOJ alleged enough officer violations to justify imposing a full-blown federal consent decree on the SPD. The DOJ refused to make public the methodology it used to arrive at its bogus results. It reviewed the cases marked for study and arrived at that absurd number of unconstitutional uses of force. Seattle University criminal justice assistant professor Matthew J. Hickman also studied the cases and concluded that a more believable 3.5 percent of officer uses of force "potentially" violated constitutional protections.

Professor Hickman wrote a bold editorial titled, "Special to the *Times*: Department of Justice owes the Seattle Police Department an apology" (*Seattle Times*, February 8, 2010). In it, he advised the SPD command staff to "call the DOJ's bluff and demand an apology." But instead of taking his prudent advice and saving Seattle's already overstressed, understaffed cops years of unwarranted anxiety, the city helped the DOJ construct the gallows and hang the nooses. Police officers were the casualties.

Many months later, with a federal consent decree in full force, the mayor and SPD leaders finally agreed with the rank and file and conceded the DOJ results were bunk. Of course, it was too late by then. In patrol roll calls, SPD relayed to its officers, through its consent decree compliance coordinator, that officers needed to cooperate quietly to "prove that the DOJ was wrong about them."

In response to a question from the editor in the Seattle Police Officers Guild newspaper, the *Guardian*, about the DOJ's bogus findings, Merrick Bobb, the federal monitor, uttered this Orwellian statement:

> *Whatever the correct figure might be [of alleged officer violations], it's not relevant to our task today. This is not the Hatfields and the McCoys. The feud is over, and past disagreements must not impede current progress. What I know for sure is that the settlement agreement embodies best practice in policing and that it's to the SPD's and Seattle's benefit it be implemented regardless of what led up to it."*
> (Guardian, August 2013)

So, apparently the lies told to get to this "agreement" don't matter. Once again with the left, the ends justi…Well, you know.

This is like a judge telling some defendants he's exonerated them, but they still have to serve their prison sentences—with a smile. Can you say "de-policing?"

Seattle is not alone in experiencing this social justice onslaught. Many law enforcement agencies around the country are suffering the same fate in the liberals' quest to quasi-federalize local police departments. San Francisco, Los Angeles, Santa Fe, Portland (OR), and many other jurisdictions have also suffered similar federal abuses.

You may ask why federalization is bad, which I'll discuss further in chapter 17. This federalism conversation is as old as the United States. In forming our federal republic, our framers set strict separations between the federal and state governments because people at the local level knew what laws served them best. The separations also serve as checks against potential federal tyranny. America is not a one-size-fits-all country. There is a reason the fifty experimental liberty labs work so well.

Look at what happened when the feds interfered in Seattle. The SPD was long heralded as a cutting edge, state-of-the-art police department. Law enforcement agencies from around the country and around the world sought out Seattle when determining their own paths to better policing. I recall attending Street Skills training with German police officers who'd come to learn from the SPD. Then the federal government came to town and found against Seattle's police officers without knowing or caring about their accomplishments or commitment to excellence. This excellence included positive community relations, which the feds helped to mutilate with their false and disparaging findings.

It's no accident that Obama's DOJ found *every* police department it "investigated" guilty of "a pattern and practice of..." violations. At last count, they'd notched up to twenty-six or so departments. From the comments I've heard from Attorney General Jeff Sessions, it seems likely the Trump administration will change this trend.

Putting political indoctrination aside, even if police were to accept social justice training, how can social justice coexist with equal justice? That's one simple question social justices can't or won't answer. Social justice favors the group. Equal justice favors the individual. How can this dichotomy reconcile with constitutional equal protection guarantees?

This is the question I asked city leaders in articles I wrote for the *Guardian*. Are the police to enforce laws based on treating individuals according to their race, ethnicity, and other nonrelevant factors to level some theoretical playing field? Isn't this in contravention to the Constitution?

Rather than answering this question, the social justices asserted I was evil. I wasn't just wrong. I was a racist, a bigot—a bad person. In his book *How to Debate Leftists and Destroy Them: 11 Rules for Winning the Argument*, conservative author and commentator Ben Shapiro writes, "The left no longer makes arguments about a policy's effectiveness. Their only argument is character assassination." Bull's-eye!

And, from the you-can't-make-this-$#!+-up file, the late large-donation Democrat Party contributor Benjamin Barber—despite being the I-know-better-than-you genius he appeared to believe he was—was stung by Project Veritas, James O'Keefe's conservative, investigative organization. During an interview with a Project Veritas undercover journalist, Barber compared black Republicans to Jewish guards who helped the Nazis murder other Jews. How can anyone reason with such an unreasonable position? It seems ludicrous to even respond to such nonsense. But, this is not isolated. Many on the left, in their win-at-all-costs approach, dismiss common sense from their strategy, and those of us who care to should respond. Even cops.

Barber said, "So there were even Jews that were helping the Nazis murder Jews in the camps. So, blacks who are helping the other side are seriously fucked in the head." (Forgive the crass language, but such absurdity deserves to be conveyed accurately.) I'd argue a Democrat who would equate black conservatives with Nazi murderers is the one who is seriously *mucked* in the head.

Seattle and other American cities are right at this moment imposing an endless propaganda barrage by leftists to politically indoctrinate their cops. In fact, the NYPD provides an apt example of this lunacy. In a police training story, Larry Celona and Bruce Golding of the *New York Post* (February 23, 2015) tell us that instructors are teaching New York's finest that they "should 'take a deep breath' and close their eyes when dealing with angry people." *Ummm*, how can anyone who utters such nonsense not be described as an idiot?

This is a part of Mayor Bill de Blasio's 35 million dollar "smart policing" training. For that money, you'd think it would be "brilliant policing" rather than merely smart—actually, it's *stupid* policing, so…

Jurisdictions are also enacting policies and enforcing laws that treat people differently based on race, ethnicity, and socioeconomic status. Seattle city attorney Pete Holmes is an avowed pro-pot, anti-cop, leftist activist elected to office by voters despite having had no criminal law experience at the time of his election. Holmes has repeatedly attempted the unjustified prosecution of police officers. Following yet another attempt by Holmes to prosecute an officer, Officer Chet Decker, former editor of the *Guardian,* titled an article, "Holmes fails again to convict a Seattle Police Officer." Holmes' campaign against the city's cops has happened often while he has actively ignored downtown street crime.

Former interim Seattle police chief and current King County Sheriff's Office Chief Deputy, Jim Pugel once wrote a letter directly to Holmes personally requesting he prosecute dozens of downtown Seattle's chronic offenders. Pete Holmes rebuffed the chief's request. Guess he was just too busy going after cops instead. Holmes turns a blind eye to laws he disapproves of, such as those against marijuana possession (prior to legalization) and naked bicycle riders (yes, some people in Seattle are known to ride in the buff, during the annual Fremont Solstice Parade and, at other times, just because) and enforces (or doesn't) a traffic crime, Driving While License Suspended 3rd Degree (DWLS3), based upon social justice criteria, not equal justice.

For all other offenses, officers give traffic tickets to violators and then forward the citations to the Seattle Municipal Court. Following the policy change, officers no longer give DWLS3 citations to offenders. DWLS3 is an administrative status: either a driver's license is suspended or it is not. Nevertheless, officers must first send all the citations associated with the traffic stop to the city attorney's office so Pete Holmes can determine who is prosecuted—and, more to the point, who is *not*.

In fact, in a July 1, 2010, interview with *Publicola.net* (now, *Seattlemet.com/blogs/publicola*), assistant city attorney Darby Ducomb said that the city attorney's office would ask the police department to send DWLS-3 cases to them instead of straight to municipal court, and the city attorneys would decide which cases merited punishment. "They're just a waste of money in our criminal justice system," Ducomb said.

Furthermore, in a video interview with Erica C. Barnett of *Publicola.net*, Pete Holmes admitted that in changing the policy on this traffic crime, social justice was his goal. When law enforcement agencies don't educate the public about what cops do, people won't understand why government-instituted social justice policy is so damaging to American liberty and why it's a major factor in de-policing.

Think about it. You're a hardworking, middle or upper income (or lower…how do they determine socioeconomic status—*guess*?) white or Asian person. An officer stops you, your license status is suspended, the city prosecutes you, and you have to pay your fines. However, if you're black or Hispanic, the city does not prosecute you. You don't have to pay the fine even for the moving violation(s) that got you stopped in the first place. Does this sound like justice or racial retribution? At the very least, it is certainly not equal justice.

If officers know that social justice means the city isn't prosecuting people equally, why should they cite anyone at all? Why would they? This is how jurisdictions cause de-policing, and it's not the cops' choice. Liberal city governments would rather enact these politically biased policies and laws than teach the public how difficult a police officer's job is. The fact is, they refuse to recognize a cop's uniquely difficult job. For the left, cops are a necessary evil; for the far left, they are unnecessary and evil.

Law enforcement agencies have been derelict in informing the public about what the police do and how and why they do it. When a high-profile police use of force occurs, many police and government leaders are more concerned with teaching the police what they should have done differently or "better." Instead, they should be educating the public about what the police did and why their actions were correct (except for the rare instances when they weren't).

Too often, an officer's actions are deemed "wrong" but only after the fact. Actions officers take are based on what instructors taught in training. Critics in the media, anti-police groups, and police and city leadership condemn the tactics because they look bad on TV. *Duh!* They always look bad and always will. Their lack of support puts police officers' lives at risk.

In my first book, *Is There a Problem, Officer? A Cop's Inside Scoop on Avoiding Traffic Tickets* (Lyons Press, 2007), I offered a brief public education on what cops do and why, using the most common police-citizen interaction: the traffic stop. I wanted to educate motorists on how not to talk themselves into tickets by misunderstanding an officer's intent or misinterpreting an officer's behavior. I felt this education would also be of interest to other officers.

Many drivers misinterpret an officer's guarded behavior as rudeness, insensitivity, or even arrogance. You need to understand that until an officer assesses you, you're a potential threat. Don't take the officer's prudent caution personally. The officer is not trying to insult you. He or she is only doing a job, a job that puts their life at risk. It's a job that liberal cities are making harder with every social justice edict they enact.

As alluded to earlier, in an event that further diminished the motivation of Seattle's cops to conduct proactive patrol activities, i.e., de-policing, the DOJ came to Seattle under the pretense of investigating the SPD for alleged excessive uses of force. Alleged by whom? By Seattle's perennial cop haters and their fellow—I wish I knew who coined the phrase—*crisis entrepreneurs*. None of the high-profile use-of-force incidents cited by critics at the time resulted in any criminal prosecution and only one in any discipline.

The DOJ conducted a brief investigation, produced a "study," and then refused to make public the methodology used in arriving at their results. This is the formula the DOJ used across America to force police departments to follow federal consent decrees. Following the acquittal of the officers in the Rodney King case in 1992, Congress granted the DOJ the authority to sue states they determine to have engaged in a "pattern and practice of unconstitutional policing." Ostensibly, this effort was initiated to discover and deal with law enforcement agencies or officers that were "bad" apples, which, if done honestly, could be a good thing. Well, President Obama's DOJ never found a "good" apple. But, how could it? Liberal Justice Department officials don't seem to believe in good apples when it comes to cops.

Liberal federal administrations use consent decrees to bludgeon police departments into "reforming" into a progressive view of how they believe policing should be done. These are contracts entered into by the federal government and local agencies, overseen by a federal judge, and monitored by a federal appointee. Some of these consent decrees can stretch on for years. SPD's has been in effect since 2012. The LAPD's decree lasted for over a decade.

According to *Newsmax.com*'s Sean Piccoll, former U.S. attorney Andrew C. McCarthy, who prosecuted the criminals of the 1993 World Trade Center bombing, says, "They've [DOJ] had their thumbs on the scales from the beginning." Piccoll continues, "McCarthy cited a string of federal civil-rights investigations into some 20 police departments, including Ferguson, Missouri's, which he said the Justice Department has approached with a presumption of racial guilt."

McCarthy's formula shows the feds come to town and investigate local police agencies, armed with a predetermined conclusion of guilt. The DOJ was using this formula against police agencies in cities such as, Portland, Oregon; Albuquerque, New Mexico; Ferguson, Missouri; and Baltimore, Maryland. The DOJ also followed this recipe when scheming against the SPD. This endeavor continues for two reasons: Obama/Holder-era consent decrees are still legally binding. And, even though a pro-police president, Donald Trump, has been elected, liberal Obama-Clinton supporters are still on the job in many offices.

As I mentioned in the introduction, following the DOJ's report, Seattle University criminal justice assistant professor Matthew J. Hickman, also a former DOJ statistician, conducted his own more meticulous and extensive study and found the DOJ's report significantly flawed. Despite Professor Hickman's findings, Seattle's government and police command rolled over and exposed its belly to an unwarranted federal consent decree. This allowed the DOJ to gain expensive, intrusive, and dangerous oversight of the SPD and its employees.

As a field training officer, I told my students that being a cop was better than working for a living. I helped people, I caught bad guys, and I put them in jail. I loved it. Now, I wonder how Seattle and federal and local social justices could have taken the best job in the world and one of the best police departments and caused such utter devastation.

Allow me to elaborate on something I mentioned in the introduction. When I first came on the job back in the early 1990s, a veteran officer—we called him Uncle Bruce—told me the worst stress cops would face wouldn't come from the blood, guts, vomit, or injuries. It wouldn't come from the verbal abuse or the lack of respect and appreciation they'd experience. Officers' greatest stresses would come from their own city and police administrations. This has proved prophetic.

Animus between rank and file and the politically tarnished brass breeds perpetual strife and a resultant rank and file frustration and apathy—even anger, which leads to de-policing. This is expressed in a facetious tip I received from one of those veteran patrol officers back when I was a rookie: "Just remember, kid. There's no call that can't be handled by a slow response." LAPD detective Mark Fuhrman once said something to the effect of, "You can't make a police officer see something they don't want to see."

I've been writing about issues affecting street cops for a long time. Sadly, I've experienced firsthand the decline in the status of law enforcement as a profession. I've spoken with officers, detectives, supervisors, managers, and commanders who admitted the police department is far worse than they've ever seen it during their careers. This included two forty-plus-year veterans who had gone through Seattle's riots and corruption scandals of the 1970s.

In a *Seattle Times* article, reporter Steve Miletich wrote the following about de-policing: "Neither [Mayor] Murray nor other officials suggested officers might deliberately be declining to enforce laws, a practice known as 'de-policing' that has been the subject of broad speculation, anecdotal discussion and a topic in the rank-and-file's union newspaper." *Wake up, Seattle! Wake up, America!* De-policing exists in Seattle—in America! The left just doesn't want to accept responsibility for it.

Miletich pointed out that between the first quarter of 2010 and the same time in 2011, calls for service had increased by 9 percent, yet officer proactivity dropped by 44 percent. During the period from 2007–2013, officers filed 71 percent fewer complaints (infractions and misdemeanors) with the Seattle Municipal Court. These cases cover minor crimes and infractions including alcohol violations, traffic offenses, public urination, and noise complaints. Between 2006 to 2013, the number of suspects booked into the King County Jail by Seattle officers decreased by 51 percent with no change in police staffing. Based on my continuing conversations with officers still on the job, it's only gotten worse.

In 2014, *Mynorthwest.com* reported overall crime up 13 percent and a 14 percent rise in violent crime. Homicides were up, aggravated assaults also up, and there was an increase in rapes. Auto thefts rose 44 percent compared with 2013.

More recently, *areavibes.com*, a company that measures the livability of over 35,000 places nationwide, based on relevant criteria including cost of living, education, and crime published their Seattle results. While Seattle scored an A+ in amenities, it received an F for crime. Are these scores also a measure of the impact of de-policing? I'll let you decide. Seattle's overall crime rate is 115 percent higher than the national average. Seattle's violent crime rate is 103 percent higher than the state average and 59 percent higher than the national average. And the property crime rate came in at 124 percent higher than nationally.

There is no doubt this decline in proactive policing is a serious problem. National and local statistics like these signify massive reductions in police proactivity (otherwise known as crime prevention). While these indicators pertain to the SPD, officers I know in various local, county, state, and federal agencies across the country show that Seattle serves as an apt example of the damage anti-police, political agendas are doing to law enforcement nationwide. The situation in other large American cities is even worse.

Chicago's response to its ongoing nightmare and lack of response to black-on-black violence defies explanation. How can city leaders ignore this problem? Liberals seem to have deference for not allowing open discussion, turning any conversation on race, including proposed conservative solutions, racist. Asking why black criminals are shooting and killing other black people in the thousands in one of America's largest cities does not make me racist. It makes me concerned for my fellow Americans who are suffering such carnage. I'll admit I don't care much about what bad people do to one another. But I do care when their actions affect the innocent. It's not just the stray bullet that finds a child playing in a yard; it's also that child's parent who can't even walk their kids to the corner store for fear of getting shot.

If the SPD is a microcosm, let's look at a macrocosm. The response of NYPD cops to Mayor Bill de Blasio after he inferred they were threats to his biracial son also illustrates a cause of the de-policing phenomenon. The mayor said, "We've had to literally train him…in how to take special care in any encounter he has with the police officers who are there to protect him." Following the comment, NYPD police officers turned their backs on the mayor at public events. More recently, in July 2017, New York City's cops turned their backs to Mayor de Blasio for choosing to go to Germany to protest President Trump rather than attend the funeral of a slain police officer.

While sitting in a mobile command post, NYPD officer Miosotis Familia was cruelly executed by cop hater Alexander Bonds. The mayor's insensitivity was astounding. What officers in their right minds would trust that man to back them if they were involved in a controversial incident? He was more interested in making an international political statement than in attending the funeral of that brave officer. This is a textbook example of the type of "leadership" that leads to de-policing in America.

As in Seattle, according to *The New York Times*, in January 2015, officer-issued court summonses in New York City dropped by over 90 percent. The *Times* believed the drop was not the result of union leaders organizing a "slow down" but of officers "apparently using their own discretion to largely ignore low-level offenses." This is the key, folks. While the effort against the police by groups like BLM may be "Astroturf" funded by leftist billionaires, officers de-policing, though unpleasant, is grassroots, organic, and done by individual cops, not organized by police unions. Frankly, much about de-policing is simply a matter of human nature. The survival instinct kicking in.

New York City estimated a revenue loss of over five million dollars from the decline in summonses. Other cities are experiencing similar declines in proactive enforcement, especially in high-crime neighborhoods—exactly where more, not less, policing is needed.

So, why should anyone care about de-policing? Anybody who remembers what New York City was like before Rudy Giuliani became mayor cares. The rule was high crime rates and a lower quality of life. The citizens who experienced the crime that occurred before America's Mayor allowed New York's Finest to actually police the city know what Seattle and other liberal and social justice-contaminated cities are in for as de-policing catches up with criminals—or *doesn't* catch up with them. Under Giuliani, the NYPD actually fought crime, which lowered crime rates and saved untold numbers of would-be victims of violent crime. Black Americans are a substantial portion of that number.

No one knows how to do police work better than cops. Still, there is no other job I can think of where average politicians and activists—and even average people—feel they know how to do police work better than the professionals trained to do it. *Just because you don't like how law enforcement is done doesn't make it wrong.*

Although I could mention numerous similar cases nationally, I'll limit my examples to a couple of officers I know and have spoken with about their incidents. Seattle police chief Kathleen O'Toole fired two friends of mine in what appeared to me to be political terminations. One was Adley Shepherd and the other Cynthia Whitlatch. I'll cover only the main points here because both cases are available for your review online.

OFFICER ADLEY SHEPHERD

I met Adley a few years before I retired. We worked different watches, but we'd say hi or chat a bit during shift change down in the parking garage. He impressed me from the moment I met him. He exuded professionalism, bearing, intelligence, competence, and kindness. This dedicated cop and family man was a walking, talking recruiting poster for the SPD. He didn't deserve the treatment he received from those who should have supported him.

Officer Shepherd responded to a domestic violence incident and arrested a drunk female suspect. He placed her in handcuffs, and while attempting to put her in the back seat of his patrol car, she kicked him in the jaw with her boot, committing a felony. Reacting to the pain from the suspect's assault, Adley punched her *once*, which resulted in a fractured eye socket. The video shows the officer did not even fully extend his arm when striking her. He didn't strike her again because this defensive tactic stopped her assault and was sufficient to bring her under control. It is not unusual for any injured person to experience a surge of adrenaline, thus increasing Adley's strength in response to the pain and danger. Yes, danger.

Some claim the critical issue was the suspect was handcuffed. These people conflate handcuffed with harmless. How could the suspect have been "harmless" if she kicked Adley in the face, causing harm?

Consider this December 13, 2016, *Fox 10 Phoenix* news report out of the Pima County [Arizona] Sheriff's Office. An intoxicated, handcuffed female kicked Sergeant Mark Bustamante in the face with her boots as he was placing her in his patrol car. (Sound familiar?) As a result of the assault, the sergeant lost his left eye. Handcuffed suspects spit at, scratch, bite, stab, shoot, kill, and even steal officers' cars all the time.

Consider this crucial element: should it matter if the officer assigned by the police chief to train you in defensive tactics reviews and assesses your actions in an incident like this as having been done "perfectly"? Apparently not because that's how the lead training officer described how Officer Shepherd performed, yet Chief O'Toole fired Shepherd anyway. Can you imagine how it feels to be a police trainer who sees an officer he or she trained, having performed as trained, fired for using that training? Imagine how Adley Shepherd feels. De-policing.

OFFICER CYNTHIA WHITLATCH

I worked closely with Cynthia in the same squad for many years at the SPD's East Precinct. Cynthia was one of the hardest working officers I've known. In fact, when writing to Chief O'Toole in support of Cynthia, I wrote that her greatest liability was her continued work ethic in the midst of such an anti-cop environment. She wasn't about to allow anti-police sentiment to stop her proactive brand of policing—but, in the end, it stopped her from policing at all. She actively resisted de-policing, and she paid the price. Although she had an exemplary record as a veteran officer—and though she'd used no force during the incident and the suspect suffered zero injuries—rather than a lesser punishment, Chief O'Toole went to the extreme and fired Cynthia.

What heinous act did Officer Whitlatch commit? She observed a man on a sidewalk swinging a golf club over his head and hitting a street sign. She circled the block. On her second pass, the man was still swinging the club over his head and then in a menacing manner toward her patrol car. So, Officer Whitlatch stopped the man about a block from the East Precinct to investigate his threatening behavior.

When ordered to, he refused to put down the club. I don't think anyone would argue a golf club can't be used as a weapon. Had the man complied with the officer's simple request the situation likely would have resolved quickly. In fact, early in the video of the incident, Whitlatch informs the man she doesn't intend to take away his golf club. Remember, she knew the incident was being video recorded. She wasn't trying to "get away" with anything. She told the man to put down the club many times, having said, "please" and "sir" over and over and having used no force during the arrest. Because Officer Whitlatch was white and the suspect was black, of course, she was accused of racism, turning the incident political. Though the chief could have easily imposed a lesser discipline, needing a sacrifice to the anti-police faction, she fired Officer Whitlatch instead. De-policing.

In August 2017, Cynthia won her case and was awarded back pay. Now, she is struggling to retain her legitimate settlement against anti-police factions who are fighting to deny a police officer any justice.

When officers saw the Obama administration swathe the White House in rainbow colors to celebrate a Supreme Court decision they support but declined to show similar support with blue lights to memorialize the mass murder of five Dallas police officers (killed while protecting leftist, anti-police demonstrators), what other result can there be than de-policing?

What are cops supposed to think when an American president invites anti-cop, BLM radicals to the White House? This is the vehemently anti-law enforcement, pro-Marxist, redistributionist, social justice group largely responsible for promulgating the Ferguson, Missouri, "hands up, don't shoot" myth—you know, *The Washington Post's* 2015 Lie of the Year. Of course, this was the incident where Eric Holder's DOJ found that police officer Darren Wilson shot robbery suspect Michael Brown after Brown attacked the officer and tried to take his gun. Officer Wilson will likely never work as a cop again. De-policing.

This BLM lie is accountable for much of the illegitimate anger aimed at America's police officers. An anger that has inspired some to kill cops. Democratic Party support provides validity to anti-police movements and encourages animosity and violence toward police officers. And you don't have to be a cop to figure that one out.

I agree with the social justices on one point. The primary issue between the public and police, causing de-policing, is trust. De-policing will not stop until trust is restored—true. *Trust*, but not as the left frames the issue. Not only trust of a community in its cops, but trust by cops in their communities that the people will support them.

CHAPTER 2

SOCIAL JUSTICE VERSUS EQUAL JUSTICE

Social justice versus equal justice is a semantic nightmare. Some people see no difference. But the problem is more than a matter of semantics. Equal justice is clear and understandable: individuals are treated equally under the law. Semantics arise when attempting to define *social justice*. Social is vague and imprecise. It could mean many things relating to society. Justice can also be subjective, as when combined with adjectives such as social, environmental, or restorative. But it is objective when treated as meaning *equal* justice. We'll discuss social justice and equal justice definitions more deeply later. For now, I'm talking about social justice as defined, practiced, and then inflicted on police officers by liberal government.

Okay, here's the nutshell version: defined by private entities such as leftist political associations and certain religious institutions, social justice often means to give preferential treatment to specific groups of people based on certain group attribute criteria, i.e., race, ethnicity, religion, and so forth. This is fine because private organizations don't have to adhere to equal justice as guaranteed to *individuals* by the U.S. Constitution.

If a government or private organization defines social justice as synonymous with equal justice, the terms interchangeable and understood to be equal justice, that is obviously as it should be. In fact, in an attempt to wrest the definition of social justice from the left, conservative scholar and Seattleite Arthur C. Brooks, president of the American Enterprise Institute, tends toward equal justice and social justice as synonymous in his book *The Conservative Heart*. However, liberal government doesn't do this.

Liberal government defines social justice as some religious organizations do: intended to help a certain sector of people. But government employing this definition cannot be acceptable in a free society. Seattle city councilmember Bruce Harrell once told me over coffee that social justice is necessary because "the playing field is not yet level." This alludes to leveling the socioeconomic playing field. To do this, government must treat people differently to give certain people benefits others don't get.

If so, then how can you reconcile this with the constitutional mandate to treat individuals equally? Even if you agree the playing field is not level (as if it ever could be; individual talents and abilities will always affect outcomes), the government of the United States *must* adhere to the Constitution by treating all people equally under the law. Or is there a liberal out there anywhere who is brave enough to say that the Fourteenth Amendment, along with its equal protection clause, is irrelevant or should be repealed or suspended? I doubt it. I suppose it's easier to ignore it.

Shall we see how this works in real life? Let's join Officer Tommy Sowell at work. He'll show us how government social justice works... or, more fittingly, how it doesn't work.

* * *

Officer Sowell is talking on his cellphone while monitoring an intersection near a grade school. School staff have complained about speeding motorists. He's saying goodbye to his wife just as a man in an older silver Buick blows a stop sign. The driver doesn't make a pretense of stopping or even slowing.

Sowell catches up to the Buick. He activates his lights and chirps his siren. The driver glances in his rearview mirror. He pounds the steering wheel before pulling over. The officer catches it all.

Sowell runs the license plate. The information comes back clear, not stolen, but the registration expired two months ago. Sowell approaches the vehicle.

"Hello, sir. My name is Officer Sowell. You are being audio and video recorded."

"Is there a problem, Officer?" the violator asks in good English but with a tinge of Spanish.

"Well, sir, the reason I pulled you over is you failed to stop for that stop sign back at Twelfth and Aloha."

"It wasn't because I'm black?" the man asks under his breath.

"Excuse me?"

"Sorry, Officer. So, I didn't stop?"

"Well, I'd be even more concerned about your driving, sir, if you don't know whether your car was stopped or moving." Officer Sowell, eyebrows arched, stares at the driver.

"I'm sure I stopped, Officer."

"Well, I guess we'll have to agree to disagree on that. License and proof of insurance, please—I have your registration on my computer."

The violator mutters and then says, "I don't have my license."

"You don't have a license, or you don't have it on you?"

"Yes, I have one."

"Okay, just give me your name and date of birth. I'll run it in my car."

The officer jots the info on his notepad and says, "Just wait here, sir. I'll be right back."

"Am I getting a ticket?"

"We'll see, sir. Just hang on a sec."

"I really can't afford one right now. I'm unemployed. I have bills."

"Then it seems silly you'd take a chance on getting stopped by running a stop sign. Wait here. I'll be right back."

Officer Sowell returns to his patrol car and runs the driver's name for license and warrant information. His license status shows suspended in the third degree. *Shit!* Sowell knows what this means. Is it worth his time to write up the citations? A civil infraction for failing to stop at a stop sign and a criminal citation for driving with a suspended license third degree.

But, due to a city policy, Officer Sowell has to treat the traffic crime of DWLS3 differently from other criminal citations and civil infractions. The violator is driving an old car, is a minority, and says he's out of work. The city attorney will determine if this driver "merits punishment" (assistant city attorney's words) according to his race, ethnicity, and socioeconomic status. It's likely all of Officer Sowell's work will have been done in vain. The prosecutor will probably not file on any of the charges.

This violator is social justice qualified—exempted from this law. He's a racial and ethnic minority and unemployed—*halleluiah*! Liberal policy makers have decided he is not adult enough to be responsible for his behavior. (What's that about the *soft bigotry of low expectations*?) So, even though the officer stopped the driver for a separate moving violation, if the city attorney determines the driver doesn't merit punishment because the social identity group(s) he belongs to has/have suffered historically, it's likely the city will file no charges.

Put yourself in the officer's place. Why should Officer Sowell waste his time writing these citations? Further, why should the officer make any traffic stops at all? Social Justice = De-policing.

* * *

Numerous factors cause de-policing. One of those is the left's attempt to replace American equal justice with liberal social justice. But, again, what exactly is social justice? It depends on who's defining it. As defined by liberal government, social justice is as destructive a concept as American liberty can face.

Social justice is a gentle-sounding phrase. It's a lexiconical wolf in sheep's clothing. It's a marriage of two words, each of which conjures pleasant thoughts. *Social*: most people enjoy being social or attending social events—an ice cream social. *Justice*: Who can argue with justice as important to society? Truth, justice, and the American way. But allow a government to join the two words and let the deception—and the de-policing—begin.

From what I've gleaned, in 1840, a Jesuit priest named Luigi Taparelli D'Azeglio coined the term *social justice*, as used in its modern sense. Yes, a Catholic priest, and this helps make the term so politically insidious. Not only is it an innocuous-sounding combination of words but also a religious tentacle tethers it culturally. If it's Catholic or Christian-based, how bad could it be if government uses it, right? Wrong!

Explore the definition(s) of social justice and you'll find the left deliberately obfuscates it. People can define it in many ways. For example, the Catholics may wish to practice social justice within their church. They may give people in certain racial or ethnic groups jobs, food, housing, or other church benefits. The church may do this because it perceives a group has suffered, therefore the individuals within it should be treated differently than other parishioners. Well, that's their private, religious-based, First Amendment-protected affair.

Problems arise when government introduces social justice, as defined above, as its policy and treats various groups of people under its jurisdiction unequally. Having been involved with the law and enamored with the U.S. Constitution, I can't understand how anyone could fail to see the inherent flaw in implementing governmental social justice. But that's one problem with conservatives/libertarians. We think the left simply doesn't understand. The sad truth is they do understand. They just want something different for America than our founders intended.

And academia is all-in on social justice. In the last couple years of my police career, I decided to go back to school and get my degree.

Toward the end of college, I took Criminal Justice 101. Why would a retired career cop take a law enforcement beginner's course? Because I wanted to see what colleges and universities are teaching today's students about criminal justice. It was eye-opening.

Check out this outlandish definition of social justice from our textbook: "Criminal Justice is the aspect of *social justice* that deals with criminal law." *Are you kidding me?* So, *social justice* isn't just one facet of criminal justice; criminal justice is a mere component of liberal-defined social justice? Is it now preeminent, having taken over an entire academic discipline?

The United States adopted the Fourteenth Amendment to the U.S. Constitution because post-Civil War, post-Emancipation Proclamation Southern Democrats refused to obey laws recognizing freed slaves' God-given equality. This amendment contains the celebrated equal protection clause. Ironically, the left often cites this clause, even lauds it—that is, until the clause fails to help their cause.

The Fourteenth Amendment forbids the states from denying "to any person within its jurisdiction the equal protection of the laws." Seattle is prosecuting suspended driver's license criminal citations according to race, ethnicity, and socioeconomic status, which blatantly violates this amendment. Social justices, many of them lawyers, mock equal justice. But they don't seem to care. For social justices it's the thought that counts. It's about feelings and the familiar ends justifying the means. To the left, any means are okay just as long as it's for society's "own good" from their perspective. Sort of a "they'll thank us later" mentality. They'll lie, cheat, and accuse their opponents of all sorts of evils. And if you oppose social justice, even on firm constitutional grounds, the left brands you a bigot for pointing out facts.

Following the 2016 presidential elections, Harvard hosted a meeting where members of the Clinton and Trump campaigns could have a rational discussion about the election. However, reason was the last thing on the Clinton campaign's agenda. In response to Trump's deputy campaign manager, David Bosse, after he praised campaign chairman Steve Bannon, Clinton communications director and sore loser, Jennifer Palmieri, said, "If providing a platform for white supremacists makes me a brilliant strategist, a brilliant tactician, I'm glad to have lost." She added, rather petulantly, that she "would rather lose than win the way you guys did." She stood there in what was supposed to be a cordial forum and accused the leaders of the opponent's campaign of having racism as its primary goal. What an abhorrent thing to say, but the ends justify the means, right?

Our American form of government declares "all men are created equal" and are endowed with God-given, not man-given, rights to "Life, Liberty, and the Pursuit of Happiness." The left's audacity is in thinking they can do "better" than America's Founders. To paraphrase Dr. Larry Arnn, president of Hillsdale College, from its Constitution 101 series, "The modern advancements of today did not give us the Declaration and the Constitution; those documents gave us the advancements."

When Thomas Jefferson (and his editors, including John Adams and Ben Franklin) wrote the Declaration of Independence, he (they) carefully selected each word. It wasn't then like it is today when folks obscure a document's real intent amidst a blur of legal jargon—Affordable Care Act, my ass. Nope, our founders wanted every word to contribute precision so the document would shine—a beacon of liberty for the world.

When they used the term *happiness*, it meant more than the face-value meaning many of us attribute to it today. In a letter of response to a question Henry Lee had written to Thomas Jefferson in 1825, Jefferson listed the authors he'd "consulted" while writing the Declaration. Among them, Aristotle.

Aristotle arrived at what philosophical scholars consider one of the best definitions of happiness yet derived. Aristotle didn't define happiness as a transient, extended, or even persistent state of enjoyment. The Greek philosopher said happiness was a condition of the soul. He defined happiness as *eudemonia*, human flourishing.

Jefferson was mindful of Aristotle's definition when he incorporated it into the Declaration.

Originally, "property" stood in the place of "happiness." You may not think the two similar, but when you consider, as John Locke did, that property includes one's life and liberty, it becomes clear. Not much happiness without life and liberty.

When Jefferson wrote the phrase "the Pursuit of Happiness," he declared that individuals had an unalienable right to flourish as human beings, according to their desires and abilities. Each individual decides what happiness or flourishing means to him or her. Remember, the founders didn't create a document that gave certain rights to the people. The founders produced a document which required government, as its most essential duty, to recognize and protect those unalienable rights God and Nature bestowed on We the People.

The Declaration's defense of our precious rights is not a frivolous concept dressed up in pretty words. Americans' natural rights mean something. In the Declaration, the colonists declared their rightful place among "the powers of the earth" as equals. About this Professor Danielle Allen, author of *Our Declaration: A Reading of the Declaration of Independence in Defense of Equality*, writes, "The colonists are not claiming to be equal and asking other people to assess their claim. To the contrary. They are 'assuming' their new station, or taking it up as already granted them." All persons are equal and should be treated equally under the law.

The term *social justice* needs to be dissected because it's at the heart of a progressive political philosophy infecting many American cities that has led to de-policing. When officers know their city's policies are to treat people differently under the law, how can this not affect how cops do their jobs? Right now, Seattle overtly enforces one law according to social justice criteria, but how long until there are others? How many other jurisdictions now enforce their laws according to liberal social justice policies?

For example, aside from the explicit DWLS3 policy, Seattle government has become infamous for ordering its officers not to enforce certain laws. I remember a city attorney edict that marijuana (less than forty ounces) was to be Seattle's "lowest law enforcement priority." (This was before marijuana became legal in Washington State.)

There are also many examples of left-wing political demonstrations where authorities have ordered cops not to enforce the law. Can you say Baltimore's Freddie Gray riots? Occupy Wall Street in Oakland? How about Seattle's Mardi Gras riots, Critical Mass (radical bicycle group) harassing motorists, and naked cyclists? All are allowed to wreak havoc unchallenged by police. Now, Seattle is contemplating *drug oases* (my term), "safe spaces" for people to inject heroin while overseen by medical personnel. Currently, the left is attempting to invalidate a citizen ballot initiative opposing injection sites by suing these citizens for practicing democracy. Leftist opponents claim, "ordinary people" shouldn't be able to vote on "public health" issues. Even libertarians who argue for drug legalization don't advocate government provide the necessary ingredients for addicts to abuse themselves at taxpayer expense.

Seattle also tolerates "homeless" people living in some parks and even on city sidewalks—tents and all. They are also considering making such behavior explicitly legal. Mayor Murray has stepped down, but the next mayor and city council will have to overcome a significant community backlash (yes, even in this liberal city) over the homeless issue. Whether it has any effect remains to be seen. That matter is competing with the inception of "safe injection zones" for heroin addicts, so...The fact the city would even entertain, never mind propose, such perversions to civil society is mind-spinningly irresponsible. Forget the Emerald or Jet City, Seattle should be known as Bizarro City.

As I and many SPD cops said during the hands-off-pot policy days, if the city doesn't like a law, repeal it. Don't pretend it doesn't exist. How in the world can cops be expected to respect the law when their leaders don't?

For those who think this ignoring of law is a simple matter of prosecutorial discretion, it's not. Discretion is used on an individual case basis. If the city used its discretion to reduce or toss out charges against defendants individually, that's one thing. To use political ideology to ignore a law or toss out charges en masse is quite another thing and compromises respect for the entire criminal justice system. Not only by the community but also by its cops. This also points out a significant difference between liberal and conservative governments. The former simply ignores laws it doesn't like. The latter tends to have respect for law and legal process even if it disagrees with certain laws. And if it doesn't like a law, it works within the system to change it—legally.

Beyond law enforcement, but tangentially related since cops enforce laws, social justice enters another realm where government presumes to dictate how much of anything—property, which includes life and liberty—a person may own or receive from government. Furthermore, leftist government also decides how much of a person's property—*money*—government should confiscate and redistribute to other people.

Social justice embraces confiscating money from the productive and redistributing it to the unproductive. Social justices may appreciate voluntary, individual charity but are more interested in the dishonest, socialist notion of compelled, collective charity. True charity describes generous individuals freely giving their property to those in need. In this sense, it is a gift from the heart. If government is the one giving somebody something (other people's stuff), it's not charity. It is an entitlement. It is welfare. It is legalized theft.

For example, if you or I (even as a police officer) stole money from one person and gave it to another person, even though our intentions might be good, it would be a felony.

For real charity to exist, first, individuals must own stuff. You cannot give to another if you don't own something—whether physical property, your ideas, or your time/labor. This is why it's so frustrating and ironic when the left attempts to co-opt religion to endorse social justice when leftists tend generally to eschew religiosity that encourages private charity. When the great religions teach people to care for one another, they mean individuals (or groups of individuals) taking care of other individuals *voluntarily*, not by government coercion. Arguing for a social justice system ignores what America's founders created—a government with a special emphasis on individual liberty.

What does this have to do with de-policing? Well, nothing happens in a vacuum and one thing affects another. We're discussing a leftist philosophy of social justice indoctrination that is infecting police departments. Just as it is important to learn how police do their jobs to help avoid what causes de-policing, it's equally important to understand how leftist ideology creates an environment where de-policing infects good law enforcement agencies.

If you give government the power over "charity," you also give them the power to determine who deserves that charity. In a related vein, look at the Obama administration. It rewarded big campaign donors with low-interest business loans, government grants, and other special perks. Many beneficiaries have defaulted on this "generosity" (taxpayers' money). For example, in 2009, the solar power company Solyndra, after getting a 535-million-dollar government green energy loan, suddenly shut down in 2011, putting 1100 employees out of work and leaving tax payers on the proverbial hook for the loan. Only a year earlier, President Obama had lauded Solyndra as being an industry leader. To make matters worse, the Obama administration made sure various federal department officials selected political opponents' businesses to close or had government agencies harass them.

After organizing two conservative-leaning groups and attempting to obtain tax-exempt status, no less than four federal agencies investigated Catherine Engelbrecht, a Texas businesswoman. Engelbrecht believes the investigations were retaliation for her organizing opposition to President Obama. The IRS delayed her groups' tax-exempt statuses, and the FBI, BATF, and OSHA investigated her business. Just a coincidence, right?

I'm the last person to question whether a liberal government would retaliate against law-abiding people who dared to express an opposing political viewpoint. I *know* it happens because it happened to me. I'm sure the feds were giving Engelbrecht special attention all in the furtherance of social justice. Incidentally, this has a similar effect on society as de-policing does on law enforcement. Cops hesitate to participate in the political process for fear of harassment or retaliation and so does the average person.

Despite its amiable name, *social justice*, it has no place in a just government. It unquestionably doesn't belong in a police department. It's bad enough when a new city administration comes into office and decides which laws to enforce and those it will ignore. But at least government is still practicing *equal* justice, as the city's not enforcing a particular law against *anyone*. But when an administration enforces a law based on what personal attribute classification a person fits into, it's undeniably stepped over the constitutional line.

Everyone—even cops—must challenge when government does this. It's a delicate issue, though, talking about cops not obeying orders to enforce certain laws. This should only rarely be done, and I argue blatantly unconstitutional laws are the rare exceptions. Police officers do not have to blindly follow orders. If an order is illegal, cops have an obligation to disobey it. And yes, sometimes suffer the consequences. For example, I once wrote in the *Guardian* that I would never enforce any law that required me to confiscate firearms from normally law-abiding American citizens. Why should this surprise anyone? I would not follow an order to abridge an American's First, Fourth, or Fourteenth Amendment rights either.

Sometimes it's difficult for the average citizen to understand why a cop would take such a stance. Here's an example, using the Fourth Amendment. Let's say I was searching a burglary suspect's home because we thought he was hiding there. After checking a few closets, my sergeant informs me the burglar is also a known drug user. During the search, the sergeant orders me to open a desk drawer. Since there is no way the suspect could be hiding in that drawer, I have no authority absent a warrant to search that drawer for drugs. As an officer, would it be my obligation to disobey that order? Probably.

Seattle is enforcing the DWLS3 crime according to arbitrary law but also unequal treatment under the law, which violates Americans' unalienable rights. But cops who choose to stand against such policies don't have to do it even overtly. Sometimes challenging means bringing government overstepping into what Ben Franklin referred to as the disinfectant known as sunlight. When you don't call people on the wrong they do, too often they get away with it. Sometimes they get away with it even if you do call them on it. That doesn't mean you shouldn't try. It's even worse with political administrations. They change every few years, and their culpability in the liberty infringement biz becomes murky as time passes.

You might say people *can't* violate the Constitution. More accurately, they're not supposed to. Murder is illegal, but people still kill people. Violating the Constitution is illegal, but people still do it—all the time. People can violate the Constitution as long as no one confronts them. Unfortunately, few dare to challenge the liberal authorities, and those who do find it an ugly path to tread. Too many people are willing to ignore lawbreaking, even federal law—if the lawbreaker is in their political camp. Can you say illegal immigration? Can you say Hillary Clinton?

The Obama administration disrespected the Constitution routinely, and it wasn't inadvertent. And even if an equal justice-promoting administration has now assumed office at the national level, it's more than likely liberal state, county, and city governments will continue to inflict social justice on American law enforcement. Why would they stop? The left wants the right to stand aside when they win, but the left never stands aside when the right wins, so de-policing will continue.

President Obama made dubious comments about the U.S. Constitution. He twice raised his right hand, put his left hand on a Bible, and swore an oath to uphold and defend the Constitution. Contrarily, in his role as a constitutional law professor, he made comments that the Constitution was a "charter of negative liberties," which disappointed him. Meaning, the U.S. Constitution doesn't dictate what government can do; it dictates what government can't do—to *you*—to *us*. What does this say about a man who swore those oaths in front of millions of Americans and God to uphold and defend this extraordinary document?

President Obama and others of similar beliefs who see the Constitution as a hindrance to socialism rather than a gift to individual liberty demonstrate why the framers had good reason to construct the document as they did. The former president has also spoken of the Constitution and Congress as impediments to his efforts to pass what seemed an imperial vision of what's best for Americans. In that scenario, rather than a system of checks and balances, the president rules by fiat when possible through executive actions. President Obama said, "We are not just going to be waiting for legislation in order to make sure that we're providing Americans the kind of help that they need. I've got a pen, and I've got a phone." This is frightening in any democratic republic that respects a system of checks and balances in a tripartite-style government.

This rule by fiat fever is contagious. When the president espouses it, liberals at all levels attempt to emulate this type of rule. Hence attempts at gun prohibition laws at the local level, as was tried in Seattle, and the unilateral suspension of the state death penalty in Washington State. It's a political mood that has good police officers wondering what happened to law and order. How can such disregard for law not lead to an environment that encourages de-policing?

Promoters of social justice bristle when someone accuses them of being unpatriotic or not loving their country. But if you dissect these anti-Constitution comments, you arrive at some hard truths. Tory colonists opposed the American Revolution and wished to stay subjects of the English king. Similarly, the social justices of today may not want a monarchy per se, but they clearly don't want the America of our founders, conceived in individual liberty. They certainly don't want limited government. They want something else.

Once again, I ask anyone who leans left politically to answer the question I have been posing to Seattle's leftist elite. How can government-sponsored social justice coexist with constitutional equal justice? You may agree the *playing field* is not level and that certain groups have suffered. This is true. But who gets to decide when amends have been achieved? Who decides how much restitution or reparations (or is it revenge) to which each group is entitled? Or, is the quest for leftist-defined social equality meant not to end—ever?

Isn't the pursuit of equal justice—equal treatment under the law—for all, the most practical and prudent way to uphold equal rights in America?

Ironically, social justices say they oppose racial profiling, but they expect police to treat people differently—unequally—under the laws cops are constitutionally mandated to enforce equally. How can this dichotomy not affect police officers? How can this liberal experiment not cause officers to hesitate when enforcing the law? How can the influence of governmental social justice on law enforcement not cause de-policing?

The U.S. Constitution, especially the Fourteenth Amendment, mandates Americans are equal under the law. Government social justice is based on treating people *unequally* under the law, as a matter of policy, according to their racial, ethnic, gender, religious, sexual orientation, socioeconomic, or other liberal-approved criteria. Equal justice is based on treating people and their actions as individuals. If the left continues with this socialist experiment, as with matter colliding with antimatter, there can be no coexistence. Only annihilation of the original idea: America.

CHAPTER 3

POLICE AND SOCIETY

C ops occupy a unique place in American society. They are among the most visible of government employees. They facilitate one of the original constitutionally legitimate government functions. They enforce the laws the People pass to help create a more secure society. This was one reason I chose law enforcement as a profession. Law enforcement, along with operating a fire department, court, and jail, are a local government's most important functions. These folks protect people and their property from harm.

Police officers serve as both protectors and enforcers—sometimes simultaneously, which can create conflict in people's minds. People call the police for help when in danger or after having been victimized. Police also detain suspicious people and then cite, arrest, or release them as appropriate.

Too many liberals believe cops are more authoritarian than guardian. These folks fall naturally into a mode that fabricates some grotesque caricature of police officers as jackboot-clad, knuckle-dragging brutes. But I'd argue that even when police use their authority, it is in furtherance of society's service, protection, and liberty. Cops allow good people to live their lives with less fear of becoming crime victims.

Cops see it all. In the course of a single shift officers may respond to a burglar alarm at an opulent mansion where fashionable shoes squeak on white marble floors. But on the next call they may be sent to some fleabag crack den where their shoes squish on the piss-saturated, cracked linoleum.

Officers flow through all strata of society. They encounter individuals of every possible human composition and attribute. Only firefighters, medics, and EMTs can claim similar access, although, their mission is a different one. One big difference between police and fire is people are happy to see firefighters. *Heroes—ugh!*

Upon seeing a patrol car, people experience the proverbial pucker factor as they bring their errant behavior into check. As many officers can attest, sometimes drivers "correct" to a ridiculous degree. Often, when it's not even necessary.

People, rich and poor, Bert and Ernie, Republican and Democrat, are generally a feel-guilty lot. This is partially due to what French historian and America observer, Alexis de Tocqueville referred to as "the soft despotism of government." People become gun-shy from too many laws and thus act guilty when authorities confront them even if they've done nothing wrong. Just look at how terrified people are of the IRS. The innocent as well as the guilty fear this government agency. Does this seem right to you in a free country?

Of course, the left doesn't advocate for the hard tyranny of a Nazi Germany, a Soviet Russia, an Islamist Iran, or a Marxist Cuba. They favor a more Fabian or Democratic Socialism where people are simply "ruled and regulated" into submission for some amorphous "greater good" individual liberty be damned. Or, perhaps, as Jonah Goldberg describes in his book *Liberal Fascism*, "happy socialism." The cover of his book displays a Smiley Face wearing a Hitler moustache—perfect.

Tocqueville's premonition back in the mid-nineteenth century is prescient and belongs in a conversation about de-policing as he accurately describes the conditions that lead to it. Tocqueville is eloquent in conveying the subtle ways big government attempts to control society. This formula also relates to how liberal governments create environments where police officers are compelled to de-police.

In Tocqueville's following quote about the nature of government, replace "society" with "police department," "man/men" with "cop/ cops," and you'll see my point:

It covers the surface of society with a network of small complicated rules, minute and uniform, through which the most original minds and the most energetic characters cannot penetrate, to rise above the crowd. The will of man is not shattered, but softened, bent, and guided; men are seldom forced by it to act, but they are constantly restrained from acting. Such a power does not destroy, but it prevents existence; it does not tyrannize, but it compresses, enervates, extinguishes, and stupefies a people, till each nation is reduced to nothing better than a flock of timid and industrious animals, of which the government is the shepherd.

Tocqueville's prescient observations in mind, let's continue. Officers are also unique in the responsibility and authority they have, serving as the sword and shield arms of their communities. Cops are expected to perform flawlessly in myriad circumstances every single time. Just look at the nightly news. You'd swear people never make mistakes the way they hold cops to account in a job harder than most people have. Many situations require cops to make life and death decisions in seconds or less. Investigators, administrators, and community activists will then take weeks, months, or years to criticize, judge, and punish police officers—well, often administrations and community activists do the judging in seconds or less too.

I remember a police academy instructor saying, "People don't call the cops because they're having a good day." Think about the last time you celebrated your kid's birthday, you got a raise at work, or you won the lottery. I'll bet your first thought wasn't, *Better call the cops*. However, if someone stole that raise or lottery ticket, or crashed your kid's party, you'd call 911 in a proverbial heartbeat.

People call the police when they're having a bad day. Sometimes the worst, or even the last, day of their lives. This is an example I wrote about in *Is There a Problem, Officer?* I would choose a different story, but this is the best illustration of a "bad day" I've had the misfortune of witnessing.

I responded to a 911 call from a panicked woman. The dispatcher broadcasted a woman was screaming that someone was attacking her. The dispatcher then said she had gotten the woman to calm down.

When my partner and I got there, the woman's ten-year-old boy met us at the entrance gate to the apartments. Fear welled in his glistening eyes, he cried, "He's killing my mom. You have to help. I can't go up there." The trembling boy waited under the apartment steps as we drew our sidearms and dashed up to the second-floor apartment. Other arriving officers made sure the boy was safe.

A broken latch and door jamb told us someone had forced in the front door. We listened. It was quiet. We stepped into the kitchen. A thin Hispanic man was standing in the doorway between the kitchen and the living room, flipping through a checkbook. A bloody knife lay near him on a kitchen counter. We quickly took him into custody without much struggle and secured him. During the arrest, we saw the woman who'd called 911 lying on her back on her bedroom floor just off the living room. She had suffered an apparent knife wound to her abdomen. She was unresponsive and had stopped breathing. We started CPR. I did chest compressions while my partner did rescue breathing. I'll never forget searching for signs of awareness in her still tear-filled eyes. I'm sure she'd been thinking about her little boy—was he safe?

Seattle Fire Department medics arrived, *thank God*, and took over care. Moving quickly, they carefully slid her out of the cramped bedroom into the living room. Before continuing CPR, they rolled her over to examine her back. Medics found multiple additional stab wounds.

We later learned several details: The reason the victim had "calmed" for the dispatcher was because she was dying from blood loss. The suspect was a family friend the victim and her husband had taken in as a favor. The suspect wanted her to write him a check. She said "no." So, he took a knife from a kitchen drawer and stabbed her. First, he plunged the knife into her abdomen, and when she turned to escape, he stabbed her several more times in the back. We also learned the victim's husband worked at the hospital the medics transported her to. And remember the victim's little boy who was waiting for us under the stairs? He told detectives that while the man was stabbing his mother, he was hiding behind their Christmas tree.

Can you imagine having a worse day than that? And whom did the victim call for help? The mayor, Seattle city council, city attorney, the DOJ, the ACLU, BLM, Antifa, or anarchists? No. She called the cops.

In September 2016, outside Jerry Ford, Jr.'s apartment complex in Texas, a gun-wielding suspect robbed the University of Houston graduate student and BLM leader of his wallet and cellphone. According to *ABC Channel 13*, at the time University of Houston police officers did not patrol off-campus housing where Ford lived. Houston PD responded to investigate. Ford stated he believed that the lack of police patrolling had to change and the area needed more security patrols—more proactive police. Imagine that. A BLM leader wanted more *hunters of young black males*—more "pigs in a blanket" in his neighborhood, now that one of those black lives had robbed *him*.

Mired in a warped ideology of hate for police, Mr. Ford is missing something. Isn't it nice to know there are people in your community you can call who will come to your aid no matter what time it is, where you live, or who you are? What a beautiful thing that is for one human being to do for another.

Police officers help *everyone*. They help people they may like as well as people they may not like—and often, people who don't like cops. Most people whom cops help are strangers. People the officers probably have not met before and will likely not meet again. Regardless, police officers risk their health, safety, and lives to help strangers.

It's not only cop-hating activists who call the cops when in trouble. Even criminals call 911 when they become victims. I remember an officer in my squad responded to the home of one of his chronic burglars. Guess what crime he wanted to report? Yep, you got it. A burglar broke into the criminal's house and stole his stuff (probably stuff he'd stolen from someone else), and do you know what? The longtime thief didn't like being a victim one little bit. Sometimes, God lets cops watch as karma whacks someone full on the noggin.

And this is what I love about having been a libertarian cop: people take for granted that a significant thing that cops do is allow them to conduct their peaceful business and leisure as unmolested as is practicable. Cops deter crime and provide some recourse when people are wronged. In other words, cops *literally* help people pursue their happiness.

The 2010 earthquake in Haiti helps proves my point. People from all over the world pulled together to assist the devastated population. In the midst of rescue crews removing the injured and the dead from collapsed buildings, some people took advantage of the lack of security and committed all manner of crimes. In the initial aftermath, officials were prioritizing that sufficient security forces were dispatched as soon as possible. As machete-wielding thugs attempted to exploit the crisis, the United Nations deployed military and police forces to keep the peace. U.S. military forces secured the airport and facilitated safe food distribution while the French military provided security forces to prevent looting.

This illustrates how domestic security—law enforcement—is essential for peaceful and free societies to exist. Providing police forces to prevent and investigate crime in the aftermath of the earthquake was the single most important priority before anything else could be done efficiently or safely.

The Freddie Gray riots in Baltimore proved this in reverse. America saw what happens when a mayor or police chief orders police officers to stand down or retreat during a riot. But Baltimore is not the only city where this has happened. In 2001, Seattle mayor Paul Schell and police chief Gil Kerlikowske similarly castrated their cops during a Mardi Gras celebration in the city's historic Pioneer Square neighborhood. This order to have police maintain a perimeter away from the crowd rather than respond to crimes in progress resulted in the brutal death of Kristopher Kime. A thug smashed Kime in the back of his head as the young man attempted to aid a woman who'd been knocked down or had fallen to the ground and whom other men were assaulting.

Seattle Fire Department paramedics were unable to provide aid to Kime because the police were not allowed to secure the scene. Eventually, two off-duty Seattle firefighters managed to carry Kime to a police car. With police, they transported him to a fire station and then drove him to Harborview Medical Center. Kime later died from his injuries. Suspects assaulted Kime and other victims, including Seattle police officers, as city and police leaders stood by on a nearby parking garage roof, contemplating what they should do. Were they more concerned with the politics of it all rather than public safety? Good question.

Did these city leaders hesitate because most of the suspects were black? Even though facts showed that most of the suspects were young black men, authorities were hesitant to slap a racial motive on the crimes. Reports suggest that while the suspects were black, they attacked victims of different races and ethnicities, including other black people. Still, regardless of race, much of the violence and damage that occurred might have been prevented if leaders had allowed the police to act.

Liberal activists, in and out of government, have been sowing the seeds of de-policing for many years. If you think about it, civic leaders in Seattle, Baltimore, and other cities holding back police amounts to a convoluted sort of de-policing. And de-policing Seattle's Mardi Gras and the Freddie Gray riots in Baltimore was intentional by their mayors and, again, sure wasn't the cops' choice. The cops were aching to be deployed. They didn't sign on to sit by and watch people commit crimes. I can tell you from firsthand knowledge that restraining the police from acting during violent demonstrations has continued in Seattle through succeeding administrations. It still occurs today.

Police should be allowed to act to reestablish order from chaos. Good taxpaying residents of cities such as Baltimore and Seattle deserve that. Still, that doesn't mean there should be no limitations on the police. If something such as the U.S. Constitution doesn't constrain the police, abuse of liberty could flourish. Power-gathering and corruption are the natural inclination of unrestrained government. America's founders were a rare group, indeed.

Consider that every country has some form of police. If a document committed to the people's security and liberty does not regulate law enforcement, police leaders could arbitrarily interpret laws, becoming tyrannical and turning into a Nazi Gestapo or Soviet KGB. A police force isn't necessarily committed to justice, and all laws are not necessarily just. What matters is from where the laws derive their authority—from freely elected legislative bodies limited by a constitution such as in the United States of America or from tyrants with few limits on their power such as in China, Cuba, and North Korea. That's why American police must serve as guardians of liberty and not allow the left to make cops despoilers of it—even through "soft" tyranny. Thankfully, the vast majority of American cops see themselves as guardians and act as such.

The best protection against police abuse is an enhanced public education effort to teach people about their rights and the police officer's difficult mission. People should know their constitutional rights and responsibilities and how cops operate under them. While it's also important for cops to know their rights and authority, it's critical they also understand their limitations and restrictions under the law. More than any other American, law enforcement officers have to apply the Constitution daily, in real life.

Too often, elected officials disregard legal limits and enact edicts that abridge the state or federal constitutions. They do this for political or ideological expediency. This is because elected officials are often judged by how many laws, rules, or regulations they manage to pass.

What if, instead, politicians were judged by how many laws they repealed? A local example of political unscrupulousness happened when former Seattle mayor Greg Nickels issued a city firearms ban in obvious contravention to both the state and federal constitutions. This arrogant executive pushed this law despite the state attorney general's contrary legal opinion. We'll touch on this topic again in chapter 18, but the audacity of the left is as remarkable as it is astounding.

As I've mentioned, my intention with this book is to provide the average person with one officer's perspective on policing (and de-policing) in America—from the street level. Too many people think a police officer's nature is authoritarian. Although some petty tyrants do exist, having met many officers from across the nation, I can say most officers are far from authoritarian. In fact, I've seen many officers contort themselves not to come across as authoritarian, sometimes at their own peril. However, since the position itself is necessarily imbued with authority, it is only natural that some people might assume cops are naturally authoritarian.

Sometimes the guardian of liberty versus authoritarian scorecard gets skewed because folks who aren't particularly pleased with an officer, such as after a cop has ticketed or arrested them, are often the ones writing the "reviews." A few people have thanked me after I've given them tickets. But that's not common. Generally, people aren't all that happy when police ticket them. I wasn't.

A state trooper once gave me a ticket and, no, I wasn't happy—*at all*. My review would have been scathing. Even if I'd deserved the citation, I wouldn't have been cheery. In fact, that ticket led to me testifying before the Washington state legislature—*against* the mandatory motorcycle helmet law, but that's another story. If you're interested, I wrote about it in my book, *Is There a Problem, Officer?*

There are many things that lead to de-policing. Cities failing to follow the Constitution is one of them. Thankfully, there are plenty of folks who revere the Constitution and our founders and still celebrate the great American experiment. However, some think my profession should have put me in conflict with being a libertarian. Nothing could be further from the truth. One of the fundamental tenets of libertarianism is that it is government's primary role to enforce constitutional laws in order to protect individual liberty, and it's the police that serve that function. Civilian libertarians also need to understand that most cops are libertarian in much of their political thinking, even if the majority consider themselves more precisely conservative.

Often, the cultural differences between progressives and liberals and conservatives and libertarians is explicit. Liberal causes seem to have no problem attracting people who don't mind missing work to demonstrate—or are being paid to do so. Also, liberals don't have to fear retribution from an angry political establishment or the mainstream media. Conversely, conservatives practically need an act of God just to have a strongly worded letter published in the local newspaper. Or, for that matter, be granted permits to demonstrate. And, conservatives have to fear retaliation from the liberal political establishment and media. Just recall the IRS targeting of conservative groups in 2013. Regardless of these obstacles, this must change. Conservatives, libertarians, independents, and Democrats concerned with the lost integrity of their party must challenge the liberal social justices because to do otherwise threatens the liberty so many fought and died to provide us.

Cops necessarily de-police when they feel powerless against a political system that marginalizes them, fails to support them, and instead supports those who hate them. Police officers need not only *feel* free to speak their minds on political issues that affect them directly, but they need to *be* free to speak their minds. Their city and department administrations and their communities need to acknowledge and respect those rights. Remember, when government chooses a path that aims to constrain Americans' liberty, it is the cops who the social justices attempt to use to enforce those laws.

Cops who believe in the Constitution and the individual liberty it protects must draw a red line *before* they are ordered to abridge any person's constitutional rights. In totalitarian regimes, police officers will raise their fists against their own countrymen out of fear of their dictator's wrath. Law-abiding Americans should never have to fear their cops or worry that their police would ever cooperate in crushing their God-given liberty.

One of the broader problems crisis entrepreneurs intentionally create that harm police-community relations and exacerbate a de-policing environment is in conflating individual racism with institutional racism. For example, as I was going through my own ordeal with Seattle's social justices, which you'll read about later, critics cited five high-profile use-of-force incidents and then called for eliminating what they call institutional racism in Seattle's police department. Curiously, they—leftist Democrats who run so many of the cities under DOJ investigation—*are* the institution and have been for decades.

There are several problems here. First, the left continues to use specific incidents as examples of police transgression even when the involved officers have been cleared of any policy or law violations. In the Seattle case of a white officer who punched a black female who was physically interfering with his writing a citation to a jaywalker, investigators cleared him of any wrongdoing. In fact, he'd probably hesitated too long to use force. Yet, that incident remained an "example" cop critics cited repeatedly as excessive force.

The cop haters so desperately need for police departments to be "bad" and especially "racist," they insist there is wrongdoing where none exists. The simple fact the left doesn't like how police work is done doesn't mean that it's wrong.

Let's say a policy or legal standard deems a use-of-force incident excessive. If the force is white on black, the left considers it racist. If it's black on white, the left prevaricates, and if it's black on black, they ignore it entirely. Although, increasingly, if it's blue on anyone, regardless of the officer's skin color, it's considered racist.

If people want to understand the nature of police work, I'd recommend they participate in police training scenarios called shoot/

don't shoot. In chapter 8 you'll read about a courageous community activist who did just that. The results were stunning. While these training scenarios will not provide the full scope of what an officer faces during a real deadly force encounter, they provide an approximation. The idea is for more people to understand that the police use-of-force scenarios that average people play in their minds come nowhere close to real life.

No doubt, people imagine high-stress police incidents occur in manageable time and always turn out predictably. Yeah, only in their heads. In reality, cops don't get much time to think about their uses of force until afterward. People need to understand the difference between assessing an incident from the comfort of a recliner while watching an edited video of a violent police encounter as opposed to figuring it out in a split second on the street. Police work is like what heavyweight boxing champion Mike Tyson once said: "Everybody has a plan until they get punched in the mouth." Until society understands this, police community relations will remain strained.

CHAPTER 4

POLICE OATH

I, _____, do solemnly swear that I am a citizen of the United States of America; that I will support the Constitution and laws of the United States and the Constitution and laws of the State of Washington; that I will uphold and enforce the ordinances of the City of _____ and applicable ordinances of _____ County; and that I will abide by the Law Enforcement Code of Ethics; that I will, to the best of my ability, diligently and impartially perform all the duties of Police Officer for the City of _____, _____ County, Washington, so help me God.

* * *

This is a typical law enforcement officer's oath. Can you think of another profession, involving people you see every day, where they have to submit to an arduous battery of physical, medical, and psychological written exams, *and* take a polygraph, *and* graduate from a police academy, *and* then—after all that—swear a solemn oath to serve the people and uphold the law? Even after a police candidate has successfully completed all of these requirements and after having sworn an oath, the rookie officer has done only what is necessary to begin several months of instruction with a field training officer along with a year on probation. Comparing a police officer's rigorous qualification requirements and the added obligation to swear an oath with the left's contempt for cops, I have to ask, should officers still be required to swear oaths?

Has the law enforcement officer's oath of office become meaningless in today's anti-police state? Many politicians swear oaths to uphold the U.S. Constitution as if they were reciting words from an alien language—not understanding the meaning and value of what they are saying or caring about it even if they did.

It's no wonder so many people give little weight to the oaths police officers take and refuse to give cops the benefit of the doubt that swearing an oath should confer. This points to a familiar theme: *trust*. Do communities trust their police officers to do the job they are well trained to do? Recent evidence says no.

An officer I worked with came up with an idea to aid officers with evaporating officer discretion and public trust. Over the years, liberal governments have implemented strict in-car video policies and misdemeanor arrest mandates. Video policies do not correlate with a cop's reality and often set up officers for discipline even if no direct incident-related issue is in question. Many officers today also get into trouble for inadvertently "violating" video policies. And arrest mandates require officers make arrests sometimes despite the flimsiest of evidence, reducing an officer's discretion. Don't you think an officer on scene is better able to determine the proper response to a fluid situation rather than some round-belly sitting behind a desk?

The officer's idea is a pocket flip flowchart. At scenes, officers could easily pull it out for reference to decide their next steps during an incident:

If suspect 1 does A, then officer 1 shall do B.

However, if suspect 2 does C, then officer 2 is prohibited from doing A or B, but officer 1 must do D.

If suspect 3 has done both A and C, then officer 1 must do B and D, and may have to do G, but only if F is not an option.

Think this idea is ridiculous? Well, believe me, someone in authority somewhere believes it would be a freakin' great idea. Liberal government, spurred by social justices, is taking discretion away from cops. This is a big problem. Perhaps another even bigger setback is that an officer's word is becoming worthless, despite having sworn an oath. The police officer's oath is supposedly so significant that agencies still distinguish their employees between sworn (police) and non-sworn (civilian).

Officers swear oaths of office when they pin on their badges. This oath means cops solemnly promise to honestly, fairly, and legally discharge their duties. This includes telling the truth as it relates to those duties in court and elsewhere. Having sworn an oath should mean an officer's word is true unless there is objective evidence proving otherwise. Apparently, this is no longer the standard. Cops need society to trust them. Instead, a segment of society spits in their cops' faces.

Some years ago, I testified in a municipal court trial where three suspects had assaulted police officers. I was one of the first officers to arrive on the scene. I saw the main suspect kick the primary investigating officer in the chest. Though there were other assaults on cops (which are all felonies), the kick was the main assault in question.

After several tussles between the various officers and the three suspects, we arrested them. I transported one suspect to the SPD's East Precinct. During the transport, I filled in the gaps in the incident for him. My prisoner had calmed and was actually pleasant. He said he thought the cop was preventing him and his friends from helping injured people after a car crash. After I'd explained to him the car that crashed had been reported stolen, his surprise was clear. He looked embarrassed. He thought for a moment and then actually apologized. Surprised? Yeah, I was too.

Still, with the able influence of his attorney and other community activists after arraignment and once out of jail, his disdain for the police and the truth returned. He rejoined the effort to sue the cops *he'd* assaulted, for violating *his* civil rights. He knew better.

The primary victim officer, other arresting officers, and I testified at the municipal trial. This was a misdemeanor trial, as prosecutors chose not to charge the defendants with felony assault, which is what assaulting a police officer is supposed to be. We told the jurors what we'd seen that day. We told the truth, not only as officers who'd sworn oaths of office but also having sworn additional oaths before testifying. We swore to provide court testimony to a judge and jury to *tell the whole truth and nothing but…* under penalty of perjury.

This Seattle jury chose to believe the suspects over the police officers. Ex-convict community agitators over sworn law officers. All the defendants had criminal records and had assaulted police officers while interfering with police duties at an injury car crash investigation involving a stolen vehicle.

This Seattle jury acquitted the suspects despite eyewitness testimony about their crimes from several police officers. I later learned that some jurors had voted to acquit because they felt the defendants had "suffered enough" because an officer had used pepper spray during the melee. *Are you kidding me?*

This acquittal resulted in a subsequent federal civil rights trial against the primary officer the suspects had initially interfered with and assaulted. After months of trial, the jury found for the plaintiffs. They may have felt they had to based on the judge's specific instructions to the jury. That happens sometimes. However, the jury awarded the plaintiffs a nominal award. Something like a dollar. Still, after the officer had lost significant weight from the stress of trial despite the defendant's Pyrrhic victory, the officer still "lost." What happens the next time the officer or the other officers are in a similar circumstance? Anyone think this might lead to de-policing?

In another wacko case of mistrust of cops, an officer told me a defense attorney had moved to dismiss his direct observations of a DUI suspect because it occurred off camera. The inference is if it's not captured on camera, it didn't happen. Apparently, the sworn police officer's word was worth little to the attorney—the court—society. I suppose the field sobriety tests would be disregarded too, if not on camera. As an officer of the court, even a defense attorney should have more respect, but they tend to be liberal too. So...there's that.

This is a dangerous trend. If an officer's word is no longer valued, then not only does the officer's professional reputation suffer but also crime victims pay a price. Let's say an officer witnesses a suspect commit a crime against a victim, but it's not captured on video. Would critics deem that crime not to have taken place? There are examples all across the nation of defendants acquitted because the benefit of the doubt is going to those with criminal records over good cops. De-policing.

America needs to return to a place where a police officer's word still means something. In those cases where an officer has given false testimony, has behaved dishonestly—has lied, the sanctions should be severe enough to match the dishonoring of the oath, but this is only going to work if society respects the oath. Is it right that an oath confers liabilities but no benefits?

Oath-taking requirements are rare among professions. For example, journalists, the folks who examine, investigate, and criticize police officers' actions, are also expected to be honest, fair, and do their jobs with integrity. However, reporters and journalists do not swear oaths, do they? I can think of a couple of *Seattle Times* editors and reporters I've dealt with who prove my point.

Many on the left accuse America of becoming a police state. I would challenge this notion: Instead, is America becoming an *anti*-police state? The nation's political slither to the left after electing Barack Obama has been devastating for law enforcement. Because of the former president's appointment of Eric Holder as U.S. attorney general and the subsequent disappointment of his replacement, Loretta Lynch, it has become an increasingly anti-police state in which we now live.

Incidentally, how has Holder followed up his stellar political career as a social justice warrior? According to Thomas Lifson of *AmericanThinker.com*, prior to becoming attorney general, Eric

Holder worked for the corporate law firm Covington & Burling representing Wall Street firms. Immediately following his departure from the DOJ, Holder is once again working for the big banks he refused to hold accountable for their part in the financial collapse of 2008. Lifson writes, "Covington literally kept an office empty for him, awaiting his return." Is that what's called having your cake and eating it too?

Both of President Obama's attorneys general have raced with armies of FBI agents and DOJ attorneys to defend the civil rights of long-time black criminals who were shot while attempting to harm police officers. However, they have ignored the plights of police offi- cers who've suffered community backlashes and have lost their jobs just for doing their duty.

The racial fraud that occurred in Ferguson, Missouri, the "hands up, don't shoot" myth, remains in the nation's consciousness. Here in Seattle, the DOJ consent decree, also a racial fraud, continues to damage what has been one of the finest police departments in the United States.

So, if America has chosen not to trust its cops, then why should law enforcement officers continue to swear oaths? To judge whether officeholders respect their oaths, you listen to what the sworn indi- viduals say and watch their behavior in office. The following exam- ples may give some insight into the lack of respect for oaths of office.

Presidents, attorneys general, and Supreme Court justices all take oaths, swearing to uphold and defend the U.S. Constitution against all enemies foreign and domestic. However, a casual skimming through constitution-related news stories over the past half-dozen years alone shows how lightly some government officeholders take such oaths, disparaging the document they'd sworn to uphold. As Speaker of the House, Nancy Pelosi brusquely dismissed a reporter who'd asked where in the Constitution Congress got the authority to force Americans to buy health insurance. "Are you serious? Are you serious?" Mrs. Pelosi asked. Yes, the reporter was serious, and the question was quite valid. She never did answer the question. And, as I mentioned previously, the left refers to the U.S. Constitution as a "charter of negative liberties" and refers to the Congress as an impediment to implementing its political agenda. Astonishingly, an American president said these things.

Based on these observations alone, is it a stretch to believe that people who don't hold their own oaths in high regard might not fathom anyone, especially cops, would uphold their oaths? Do some politicians project the disrespect they have for their own oaths onto others? Could it be that some politicians don't trust that cops are honest because those politicians are not honest?

Today, we exist in a video-inundated world. More departments are mandating videos in police cars, in holding cells, and now, even on officers' uniforms. How many politicians would last even a minute in office if they had to wear body cameras at work? There is nothing wrong with video technology in itself. Like the gun, it all depends on how it's used. However, the reliance-on-video culture is becoming dire. Unless video of an officer's actions exists exonerating him or her, the officer is presumed guilty. I don't have to tell you how this contributes to de-policing.

Think about the motivations of cops and criminals. Police officers act nobly on behalf of the community. Criminals act selfishly on behalf of themselves. Cops aren't psychic. They don't target young black males as a matter of course. More often than not, police target a suspect's actions or a description a witness or victim provides. I can't remember ever looking for a black person when the description said a white person did it—or vice versa.

When high-profile incidents occur, such as in Ferguson, Missouri, the new anti-police state gives the benefit of the doubt to the criminal despite President Obama's DOJ finding that Officer Darren Wilson's use of force was justifiable. This good police officer, in a life and death situation, was found to have performed properly in service to his community, as he'd sworn an oath to do. Despite this, he wasn't the one invited to a political party's national convention. But the mother of the man who very well may have tried to kill Officer Wilson if he'd been successful in taking his gun was invited.

At their national convention in 2016, the Democrats recognized Michael Brown's mother, Leszley McSpadden, including her as one of the mothers who've suffered from what BLM fraudulently promotes as an "epidemic" of cops shooting young black males. While tragic for any mother, what does honoring a mother whose son committed a robbery and then tried to take a cop's gun say to the nation's police officers? What does it say to young black men?

The myth that cops are hunting down young black males in the streets has been debunked—many times—but Democrats ignore the facts because they don't conform to how the left *feels*. Democrats can read, right? Well, in talking about a study he conducted, an economics professor and Harvard researcher, Roland G. Fryer, Jr., said, "It's the most surprising result of my career." What was the surprise? Professor Fryer studied one thousand shootings in ten major cities in three large states. According to Quoctrung Bui and Amanda Cox in *The New York Times*, Fryer found "officers were more likely to fire their weapons without having first been attacked when the suspects were white." FBI statistics also confirm there is no such epidemic. The Democrats know it, which makes their perpetuating the myth all the more heinous. Willfully harming the nation's cops, black people, and civic unity for political expediency? Especially during a time of increased terrorist threats? Who does that?

President Obama, Attorney General Holder, and Missouri Governor Jay Nixon spoke out for justice in Ferguson. But they did so *only* for Michael Brown and his family, *not* for Officer Darren Wilson—the actual victim—and his family. Ironically, it was Holder's DOJ that showed, I'm sure reluctantly, that events unfolded in such a way that Officer Wilson acted as he swore to do when he took his oath. Wilson should have been honored, not demonized by his government leaders. And yet his life, as he once lived it, along with his career ambitions and goals, is essentially over.

Have any leftist politicians, activists, or media pundits—let alone the DOJ—apologized to Officer Wilson? Hell, President Obama went on a worldwide "apology" tour. What's one more? Will they ever apologize? As the Brits say, "Not bloody likely!" Anyone think it would have helped Officer Wilson, not to mention help heal a nation and stave off de-policing, if Attorney General Holder, President Obama, Governor Nixon, or any leader on the left who'd been wrong about *hands up, don't shoot*, had made public comments noting Wilson's heroic police work? Of course it would have. This lack of support can be staggering for police officers. It's likely Darren Wilson will never work as a cop again—his reward from liberals for doing his job.

No, they didn't invite Officer Wilson, but the Democratic Party did provide Michael Brown's mother with an aura of victimhood, inviting her into the glow of its party's national convention spotlight. If this isn't more proof of today's American anti-police state, what is? And when the presidential candidate of a major political party honors the mother of a suspect who assaulted a police officer and tried to take his gun, cops are only smart to back off proactive policing. This all contributes to de-policing, folks. If an officer fails to investigate a potential burglar roaming in your neighborhood because he might be called a racist, and the criminal breaks into your house, you'll know who to thank.

If an officer gains nothing by taking an oath because society no longer values such solemn pledges, then maybe the law enforcement oath's time has passed. If a police officer cannot earn the benefit of the community's doubt, then who else in society deserves it? Too often, it's criminals such as Michael Brown who have earned the liberal's benefit of the doubt.

The vast majority of police officers do the job so people can live in safe communities and can pursue their happiness. Law enforcement is one of the noblest of all professions and one without which peaceful society cannot exist. Racial agitators would have you believe black Americans live in a police state where white cops and their

"Uncle Tom" black colleagues are gunning down black teens in the streets. However, the statistics show that out of twelve million arrests per year, over thirty thousand per day, 99.9 percent occur without a suspect being killed. And of that one-tenth of 1 percent, the vast majority are justified police shootings of a dangerous criminal. Hardly the bloodbath some describe.

Are we witnessing a time when the most qualified people will no longer be willing to pin on the badge? Are we witnessing the inception of an American anti-police state? Are we witnessing the age of de-policing and the end of any meaning to law enforcement officers swearing an oath?

CHAPTER 5

BADGE OF HONOR

Inside the old Starbucks in Seattle's
Madison Park neighborhood:

"So, what do you think of the job so far?" the crusty old veteran, Ron, asks Mark, the crisp new rookie. I sit next to Mark. On the other side of the table, Ron sits next to Rhonda, Mark's field training officer (FTO) and Ron's partner when neither has a student.

"It's fun, but there's a lot to learn," Mark answers.

I was a few months ahead of Mark and though I had completed my FTO training, I was no veteran, either. "I agree with that," I say.

Ron grows serious. He looks at Mark and me and says, "Well, I can guarantee you'll see things in this job you never thought you would." Mark and I would eventually become partners, working in patrol and on the Community Police Team (CPT). Yes, we would see a lot of strange stuff.

Just then, there came a loud clank. Other patrons' heads snap toward us. Then silence reigns. As what happened settles into our awareness, Ron looks down at the table and says, "That can't be good." We chuckle and then all start laughing.

All of a sudden, Ron's badge had fallen off his uniform, clanking onto the table. Apparently, the pin lock had chosen that moment to give out. Ron was sure right about us seeing odd things. We added that incident to things we never thought we'd ever see as police officers. But that defective badge didn't approach the strangest or most disheartening things we'd see over our careers, including things that would contribute to de-policing.

* * *

The badge law enforcement officers wear can be intimidating. Whenever I spoke with someone while in uniform, I notice two things: their hands and their eyes. Hands and eyes tell me what I initially need to know to keep both of us safe—well, mostly me.

First, I look at their hands. Are they holding something that can hurt me or are their hands balled up into tight fists? Second, I look at their eyes. Eyes betray clues as to what someone may be thinking or planning. I've noticed over the years people stare at two things they need to get past before they were comfortable with me: my badge and my gun.

A badge may be intimidating to some; a gun is intimidating to most. It's meant to be. It's a deadly weapon. If cops can prevent bad guys from doing something illegal because they're wearing guns, that's better than having to deal with the aftermath of a violent crime. If the gun helps to do that, good. For many people, especially in urban areas, guns are a novelty they rarely encounter. To the average person, a gun is huge and intimidating. To the cop, it's one of his or her tools, like a laptop is to a businessperson or a hammer is to a carpenter.

The badge is not a tool. It's a symbol our culture has imbued with power. Practically speaking, the law enforcement badge is only a piece of metal pinned to the left breast of a police officer's uniform shirt. Shiny though it may be, it's still a trinket that'll someday find its way into a family display case, be melted as scrap, or one day lie at the bottom of some relative's drawer collecting dust. But symbolically, a cop's badge is different. It may seem like an inanimate and innocuous symbol, but for many it's infused with a mystical power. Police badges evoke interesting reactions in people. Most people seem fascinated. After I was sworn in as a police officer, the first thing my kids wanted to do was look at my badge. Parents with young children know that see often morphs into touch. My kids fondled it or pinned it to their shirts—a new sheriff in town.

The first time my wife and I went out to dinner after I finished the academy, it was with one of Jody's fellow firefighters and his wife. The first thing his wife said was, "Let me see your badge." She didn't pin it to her shirt, but she did rub it solemnly as if a genie might appear. My wife commented that our friend's husband also had a badge but, not to be outdone, I noted that mine was bigger than his. Tequila was involved, so...

There are conflicting opinions about how the police badge came to be, but it seems generally accepted that police first used uniform badges in London in 1845. Sixteen years earlier, Sir Robert Peel had established what is considered the first modern police force. Peel oversaw a staff of 160 officers under the auspices of Scotland Yard. It didn't take long for people to tag police officers with nicknames. "Peelers" and another nickname that has stuck to this day, "Bobbies," derive from founder Robert Peel.

And since we're waxing historical in this chapter, allow me to digress. Why police uniforms are blue comes from the same era. It seems the British Army soldier's red uniform (i.e., redcoats) struck terror into the hearts of British subjects, as the government used soldiers, sometimes brutally, to quell public disturbances. On the contrary, Royal Navy sailors, popular with the average Brit, wore blue uniforms. So, the police adopted "navy" blue.

Back to the subject of nicknames—but still related to badges—manufacturers used copper to make the first police badges. Many historians believe this is how the early police nickname "copper" derived. Copper, shortened to "cop," is still used in English-speaking countries. Another theory holds that the word "cop" is an acronym for Constable on Patrol.

From where did the idea for using a badge to identify a police officer as a person with the authority of law come? Based on early badge designs (that police still use) such as circular or oval shapes, some speculate the badge may be a miniature facsimile of the medieval knight's shield. Others lean toward this idea coming specifically from the Arthurian era. I'm not making a claim to any historical facts in suggesting such a connection. However, it cannot be denied that the legendary King Arthur and his Knights of the Round Table are associated with honor, integrity, and bravery—the best of police traits.

Knights carried their shields with pride to the left to protect their hearts. Police officers today proudly wear their badges on the left over their hearts. A shield displayed a knight's "colors," the symbols and hues that identified his heritage. Some police departments today refer to their badge as a shield.

Do Arthur's knights qualify as an early police force? In a sense, maybe. As with modern police officers, Arthur required his knights to be of sound moral character, trustworthy, honest, and brave. The king also charged the knights with enforcing the laws of the land. Just what cops do today.

Specific to the badge, most modern police badges (beginning in 1845 London) retain the general shape of a knight's shield. The modern police officer's badge also conveys much of the same information as the knight's shield, containing colors, texts, and symbols representing an officer's jurisdiction.

In this age of de-policing, I fear the badge no longer possesses the symbolic influence it once did. Along with a lack of respect for the officer naturally follows a declining deference for important law enforcement traditions and symbols of authority. To those who refuse to appreciate the police as a positive force, the badge is a symbol of oppression. For people who appreciate police officers and understand what they represent, the badge is a symbol of good.

I was once checking the grounds of an apartment building for a reported suspicious male looking into windows. As I approached a corner, a young woman rounded it from the other direction. She was obviously startled, and her fear was palpable. But within a second or two I noticed her eyes locked onto my badge before she took in my uniform and realized I was a police officer. Her fear dissipated. She relaxed, smiled, and asked me what was going on. We had a nice chat before I walked her back to the front door. This incident represents one of the things I enjoyed about being one of the "good guys." That look in people's eyes when they knew they were safe with me.

CHAPTER 6

U.S. CONSTITUTION BEHIND EVERY BADGE

I am not a constitutional scholar (what a way to begin a chapter on cops and the Constitution, eh?), but I'm at least as familiar with the U.S. Constitution as the next cop. I'm one of those nerdy cops who figuratively carried the U.S. Constitution behind my badge and literally carried a Constitution booklet with me on duty. Still, poring over each word and phrase in our nation's blueprint hasn't been my life's work. But I suppose that's one point of this book: this isn't a scholar's point of view. It's a patrol cop's perspective from the street level.

Researchers and academics write and lecture about what cops do. Students read the textbooks the experts write, listen to their lectures, and participate in discussions and debates about what cops do, should(n't) do, or should(n't) have done. But there isn't a textbook on earth that can anticipate every changing detail that occurs in the myriad situations police officers face daily. Non-cop academics may put incidents into neatly packaged scenarios where everything happens with sufficient time for the officer to react "properly." But it doesn't work that way for cops.

Critics and investigators study, discuss, debate, and criticize, over days, weeks, months, and sometimes years, confrontations cops faced with only split seconds to react. Cops deal with these situations while also contending with inclement weather, piles of garbage, screaming kids, foul-mouthed families, and agitated bystanders. You can often add to that the stench of piss, shit, vomit, or death. Those ancillary aspects provide a unique ambience for cops while trying to handle crises. It's important the public learn to put a police officer's actions into proper context. But the average person finds it difficult to imagine working under such distracting conditions.

Back to something I mentioned previously, it is important that every citizen become familiar with the U.S. Constitution. This includes police officers. One way cops employ the Constitution is when folks tout their peculiar understanding of it (e.g., "I know my rights!"). People should temper their theoretical constitutional knowledge when dealing with cops. It's great when people know and even assert their rights, but only if they are *right*.

Sometimes folks assume the worst about cops and freak out at the least perceived violation of what they believe are their constitutional rights. In my first book, *Officer*, I tell a story about a misunderstanding that addresses this point.

My partner and I pulled over a young man because one of his car's rear wheels was wobbling as if it were about to take its act solo—literally. We assured him he'd done nothing wrong and told him about his wheel. He explained he'd just changed the tire but admitted he didn't know what he was doing. We had the kid pop the trunk so we could access his tools to help him fix the tire.

As the three of us were peering into the trunk, a fifty-something, frumpy, ponytailed man approached us and stopped. He stood on the sidewalk staring at our drama. He had an iron gaze fixed on us, his facial muscles tense. He appeared a land mine about to detonate. Apparently unable to contain himself any longer, the man exploded. "They need a warrant to do that," he said, pointing a finger, shaking his head, his entire body vibrating.

The kid cast a confused expression at his bystanding would-be barrister. Then we three looked at each other and then back at the man. With more sarcasm than I should have, I asked, "Why do we need a warrant to help this young man *change his tire?*"

The man paused. His stiff expression and rigid composure persisted, except for his eyes, which dimmed. Finally, his shoulders drooped, he expelled a rough breath, and he trudged off. I followed him a few steps until he got to his home only a few yards away. He fumbled for his keys. It seemed his civil rights rescue hadn't gone as planned.

I asked him what the police had done to give him such a negative view of us. He said something about cops kicking in a friend's door, and then he slammed the door in my face. I'm not sure if that was the real reason. I sensed it wasn't, but he had a hair trigger and evidently viewed cops as a neo-Gestapo rather than the affable, people-helping coppers we were.

Police academy instructors teach student officers constitutional law. Many officers have also studied the subject in college or through self-education. Some cops have degrees in criminal justice where they learned about the U.S. Constitution. Few grade schools and high schools offer more than a brief perusal of liberty's greatest document upon which our legal system is based. And, sadly, many college courses focus primarily on its flaws—as they see them—and not its many blessings.

This lapse is important because, according to the Lumina Foundation, 60 percent of working-aged Americans do not have a two- or four-year college degree. If these people aren't exposed to the Constitution in K-12, they aren't likely to gain any greater understanding of this important American birthright later in life. However, institutions such as Hillsdale College offer free online courses, including on the U.S. Constitution. It's a shame and it shows how the schools no longer teach American history or civic pride. This deficiency deprives Americans of the capacity to think critically about the law of the land and consider events, such as police uses of force, in their correct context. I'm convinced that this lack of education is partially responsible for the conditions that have led to de-policing.

Adhering to the Bill of Rights is a police officer's necessary priority during enforcement duties because this is the primary aspect of constitutional law cops deal with daily. While people discuss, cite, and assert their constitutional rights, both accurately and inaccurately, cops have to apply the Constitution correctly in real life. Hell, it becomes second nature.

It's remarkable how many people shriek like wild boars caught in a trap if they perceive a constitutional violation but are ready to overlook it if violating the Constitution helps them. For example, you wouldn't believe the number of folks, regardless of politics, who ask cops to violate people's constitutional rights. Are these folks anti-Constitution? Not necessarily. They make these requests with little thought, which is one reason the Constitution is such a brilliant document. It protects us regardless of whether we respect or understand it.

The framers clearly created the Constitution to protect individual rights. It's what makes us so different from other countries. America was explicitly designed to advance individual liberty. Still, leftist government in America resists the preeminence of individual liberty in the Constitution. They redistribute peoples' income, force people to purchase health insurance, and continue to find ways to weaken or destroy the peoples' Second Amendment rights.

The founders created a document resistant to the fog of transient emotions that people experience during passionate debate. Officers show up on scenes as dispassionate parties with only the goal of restoring peace while adhering to the Constitution—and getting back to coffee.

A complainant may say, "I don't want that guy sitting on that bench in the park across the street. I think he's a drug dealer." Without proper cause, they expect the police officer to force a person to leave a place he has a constitutional right to be. Perhaps that individual *is* a drug dealer who *has* been dealing drugs. The complainant may *know* and even the cop may *know* a crime is occurring, but the Constitution protects even criminals, creating a high standard that cops must meet before they can act. An officer must find evidence, establish proof, etc., that a crime is being or has been committed. Only then do the police gain the constitutional authority to force a person to leave an area or arrest the person.

Whether an individual is driving, walking, or sitting on the couch, the Constitution is an invisible cloak enveloping all people in America under its protection. How? The officer flips through a mental Rolodex of an individual's constitutional rights. This informs the officer as to what he or she can do legally or must not do.

First, can the officer legally contact the individual? Anyone, including a cop, can peacefully approach and speak to any person in a public place. People aren't obligated to listen, talk back, or even remain. Absent probable cause or reasonable suspicion of a crime, the officer cannot force a person to stay or order a person to leave. He or she may ignore the officer and stay or politely or rudely walk away.

People don't have to speak with the police. For cops to compel an action there has to be a legitimate legal justification. And to what do we owe such liberty, such protection? We owe our thanks to the framers and the brilliant Constitution within which our natural rights and government's strict enumerated limitations are inscribed. Shouldn't every American know this?

If American schools taught students as much about the U.S. Constitution as they do global warming, people would know their rights. And since we're on the subject, it wouldn't hurt to add some education in our schools about how the police do their jobs. Consistent education from a young age would be a lot easier than playing catch-up with world-weary adults ignorant of police procedures. People constantly hear public service announcements (PSAs) on radio and TV about things like child car seat use, drunk driving, voting, or joining the Peace Corps. How about PSAs about what to do when interacting with police or about how and why officers have to use force? How useful would that be in fostering understanding and trust if we'd been doing it all along?

Once officers have determined they have reasonable suspicion to believe a person is involved in criminal activity, they may make what is called a Terry stop. *Terry v. Ohio*, a 1968 Supreme Court decision, gives officers the authority to stop, frisk (for weapons), and detain for investigation "suspicious" people for a reasonable period of time if officers believe, based on objective facts, the person had committed, was committing, or was about to commit a crime.

What's odd about New York City's current issue with "stop, question, and frisk" is it's based on a current legal ruling that states it's still legal. The left became upset when Republican Rudy Giuliani actually had his police use it effectively. Liberal politicians and judges are attempting to, de facto, overturn a Supreme Court decision by judicial and political activism.

Objective facts: factors that push police officers' suspicion buttons are things such as the following:

Location: Is the area/building known for criminal activity?

History: Does the officer know that the suspicious person has a criminal history?

Prior knowledge: Has the officer arrested that person before, especially for that specific criminal activity? Example: a known burglar.

Clothing: Is the person's manner of dress consistent with environmental conditions, e.g., heavy coat in hot weather or light dress in frigid temperatures?

Furtive behavior: Does the person appear to be concealing something, or did he or she duck into an alley upon seeing the police officer?

This isn't a comprehensive list. Each officer has triggers as to what alerts his or her "spidey senses." What's important is if officers can articulate in reports or when testifying in court that the person's suspicious activities were sufficient to convince a judge or jury that the officer acted appropriately under the Constitution. Officers need to convince all who will read the report and listen to testimony that they honored the person's constitutional rights—in particular, Fourth Amendment protections against unlawful searches and seizures. As officers build their investigations they must adhere to the U.S. Constitution during every step.

This subject always reminds me of a line in the Demi Moore movie *G.I. Jane*. U.S. Senator DeHaven is speaking to Captain Salem, commanding officer of a U.S. Navy base, about media taking photographs off base with telephoto lenses.

Senator DeHaven asks, "Can't you get rid of these photographers?"

Captain Salem answers with biting sarcasm, "There's nothin' I can do about it unless you want me to infringe on their civil liberties, which I'll be glad to do if you'll just trim a little fat off the Constitution."

This scene illustrates how the Constitution protects We the People, people who may never realize they've just profited as James Madison's beneficiaries, protected by the First Amendment. And as I mentioned earlier, folks who act without thinking are quick to abridge other people's rights when it's expedient—for them. But dare to even approach violating their rights, and you can imagine the Pandora's box of invectives they'd unleash. I know. I've been on the receiving end—many times.

Constitutional law, both federal and state, also applies when cops deal with the courts. You know, those lofty folks who set jurisprudential precedent from the protected, comfort of their cozy courtrooms that cops then have to apply on the streets in warp-speed reality.

Not very long ago, a court handed down a decision that ensured de-policing would increase in Washington State. It folds the social contact, noncustodial interactions between officers and citizens, as mentioned above, inside out. Prior to the ruling, officers could ask people to keep their hands out of their pockets while speaking with them. This is a prudent safety request, not a demand. Most people comply. Officers can see what's in a hand, not what's in a pocket.

A Washington State Supreme Court ruling put an end to that. Now, if officers stop to talk to people and ask them to take their hands out of their pockets, Washington State considers people "seized." This ruling essentially nullifies an officer's ability to socially contact people in high-crime areas where the likelihood of encountering dangerous people is increased. In training, officers are taught there is no such thing as a routine contact. And what about if someone approaches the officer to chat? If the officer asks a man to remove his hands from his pockets, has the officer seized that person? Did the court think about this?

A diligent officer knows suspicion may increase as conversations with people evolve. Social contacts serve as preventative anticrime measures that protect the community. This involves officers requesting people keep their hands out of their pockets during a chat. There is no compulsion involved. This used to be called good police work. Keeping hands out of pockets reduces the risk of a misunderstanding should the person suddenly withdraw any object from his or her pocket—especially in low-light situations.

Remember, when officers contact people socially, people can refuse to talk and can even leave unless the cop has a valid reason to order them to stop. The officer isn't responsible for a person's ignorance of his or her rights if they do not realize they are free to leave. I suppose that "ignorance of the law" thing applies here too.

If people do walk away, either they are rude, don't like cops, know their rights, or may be up to no good. These are things cops file away in their mental notes. If a person is caught later committing a crime, officers can relate in their report having seen the person loitering in the area. If the person walking away is a criminal and is concealing an illegal gun, *that* would definitely pose a future threat to the entire community.

Liberals are always touting community policing, which involves cops getting to know the people on their beats. Well, not all neighborhoods are like Mr. Rogers's. Because of the court ruling, if an officer wants to chat with a person to get a feeling about what they're up to, officer safety is no longer relevant. Why should police even try to get to know people in traditionally high-crime areas when some of those people will be violent criminals and cops can no longer take certain basic safety precautions?

A police seizure occurs when, during a police contact, a *reasonable* person does not feel free to leave. (Things like police cars with lights flashing or officers blocking a person's path.) During a noncustodial stop, it is often prudent for officers to ask people to keep their hands out of their pockets. How is a police officer *asking* people—some potentially violent—to take their hands out of their pockets a "seizure" if people are free to leave? If they choose to stay, it's only prudent that an officer reduces threats—to *both* parties. This way, officers are safer and people are safer because cops don't have to worry as much about a concealed weapon. Disallowing this safety tactic guarantees an increase in de-policing.

This hands-pockets court decision offers a precise formula to increase de-policing. When officers see someone, who appears to be planning a crime but hasn't made an overt criminal act yet, they can no longer speak with that person unless they wish to compromise safety. The court has taken away a critical tool with dubious public benefit. It seems this decision helps only the criminal. It's crucial to reiterate that this action denied no one their liberty because the people were free to leave. Can you say de-policing?

People criticize the police as Nazis, fascists, and jack-booted thugs (yes, people have called me all of these clichés—and worse). Most officers resemble none of these. I came to law enforcement later than many, so I started with a more real-life perspective. I have no doubt the vast majority of cops respect the Constitution. They'd no sooner violate it against someone else than they'd want it violated against themselves, their friends, or families.

Now, I'm not saying there aren't officers who occasionally, a few even intentionally, violate people's constitutional rights. We know there are. But contrary to the cop haters' view, they are exceedingly rare. FBI crime stats support this point. In fact, I like to think police officers carry a tiny, rolled up U.S. Constitution behind their badges.

Corny? Maybe, but I think it's true. Nevertheless, it doesn't take many bad officers to singe lots of folks' opinions of the cops. This is especially true if the incident gets media attention. Then the police gain an army of new detractors aided by the 24/7 mainstream media news.

And then there's Hollywood. Tinseltown has been guilty of highlighting police officers' bad behavior even in shows where cops are the good guys. I enjoy shows such as *Chicago P.D.*, *Shades of Blue*, and *Justified*, but, being a cop, I know many of these cops' actions are pure fantasy—even if they are touted as "reality" based. TV cop bad behavior, even though it makes us feel good when a bad guy gets a wood shampoo or a waffle-face, has to have an effect on a culture glued to the TV. Even subconsciously, if people expect fake cops to shoot to wound or shoot the gun out of a bad guy's hand, why wouldn't they expect real cops also to routinely slap criminals around in real life?

Police intentionally abusing people's civil rights are few. During my career, I learned that a large segment of those who allege police abuses are veteran criminals seeking victim status. *You* sit in your living room watching the nightly news. *You* sympathize with that "poor" guy or gal whining about terrible treatment at the hands of the big bad police. At the same time, *officers* sit watching the same newscast and grumble about how many times they've arrested that "poor" scumbag. This is another example of theoretical versus real life.

In my experience, most street cops lean politically right, and some, like me, are libertarian. Even the more liberal street cops lean more conservative on constitutional and officer safety issues. The vast majority of police officers do not normally intentionally violate the Constitution. In fact, it's quite rare. Police officers defend and uphold the Constitution every day. And when politics interfere with this defense, officers become frustrated at the abuse heaped on them due to incompetent leaders and flawed policies that enable criminals. Again, from Taleeb Starkes's *Black Lives Lies Matter*: "There's an unholy matrimony between thugs and thug enablers." When government and community leaders back criminals over their own police officers, how can you not expect de-policing to happen?

CHAPTER 7

GUNS

Badges, and bullets, and guns, oh my!

Officer Sean Hannity notices a middle-aged, thin, nonthreatening man staring at him. Staring not so much at him as at what he is wearing on his left hip. "Can I help you, sir?"

"Oh, I'm sorry, Officer. I was staring, wasn't I?"

"Sure looked like you were, sir," Hannity says with a smile. "Staring at an officer's gun puts us on edge, if you know what I mean."

"Sorry…It's just…Oh, never mind," the man says, sheepishly, but not angrily.

"If you have a question, sir, ask. I don't mind."

"Okay," the man begins. "So…Isn't it scary to carry a gun around every day?" The man looks as if he'd swallowed a fly—a bitter, lemon-coated fly—his nose scrunched up between squinty eyes.

This exchange is where many experienced gun enthusiasts might roll their eyes and treat the questioner with all the condescension such an ignorant question may seem to deserve. But Officer Hannity must put the situation in context. He needs to view the question not from his own perspective, familiar with firearms, but from the man's perspective, knowing nothing about guns.

"Let me ask you," Hannity begins. "Do you remember back when you first learned to drive?"

Head cocked and eyebrows furrowed, the man says, "Yes. But what does that—"

"Hang on a sec," Officer Hannity says. "Think how it felt to be in control of such a powerful and potentially deadly but useful object. Think of the first time you shifted into gear, took your foot off the brake, and depressed the gas pedal. Think about the lump in your throat and your stomach churning as the big machine lurched forward—so much power under your control." Hannity pauses, and then says, "Was it like that for you? Was driving a car scary at first?"

"Yes," the man answers. "A lot like that, but..." The look on his face let Hannity know that the man may have begun to comprehend his point, but they weren't there quite yet.

Hannity holds up a finger. "I'm getting to it. How long have you been driving?"

"Oh, I don't know. Twenty-some years."

"And how do you feel about driving cars now? Are cars scary to you?"

"No." A grin begins to form.

Now, the point is settling in. "It's the same with guns. The main reason many people are afraid of guns is they don't know about guns. They're not comfortable with guns because guns are powerful, potentially deadly, but useful objects. Sound familiar?"

The man's face un-scrunches, and he smiles broadly.

Officer Hannity continues. "If you were exposed to and used guns, you'd become accustomed to them. They'd no longer scare you. You might decide you still don't like them, like some people don't like cars, and don't want to use them, but it would be an educated decision based on reason and experience, not emotion. Make sense?"

"You know, Officer," the man begins. "I never thought of it that way, but I have to admit it does."

* * *

While the cop's mere presence in our communities reduces some crime, it will never prevent it all. However, without the police, normal society would cease to function. Still, street cops know better than anyone that at the moment a criminal physically attacks an individual or steals his or her stuff, the police aren't likely to be there to prevent the crime.

As John R. Lott, Jr. writes in The War on Guns: Arming Yourself Against Gun Control Lies, "The U.S. data is clear: laws that restrict gun ownership adversely affect people's safety. Police are extremely important in reducing crime—my research indicates that they are the single most important factor. But police themselves understand that they almost always arrive on the crime scene after the crime has occurred. Behaving passively is definitely not the safest course of action to take." In other words, police can get there in time to investigate your murder or your self-defense.

This is why guns play such an important role in American society for both individuals and police. And, this is also why most cops, especially street cops, are fervent supporters of the Second Amendment. In fact, law enforcement organizations have sprung up exclusively comprised of lawmen and women who strongly oppose liberal government's attempt to dilute or subvert the Second Amendment. The Constitutional Sheriffs and Peace Officers Association lists fifty-nine county and state sheriff's associations across the nation that advocated against President Obama's gun control measures. How can people have a right to self-defense if government makes it virtually impossible for people to possess the most practical means to that defense? It makes no sense.

Guns in America have suffered undeserved vilification over the past half century. That's a shame. Guns in the hands of patriotic Americans were largely responsible for achieving and then sustaining our unique republic from 1776 onward. No citizens with guns: no America. Some irresponsible Americans have imbued the "evil" gun with agency. As if a gun has its own soul, animation, and motivations. Last I checked, the gun I carry sits in its holster until I pull it out. It is an inanimate object, like a stapler or label maker, which lays inert until I make it, um, ert.

It's disconcerting when society disparages an essential tool of the trade I plied proudly. What do children learn about guns when they see Gun-Free Zone signs plastered all over their schools? Even subconsciously, the signs convey to kids that guns are inherently wrong, bad, or even evil. In August 2016, Apple did something profoundly silly. It got rid of its pistol emoji and replaced it with a plastic squirt gun. Once again, liberals deem the tool police officers carry every day as evil. If guns are evil then the cops who carry them must be too.

In a police officer's or law-abiding citizen's hand, a gun serves the good. In the hands of a criminal, a gun serves the bad. In either case, the gun is just a thing. It's how a person uses it that matters. Is the Chevy SUV the bank robber used as a getaway car bad? Is the Dodge van the Red Cross volunteer drives to the relief center good? Jack the Ripper's knife is bad, but Julia Child's knife is good? Each item is neutral until put to use for good or bad.

Think about it. Does anyone believe Gun-Free Zone school signs prevent gun crimes?

* * *

Imagine a man arrives at a school, intent on committing an atrocious act with his guns. He's dressed in military fatigues. His hat is pulled low over his brow where the brim meets his dark sunglasses. He's got two pistols holstered on his hips, a combat knife in an ankle sheath. His vest is laden with extra ammo. He has a fully loaded AR-15 rifle slung over his shoulder.

He parks in the lot outside the main building. He scans the area. The coast is clear—no good guys with guns. He assumes the unarmed teachers and kids must be busy in their classrooms—unprotected and helpless. He steps from his pickup, inhales, and then lets out a hoarse breath. In his warped mind, this must be done. He adopts a thousand-yard stare and marches stoically toward the school doors.

But there's a glitch. As he steps up onto the front sidewalk his thousand-yard stare falters by something in his periphery. He turns and locks shocked eyes on it. A small black and white sign declares: Gun-Free Zone. He hesitates before another sign to his left catches his attention. This one has a black gun silhouette inside a red circle with a red diagonal line slashing through it. He finds this sign particularly threatening. He begins to shake. His breathing becomes shallow. He sops his soaked brow with a camo shirtsleeve. His furtive glances betray wide-eyed terror. What to do?

The man's expression morphs from resolve to regret. He hadn't done his homework diligently enough when planning his mayhem. How could he have missed something so obvious? His head hangs low, his shoulders droop, and he lowers his weapon. He turns back toward his truck and trudges away in a state of profound dejection, the rifle's muzzle dragging on the asphalt. He removes his weapons, places them in his truck bed, and then drives off in search of another target. One that is not in a dreaded Gun-Free Zone.

Oh, and it was also good for Mr. Sekulow, a third-grade teacher and former Marine. Complying with the school's "Gun-Free Zone" policy, he'd left his Glock 27 locked in his car's trunk.

Ridiculous, right? It is for anyone who thinks about it with a modicum of intellectual honesty. The only pistol-packing person this sign is likely to keep out is the law-abiding citizen—you know, like Mr. Sekulow. This policy is designed to malign firearms and abuse your Second Amendment rights. While you—presumably—maintain your right to self-defense (and defense of other innocents), these school officials, like liberal politicians, abridge your right to the most practical means of defense. A firearm.

And, what about your right to protect yourself? Whether you are a parent visiting or a teacher working, what is the school's responsibility to protect you if they won't allow you to protect yourself? The criminal won't heed the signs, so if someone with a gun harms you while at the school because you obeyed the rules and left your gun at home or in your car, what sort of liability does the school have for effectively disarming you? Something to think about, isn't it?

Tragically, many human vermin have made my point. In 2008, in Pierce County, Washington, Jed Waits brought a gun onto an elementary school's property. Somehow, he penetrated its formidable Gun-Free Zone defenses. Then he waited for Jennifer Paulson, a special education teacher whom he'd been stalking.

He found her and shot her twice, killing her. Sheriff's deputies—good guys with guns—killed Waits a short time later while attempting to apprehend him. Good riddance. The victim had a court restraining order in effect against Waits, but it's only a piece of paper. I don't know if the victim had a permit or was inclined to carry a gun, but it wouldn't have mattered. School policy prohibited her from doing so. So, while a court order can be a useful tool, a piece of paper signed by a judge is useless against an armed person intent on taking your life.

If anyone can show me how any sign—a placard displaying words—does anything other than suggest voluntary compliance, I'm listening. Antigun signs serve to demonize guns and attempts to circumvent the Second Amendment, preventing good people from protecting themselves and others.

The guns cops carry serve as safeguards not only against attacks on the officer but also in protecting the public against criminals. The pistol is the single most effective deterrent against street or home criminal assaults. Using a handgun is easily learned, it's easily concealed, and easily retrieved if needed. Even a minute is a long-ass time when a criminal has kicked in your door and is pummeling you. Police responses are likely to take at least four times that, probably longer, to come to your aid.

Try an experiment sometime to see how much damage can be done during a four-minute wait for police. Get a stopwatch, a one-minute egg timer, or a sundial. Next, grab a hammer and a block of wood. Click the stopwatch and then hammer on the board as if hammering a nail and count the strikes. When one minute has passed, after catching your breath, ask yourself a question: If the board had been you and the hammer a criminal's fist, knife, or gunshots, how much injury could the attacker have inflicted on you before the police arrived? How many times could a bad guy punch, stab, or pull the trigger in only one minute? How about four minutes? Most criminals would run out of ammo long before even a minute ran out. Unless a police car happens to be passing your house as you call 911, you're essentially on your own.

People can't count on the police for their total protection. In fact, courts have ruled that there is no individual expectation of protection from the police. No, really! The U.S. Supreme Court stated that the "fundamental principle of American law is that a government and its agents are under no general duty to provide public services, such as police protection, to any individual." Tough sounding, but it makes sense when you think about it. After all, there are roughly 900,000 police officers serving a nation of nearly 330 million people. That's about 366 cops for every 1,000,000 Americans. The numbers alone preclude any expectation of individual protection.

How does this tie into de-policing? Remember the other facet of this book: to educate the public. Many of the conditions that lead to de-policing come from a fundamental misunderstanding of how cops do police work. If people recognize the limitations police officers face, they are more likely to give them the benefit of the doubt they deserve. Another limitation is there's just not enough of them.

Police can only prevent crime by being intentionally, incidentally, or even unknowingly in proximity of a criminal who's planning a crime but aborts after seeing an officer. More cops, less crime. And while this is good preventative police work, most times cops won't prevent your murder. But they will investigate—after you're dead.

Responsibility for protecting yourself and your family lies chiefly with you. Whether you like it or not, the gun is one of the best ways to protect yourself and your family. This brings to mind those security company commercials. You know, the ones that aim to scare the crap out of you so you'll buy their products. They show a woman playing in the yard with her child. Just after going into their house, Mom sets the alarm. A criminal smashes through the front door but runs away when the alarm siren wails.

The woman sprints to another room and grabs the phone. Most people may accept this as normal and as what they'd do in a similar situation. But you know what most cops think when they watch that commercial? Mom should be grabbing a gun out of that nightstand, not using a telephone. The criminal may or may not run away as in the commercial. If he doesn't, imagine the harm he could cause before the police arrive. That's unacceptable.

Remember, not everyone has a home alarm, and a criminal aiming to hurt people isn't necessarily going to run away even if the house is alarmed. Depending on where you live in urban and suburban areas, average response times to panic alarms might be one to two minutes but are more likely three to four minutes or longer. If you live in a rural area, as Tony Soprano might say, "Fuggedabboutit!"

It's been my experience that the vast majority of alarms are false, including panic alarms. False alarms tend to garner a slower police response to avoid patrol cars causing property damage or injury en route.

Concerned with police-involved collisions, many police agencies have amended their policies to mandate slower responses to certain types of alarms. Police may not arrive as quickly as you expect. It's not like on TV where it seems every call warrants lights and sirens. If there's no additional evidence of violence or a crime in progress, other than the alarm, officers will respond but routinely. Meaning, no lights and sirens, obeying all traffic rules.

I don't mean to imply that cops aren't necessary for your individual protection. Would I do that? Fear of arrest does inhibit some would-be criminals. But I'm realistic. Call the police if you need them. Sometimes cops do get there in time to prevent crime and arrest criminals. Still, people should know the reality of police response times. And that reality is to count on yourself first, especially against violent crime. Sometimes that might mean hiding in your house from a criminal until the cops come. But tell me this: Would you rather be hiding with a gun or without a gun?

What about your little girl, shaking, clutching your waist so tightly you can barely breathe? What is she thinking as she hears a stranger's footsteps and breathing on the other side of the closet door? Wouldn't you like the chance to protect her? Don't you have an obligation to protect her? Victims don't choose the time for crimes; criminals do. You never know what you'll be doing at the time you become a victim. Be as prepared as you can be.

I was once called into a lieutenant's office and scolded for telling upset complainants the truth about police response times. I'd cited the high percentage of false alarms and the lack of police officers available to respond due to inadequate staffing and irresponsible personnel deployment. Several times over my career, I was the only officer for an entire shift. (I'll discuss this more in chapter 25.) Think this might cause de-policing?

There I go again. We were talking about guns, right? The founders of our great nation knew how important an individual's right to keep and bear arms was—not only for hunting but also to ward off criminals and, in extreme cases, prevent government abuses. When James Madison and others created the Bill of Rights, they placed the People's right to keep and bear arms at number two of ten amendments. Many people have referred to the Second Amendment as the unalienable right that protects the other rights the Constitution guarantees.

Some states, such as Washington, have also placed the right to bear arms early in their state constitutions. Washingtonians' right to bear arms is expressed in Article I and is more explicit than the federal constitution: "The right of the individual citizen to bear arms in defense of himself, or the state, shall not be impaired..."

Think about it. Antigun zealots attempt to mangle the Second Amendment with arguments about commas and employ presentism with regard to an eighteenth-century lexicon. Did the framers mean "the People" with regard to Amendments I, IV, IX, and X but not mean "the People" as it pertains to Amendment II? I may harp on this, but just ask yourself this question again: would the founders have recognized the People's right to self-defense but then expect politicians would make illegal the most efficient means to that defense?

Again, your protection against criminals doesn't rest solely with the police. Take responsibility and choose a protection method that suits you according to your particular circumstances. A gun is an excellent means of security. For you, maybe it's another deterrent like pepper spray, a stun gun, or even a big dog. Either way, choose something effective, train yourself, and be prepared to use it. Remember, it's better to be prepared than paranoid. To have a gun and not need it is a secure feeling. To need a gun and not have it is one of the most helpless feelings you could ever have.

If you choose not to arm yourself, that is also your right. This is still a free country. But please don't blame the police for not getting to you before a criminal kicks in your door, cocks the hammer, and pulls the trigger.

How long did it take you to read that last sentence? Probably about as long as it would take a criminal to kick in your door, cock the hammer, and pull the trigger. You'd have been lucky to have enough time to pray, never mind dial 911.

Let's wrap up this discussion with cops using guns. People ask me if I ever had to use my gun in the line of duty. I tell them, "Yup, all the time. In fact, I used it every day." When they appear confused, and they always do, I'd reassure them: "No, I didn't shoot people every day. In fact, fortunately, though I came very close, like most police officers, I never had to shoot anyone." So, what do I mean when I say I used my gun every day?

When you wear a seat belt, do you say you "used" it only if it prevented an injury in a crash? Or, are you using it every time you fasten it? See where I'm going? A police officer is using the gun whenever he or she carries it. Like a seat belt, the gun is an insurance policy against injury and death. For a police officer, the gun also functions as a deterrent to those who intend harm.

So, police officers "use" their guns even when holstered. Officers use them when they draw them to check a house for a burglar, when they point them at a felon they're taking into custody, and when they're forced to shoot a dangerous suspect. In a cop's hands, a gun is nearly always a good thing. In your law-abiding hands, the same is true.

CHAPTER 8

"LESS-THAN-LETHAL"

*"OOOHHH, OUCH!" a fire department para-
medic shouts and recoils as the police officer in front
of him fires his Taser at the naked, bloodied, suicidal
man holding a razor blade.*

* * *

In a dual response, police and fire personnel arrive at a reported
suicidal person cutting himself with a razor blade. On arrival,
fire department paramedics stage in the hall near the suicidal
subject's apartment door. Officers get a key from the manager, open
the door, and enter the apartment.

"Seattle Police. Anyone here?"

A male whimper comes from a room toward the back of the
apartment. Officers move toward the noise while the paramedics follow from the hall to the doorway.

"Seattle Police. Come on out and let's see your hands."

"No! I'm not coming out. Leave me alone!"

Officers can now see the thin, naked man holding a razor blade,
blood coursing down his arms and belly to his legs. He's standing in
a small bathroom. The two officers in front draw their guns and hold
them at a low-ready position (pointed forward but toward the floor).

"Drop the blade. Drop it now! Do it now!" an officer commands and then adds, "We're here to help you."

"No! I don't want your help. Just leave me alone."

"Sorry, we can't do that."

The subject holds the razor up but makes no move toward the officers. This can change in a heartbeat. The second officer signals the first officer that he is going to holster his gun and deploy his Taser. The first officer nods. He knows he will now be lethal cover for the Taser officer should the man suddenly attack. The apartment is small, so only two officers can speak directly with the subject. The two other cops wait behind them. By this time, the paramedics have sidled into the apartment and have moved behind the two officers at the rear. All present can see the unfolding drama.

The second officer, Taser ready, nods to the first officer, signaling he's ready to fire. The first officer signals the Taser officer to wait as he tries one more time to get the subject to comply. "I need you to drop the blade. You don't want to hurt anyone."

"No. I just want to hurt myself. Leave me alone!" he yells, moving the razor blade toward his arm.

Before blade touches skin, the officer pulls the Taser trigger and two darts, trailed by electrically charged wires, pop and fly toward the man. Thwack! They arrive on target and penetrate, one high, one low, into the subject's upper chest and pelvis area.

"OOOHHH, OUCH!" a paramedic winces and yells from behind the officers.

The man freezes, convulses, drops the blade, and then crumples to the floor. Officers take control of the bloody man. Once in custody, and no longer a danger to himself or others, the paramedics move in to remove the Taser darts and provide medical care.

Had there not been a less-than-lethal weapon (LTLW) option, and had the subject moved with his weapon toward the officers, this incident could have had a more tragic, lethal, outcome.

Nevertheless, it's three weeks later and Sergeant O'Reilly calls the Taser officer, Jim Madison, into his office. Sarge informs the officer the department has received a complaint from the suicidal man (and his lawyer) that Madison had used excessive force when he tased the man.

"The man is alleging you 'tortured' him with excessive zaps from your Taser."

"That's ridiculous."

"Like that matters these days," Sarge replies.

Despite the fact the Taser is computerized and automatically records how many shocks an officer gives during use the department will investigate the complaint with vigor.

Does it matter that the officer deploying the Taser probably saved the man's life? Not as much as it should. In fact, he saved the man in two ways: the man didn't kill himself, and an officer didn't have to shoot him—with a real gun.

Following the officer's meeting with his sergeant, he drives down to the quartermaster's office and turns in his Taser (yet another form of de-policing). What will happen the next time the officer faces an armed, suicidal person? Ultimately, and ironically, he won't have that LTLW force option available.

Again, does it matter that the officer likely saved the man's life? These days…no. It doesn't matter. De-policing.

* * *

So-called LTLWs came to law enforcement, in part, due to critics' concerns over police shooting criminals when they might have avoided it. Today, those same critics criticize LTLW alternatives and use controversial incidents to attack police officers who deploy them. For example, if critics deem the application "excessive," some critics accuse officers of "torturing" a suspect when deploying a conducted electrical weapon (CEW) such as a Taser. Or people accuse cops of racism when white officers use LTLW on minority suspects.

Cops can't win. Bottom line, LTLWs exist and are here to stay. People should understand a police officer's capabilities, limitations, how LTLWs correlate to the use-of-force continuum, and the rules for deploying these tools. It might seem a Taser would be high on a use-of-force scale. On the contrary, it can be deployed relatively early, not only as an alternative to lethal force but also to other forms of physical force. An impact weapon or joint manipulation technique can cause injury beyond transient pain. A Taser is painful only during the few seconds of its application. There are normally no lingering effects. Let's take a look at an officer's use-of-force options.

USE OF FORCE CONTINUUM

SUBJECT IS...	OFFICER CAN...
Combative (Severe Injury or Death)	Deadly Force (Gun, Lethal Strikes)
Assaultive (Physical Injury)	Impact Weapons (Baton, Asp)
Resistant (Active)	Physical (Hard) (O.C. Spray, Punch, Taser)
Resistant (Passive)	Physical (Soft) (Wrist Lock, Arm Bar)
Compliant	Verbal (Warnings, Persuasion)
Behaving	Officer Presence (Uniform, Marked Patrol Car)

Agencies teach their officers a use-of-force continuum. These scales begin with the minimal force level and escalate up to lethal force. Levels of force along the spectrum include officer presence (symbol of authority), hands-on (compliance holds/joint manipulation techniques), pepper spray, Taser, impact weapons (baton, asp), and firearms. It's also important to realize that the continuum does not limit an officer's options. Since circumstances vary greatly, officers may need to improvise to survive a deadly encounter.

People need to understand that officers need not go through each force level before moving to the next. It is the suspect's actions that will determine the force level an officer will use. If a passive suspect suddenly threatens an officer with a deadly weapon, the officer must leap from officer presence to lethal force.

For example, the officer is approaching a car he or she has stopped for a traffic violation. As the officer nears the driver's door, the driver jumps out and points a gun at the officer. The level of force necessary should be obvious. If it is not, you cannot be reasoned with. Get out!

Another thing that mucks up use-of-force issues are the myths surrounding force. This partially results from cops being terrible at educating the public about what they do, how they do it, and why they do it. For instance, everyone is familiar with the person who says, "Why didn't the cops shoot the gun out of the robber's hand or shoot to wound?" The moment this person ever fires a gun, the absurdity of the comment will become clear. While some may have innate abilities with firearms, and while pulling a trigger is relatively easy, shooting well is an acquired skill, and it's difficult to become proficient.

It's not that it's not possible to shoot a gun out of a person's hand. Nevertheless, in a real-life scenario, only the most expert marksmen could attempt such a shot with a handgun with any hope of success. Most cops do not train at the level of military Special Forces or law enforcement SWAT. If they did, they'd never have time to handle 911 calls. Even those with special training rarely find themselves in a situation where taking such a shot would be prudent.

Once again, I'd recommend everyone take part in shoot/don't shoot police scenario training. As I mentioned earlier, this will not provide the full scope of what an officer faces during a real deadly force encounter, but it will offer a useful approximation. The idea is for people to understand that the police use-of-force scenarios they may play in their minds come nowhere close to real life. I think many people imagine these incidents occurring in manageable time— meaning, time to react perfectly—like in the movies.

In reality, cops get little time to think about their uses of force until afterward. People need to understand there's a difference between assessing an officer's use of force from the comfort of a recliner while watching an edited, unending video loop on TV news and figuring it out in split-second, life and death reality.

I'd urge everyone to look up the YouTube video of Reverend Jarrett Maupin, an Arizona civil rights activist, who agreed to take part in shoot/don't shoot training scenarios with the Maricopa County Sheriff's Office. In the first scenario, Reverend Maupin, in the role of police officer, arrives to deal with two men fighting in a parking lot. As he approaches, one man refuses to comply with Maupin's commands and advances on the "officer." Maupin draws his (training) weapon. When the "suspect" comes within ten feet of Maupin, the civil rights activist shoots the unarmed suspect. When the training officer asked Maupin why he shot the suspect, the activist said the suspect "walked up on me" and came within "that space."

Remember, every time a suspect fights with a police officer, it is a gunfight. At least one gun is always involved—the cop's. If a suspect attacks an armed officer, especially when the officer has his gun drawn, the officer can only conclude that if that suspect were to get the gun, the suspect would use it to shoot the officer. Even though a suspect may appear unarmed, if the officer has not made a physical search, he or she must assume the suspect is armed. To do otherwise would compromise officer safety, not to mention be foolish.

Cops should have alternatives to lethal force, but that doesn't mean that the alternatives are never lethal. People need to know that LTLWs, though rarely, can be lethal—death can occur. Police armed with these weapons have killed people unintentionally. Some people suffer a severe, adverse reaction to the ingredients in pepper spray (oleoresin capsicum), which can cause cardiac, respiratory, and neurologic reactions, in rare cases leading to death. Some suspects may suffer significant injuries from the impact of a nightstick to a vulnerable area. With others, Tasers have triggered heart attacks.

Again, cops are damned if they do and….well, you know. Anti-cop activists screamed for police to get LTLWs—weapons such as pepper spray and Tasers. Specially trained officers and units also deploy other LTLWs such as beanbag projectiles, pepper ball shotgun rounds, and rubber bullets. Once implemented, those same critics then screamed to ban LTLWs such as pepper spray. According to PBS.org, "Some human rights and civil liberties groups championed the cause of ending all police use of pepper spray in the mid-1990s, after law enforcement agencies adopted the weapon en masse."

Only God is perfect, so tragedies will occur. In 2004, a Boston police officer accidentally killed Emerson College student Victoria Snelgrove when a LTLW beanbag round struck her in the eye. She was a fan celebrating the Red Sox win over the Yankees that propelled Boston into the World Series after an eighty-six-year drought. She and her family can thank unruly revelers for causing police to have to quell the violence that turned celebration into tragedy.

Nothing is foolproof and everyone is different. While the vast majority of people can eat peanuts without incident or suffer a bee sting with only temporary pain, some people can die. According to Amaury Murgado, writing on Policeone.com, "Critics of the weapon [Taser], like Amnesty International, are quick to point out that in the United States there have been 500 documented deaths after a CEW [Taser-type weapon] was deployed." This may be true, but if the alternative was to use a firearm thus increasing the odds of serious injury or death, then what is their point? It's not like the alternative was to tickle these folks with feather dusters. The alternative would have been more likely to lead to people's deaths. The LTLW at least provided a better chance of survival. Obviously, the number of people who have survived a Taser application, rather than having police shoot them, is the true story of the LTLW. Faulting the lack of perfection is unreasonable.

Still, the public demands cops be perfect every time (perfect as defined by cop critics), so every unintended consequence of a LTLW use is judged to be a possible policy violation, criminal act, or even torture. And officers can't count on Tasers in every circumstance. Murgado again: "Statistics reveal that they [Tasers] are only successful approximately 60% of the time. An officer still needs to train in combatives [sic] and hands-on controlling techniques." Always have a backup plan—even for your backup plan.

This call to restrict the Taser as a compliance tool has occurred to the detriment of public safety. In Seattle, the Taser deployment protocols became so onerous that many officers have turned in their Tasers. Today, the standards for LTLWs often resemble those for firearms. Officers have to wonder why they'd want to have to decide between two weapons if the criteria for use are nearly identical. Does it make sense to require rigid lethal force protocols for less-than-lethal weapons? Confusion causes officers to delay, and delay causes injury and death. If the situation demands lethal force, use lethal force. De-policing.

People should realize that LTLWs are not flawless. In fact, there have been cases where officers in high-stress situations have mistakenly drawn their firearms believing it was their Tasers, with tragic results. Many officers I know carry their Tasers on the opposite side of their guns to avoid confusion. As mentioned previously, sometimes, on some people, LTLWs don't work. People are different and have varying tolerances to pain and substances. People should also appreciate that LTLWs are not directly or automatically deployed instead of lethal force; each type of force has its place. If an alternative to lethal force exists, it could affect the outcome, avoiding death. But should society demand perfection from the imperfect—LTLW or cop?

For example, it would not be appropriate for a lone officer, faced with a suspect armed with a knife, rock, or club, to use a Taser. This situation likely requires lethal force. This surprises people, and I still get pushback from those who believe cops should use a Taser with any suspect who doesn't have a gun. I guess in their theoretical world cops can't be hurt or killed with knives, rocks, or clubs.

A Taser might be appropriate against an aggressive but unarmed suspect. On the other hand, for an officer to know a suspect is unarmed is not as easy as you may think. Here in Washington State, an "unarmed" naked suspect attacked an officer, wrestled away the officer's gun, and then used it to kill him. Was this an example of an officer hesitating to use sufficient force because the suspect was "unarmed"?

In October 2016, following a traffic collision, twenty-eight-year-old Parta Huff, allegedly high on PCP, savagely beat a Chicago police officer, pounding her head against the pavement.

According to CBS News, Chicago police superintendent Eddie Johnson said, "She [the officer] looked at me and said she thought she was going to die, and she knew that she should shoot this guy, but she chose not to because she didn't want her family or the department to have to go through the scrutiny the next day on national news."

Johnson added that the officer's body camera shows Huff, during the several-minutes-long attack, "holding on to the officer's hair, as other officers attempt to subdue him. Huff admitted in court Friday that he slammed the officer's head into the pavement. The officer went unconsciousness during the attack." Oh, and Huff was "unarmed." De-policing.

If you take nothing else away from this chapter, understand that nothing a police officer does while conducting his or her official duties should be taken at face value. There are many factors to consider. LTLWs are not always less than lethal for everyone, every time. Occasionally, people will die. This shows another reason police officers deserve your benefit of the doubt when things go "wrong." And remember, "unarmed" suspects kill cops—all the time!

CHAPTER 9

DISCRETION

The driver asks, "Can't you give me a warning, Officer?"
The officer replies, "The city already gave you a
warning, sir. It was that 30 MPH sign you passed
up the road."

* * *

"Can't you give me a warning, please?" the woman asks from the seat of her Toyota Prius, her silver hair pulled back.

"I'm sorry, ma'am. Our bosses want us to focus on dangerous drivers," says the officer, the woman's reflection mirrored in his sunglasses.

"Well, I understand the need to drive safely. You know that. I've never had a ticket. I have a perfect record."

"Until today, ma'am. You should know better."

"I wasn't driving dangerously. So, I didn't have my seat belt on when I backed my car out of the grocery store lot. I didn't even make it to the road yet."

"So, you admit it."

"I'm not admitting anything to you," the woman says, sneering.

"I don't appreciate the back talk, ma'am. Can I please see your license, registration, and proof of insurance?"

The woman sighs and fishes the requested documents out of her massive, flowered purse. "Here you are. Are you sure you can't give me a warning? I promise to drive more safely."

"Is this your current address, ma'am?"

The woman glares at the officer and nods.

"I'm sorry, ma'am, but what if I gave everyone a warning?"

"That's okay with me."

"Not funny, ma'am."

"Can't you use your discretion?"

"No, ma'am. Discretion can only get me in trouble these days. You're white. What if I give you a break but not the next minority driver I stop? They'd accuse me of racism. Is this your current registration, ma'am?"

"Yes. And stop with the ma'am stuff." The woman rolls her eyes.

"Can I get your current phone number, please?"

She stares at the officer like a kindergarten teacher at an errant student, pauses, and then recites her phone number on an exasperated breath.

"I'd think you of all people would be more considerate of the tough job cops have. I'll be right back, ma'am. Please, wait here."

A few moments later the officer returns. He hands the woman a copy of the citation and explains her options: pay it or contest it.

"Any questions, ma'am?"

"No, but I have a suggestion, Officer."

"And what would that be, ma'am?"

"You can kiss my ass!" The woman exaggerates putting on her seat belt. Click! Then she drives away.

Stunned, the officer stares at the departing Prius. Finally, he says, "Oh, nice language, Mom!"

* * *

What concerns me is how partisan politics affects officer discretion. An officer's discretion can get a cop labeled racist, sexist, homophobic, or what have you. What if the officer warns a white driver but cites a black driver? Should it matter if the white driver, driving slowly, merely didn't signal a right turn, but the black driver was speeding and nearly struck a pedestrian in a crosswalk? What if 50 percent of the drivers an officer cites are black while only 30 percent are white? What if the officer's beat is 80 percent black, 20 percent white, and 20 percent other minorities? Cop haters don't care about the relevant details.

I remember a roll call when sergeants advised us of a city policy change. Possession of forty grams or less of marijuana would be Seattle's lowest law enforcement priority. (Marijuana possession is now legal in Washington State, although it remains a federal crime.) The mayor and city attorney replaced officer discretion with unilateral, municipal fiat.

Elections have consequences. I get that. I'm not even saying marijuana shouldn't be legal. I'm saying that political nullification by executive order seems dangerous. It subverts our legal system and encourages disrespect for laws and law enforcers. If a mayor directs police officers to ignore city laws with which he or she disagrees, what value does any law have? Laws must apply to everyone equally, or they should apply to no one. If you allow one group of people to violate a certain law, shouldn't society question if that prohibition or mandate should be a law at all?

When Mayor Mike McGinn was in charge, his administration took the pot enforcement ban one step further. City attorney Pete Holmes dismissed all minor marijuana cases from the court's docket. Thus, they not only disregarded officer discretion but also undid the work officers had done to enforce an existing law. How much do you think this public policy affects police work? I don't know about you, but I don't know anyone who enjoys doing work only to have it undone on a politician's whim. De-policing.

I'm libertarian on most drug issues. While I tend to personally oppose "recreational" drug use, for health and life quality reasons (although I make exceptions for a Mack & Jack's microbrew or a 14

Hands merlot), people are sovereign over their bodies and should have a right to ingest what they will. Having said that, a person's behavior is what society must hold him or her responsible for when voluntarily overindulging—with any intoxicant.

Officer discretion is one of a free society's checks on soft tyranny. How many cops enforce Washington State's ordnance against smoking within twenty-five feet of the front of a business? I never got one call to enforce it. What about must-have-a-trash-bag-in-your-car laws? A lack of discretionary enforcement of silly laws can lead to eventual repeal. Noncompliance and nonenforcement is a sign that a community feels their government has overstepped. But this can only happen if cops have discretion.

On the first day of marijuana legalization, Seattle city attorney Pete Holmes (Pothead Pete) dashed down to Cannabis City and scored two grams of OG's Pearl marijuana. Holmes said he wanted to enjoy this new "freedom" and that he would save one bag for "posterity" and the other for "personal enjoyment when it's appropriate." It's pretty clear where this man's priorities lie. He actually brought his weed to work.

According to the Seattle Times, "Kimberly Mills, the City Attorney's office's spokeswoman, said in an email Holmes is not exempt from city workplace rules, but that he 'never intended to use (the marijuana he brought to work) anytime soon.'" Mr. Holmes, what would happen to any police officer who was caught with a bottle of alcohol while at work? Would you, Mr. City Attorney, be lenient with an officer who offers this defense: "Yes, I had it at work, but I didn't plan on drinking it any time soon."

What wasn't appropriate was the city attorney taking dope to work—at city hall, a "drug free" workplace. Holmes defended bringing the pot, still a federal crime to possess, into a city government building. He said he was "trying to keep up with a busy schedule." Well, I guess not too busy that he couldn't make a stop at the pot shop.

Officer discretion is important in a free society. How would you feel if on your way to work an officer stopped you for a minor traffic offense, but regardless of how polite and contrite you were, the city does not allow the officer to warn you? By policy, the officer must issue you a ticket. By contrast, let's say police nab your coworker with thirty-nine grams of pot. However, city policy says the officer must not cite her. You get cited, she doesn't. How important is officer discretion to you now?

Although officer discretion occurs in all law enforcement areas, let's use minor traffic infractions as an example, since it is the most common way people and police interact. You can imagine how an officer might apply discretion in other facets of law enforcement. For example, not immediately handcuffing a cooperative suspect while his or her children are present. Or, choosing not to arrest a cooperative suspect for a minor warrant because that suspect has provided valuable information about a neighborhood crime wave.

Anyway, back to traffic enforcement. A civil infraction is not a criminal violation. It cannot result in jail time. It is punishable by a penalty such as a fine. Officers can issue offenders warnings, either verbally or written in most places, or citations. Even with warnings, drivers still prefer a friendly "please, don't do that again" to a stern "please, press hard, four copies," regardless that written warnings carry the same fine as the verbal—none.

Along with a warning the officer may also add a mild to stern lecture depending on the offense and the driver's demeanor. One traffic enforcement training tenet instructors taught in the academy was if you cite, don't lecture; if you lecture, don't cite. This good guideline is also a matter of propriety.

You might take offense at a rookie officer lecturing you. But it's hard to say the officer mistreated you when you only got an oral warning. In fact, the way social justices are condemning officers these days, accusing them of racism even when they've issued only verbal warnings (verbal warnings are no longer allowed in Seattle), the officer may be better off citing everyone or, better yet, stopping no one. De-policing.

CHAPTER 10

GUARDIANS OF LIBERTY

I f you go to the Washington State Criminal Justice Training
Commission website, in the "How to Become a Police Officer"
section you'll find a heading: "Guardians of Democracy." Police
officers serve America as guardians of the people's freedom, democracy, and liberty.

Without the security police officers provide, society couldn't
conduct its business or leisure without increased threats and assaults
from criminals. Whenever human catastrophe hits, some of the first
things that too often occur are property damage, looting, assault,
rape, and murder. When this happens, the first government responsibility is to establish security. Until a community is secure, it cannot
progress, succeed, or sustain any meaningful liberty and prosperity in
the long or short terms.

Infamously, in 2015 in Baltimore, Mayor Stephanie Rawlings-
Blake withdrew her police officers from attempts to quell rioting over
the Freddie Gray incident. Without the security police provide, the
thugs that exploited the riot and police nonresponse overwhelmed
the city and stole or destroyed its good residents' and business owners' stuff.

If you doubt that American cops are our society's guardians
of liberty or think I'm overstating it, hang on a second and let me
explain. Generally, our military servicemen and women act as the

guardians of liberty at the external or international level, thus domestic law enforcement officers guard the people's liberty at the internal or national, state, and local levels. The local guardian's—the police officer's—purview is the liberty and security people enjoy and experience in their daily lives.

Unfortunately, even though cops protect liberty every day at the community level, police often go unappreciated due to a lack of understanding of law enforcement's duties and responsibilities in a free society. After all, how many people are happy after a cop conducts many of his or her essential duties, even when done properly and according to policy and law? "Thank you for the ticket." "I'm happy you arrested me." "Thanks for kicking me out of the park for drinking alcohol." Not likely. When folks who've had the law enforced against them are not happy with the police, does that mean the cops have done their jobs poorly? Today, a lot of cop critics and even some police leaders would have you believe police officers have failed anytime anyone complains for any reason.

It's natural that we don't think about what cops do to secure our liberty or even put a police officer's job in that context. In fact, if cops are doing their jobs well, people's ability to pursue their happiness free from criminal interference almost seems designed to be taken for granted. Society gets lulled into believing security is the natural state of existence. It's not! Even if the vast majority of people are self-regulating and honest, there are still plenty of predators who are not. It's also natural for society to take cops for granted—until you need one. We call the police when someone commits a crime against us. Even criminals call cops when they become crime victims. Cops make liberty possible in a real-life, concrete way every single day.

Most folks are law-abiding, productive people who want to live in peace and allow others to do the same. However, it doesn't take many criminals to make life difficult. And while there will always be criminals, their numbers are kept lower when a community has robust law enforcement. Fewer criminals logically correlate to fewer crimes and victims.

But what happens when those criminals proliferate in a community due to lax law enforcement? Administrative incompetence, lack of support for police, or the advancement of some progressive political agenda such as government-defined social justice can cause officers to avoid self-initiated activities. These are classic causes of de-policing.

Back to Taleeb Starkes, and his book *Black Lives Lies Matter*. He writes that in response to the lack of support from city leaders, the Memphis (Tennessee) Police Union sponsored billboards warning, "*DANGER: Enter at your own risk. This city does not support public safety.*"

There are jurisdictions with social justice agendas that place criminals' rights over those of law-abiding people and certainly above police officers. Just look at the so-called "sanctuary city" movement, of which Seattle is one. In Seattle, cops can get into more trouble asking a criminal if he or she is in the U.S. legally than an illegal immigrant can by committing a crime or by being in this country *illegally*. In fact, Seattle's social justices are more likely to conduct paperwork gymnastics to allow an arrested illegal alien to escape justice than they are to protect their own community. Interestingly, even American criminals don't get this kind of help from liberals. Does Seattle have a Kate Steinle tragedy in its future?

Here's another example of government choosing criminals over the law-abiding: Americans witnessed a demonstration of the social justification of anarchy in Baltimore. Reports surfaced that social justice warrior Rawlings-Blake ordered police not to enforce laws or make arrests during the rioting that ensued following the in-custody death of arrestee Freddie Gray. The mayor ordered this pullback despite the crimes committed being serious felonies, including arson, looting, and assaulting police officers. Before the mayor ordered the cops to retreat, rioters were throwing rocks and chunks of bricks that injured several officers.

Regardless, the mayor commented that she was satisfied since no one died. Michael Daly of the *DailyBeast.com* wrote a column titled,

"Baltimore Mayor Gave Permission to Riot." Hyperbole, one might argue. However, he quotes Mayor Rawlings-Blake, who said, "We also gave those who wished to destroy space to do that as well." Her Honor has not refuted or clarified the comment to reflect any other context than that which is apparent as stated.

Harvard law professor Alan Dershowitz wrote in *The Boston Globe*, "When Baltimore's state attorney Marilyn Mosby announced charges last week against six officers in the death of Freddie Gray and proclaimed to the city that 'I heard your call for "no justice, no peace," it's possible that her decisions were based, at least in part, on the understandable goal of preventing further riots. This goal is commendable, but the means selected to achieve it—'hearing' the calls of demonstrators—raises fundamental questions regarding the due process right of those charged with serious crimes."

Dershowitz's argument contends the mayor traded a current peace for a future riot. Dershowitz also wrote, "Jurors should not have had to worry that if they decided to acquit, they would have been placing businesses, homes, and even lives at risk. Jurors should have had no stake in the outcome of the case beyond doing justice based on the law and the facts." This seems like common sense, but common is the last thing it is in some political corners where the ends justify the means. Dershowitz finishes with this: "There is also a strong case for substituting a prosecutor who does not appear to base her discretionary decisions on the call for 'no justice, no peace.'"

Many people called on Ms. Mosby to release the number of those arrested and charged with crimes committed during the rioting. City and state attorneys' offices routinely request this information be made public. Mosby refused to release this information immediately, citing the difficulty involved in collecting the data but promised to release it within thirty days. It probably happened at some point, but from the way she was filing protective orders to prevent the release of other documents related to the case, I wouldn't make any bets. At this point, it doesn't matter. The initial, unnecessary delay was the point—to obfuscate the charging of criminals.

It speaks volumes that when I did a bit of research to find out how many Baltimore rioters were charged and prosecuted, I found scant information regarding charging and prosecuting rioters. However, I found article after article about Mosby prosecuting Baltimore cops. By the way, none of the cops were convicted. In a related story, the *AP* reported that George Washington University law professor John Banzhaf, III filed a complaint against Mosby. Citing her mishandling of the Freddie Gray case in charging six Baltimore police officers in Gray's death, Banzhaf accused Mosby of violating Maryland's rules of professional conduct. What was his point? Mosby had no probable cause to charge the officers. Ironic because the rioters seem to have provided Ms. Mosby with plenty of probable cause to charge them for the havoc they wrought. But, she showed us quite clearly, she had no stomach to prosecute those poor "victims." Social justice = De-policing.

Those in positions to know have surmised that an intern in Mosby's office could have gathered that data in a matter of moments from the county computers and disseminated it to the press—as they do all the time. It seems the prosecutor is not particularly interested in the public knowing how little she appears willing to pursue criminal charges against the "poor victims of racism" who trashed Baltimore. The mayor showed utter contempt for the city's hardworking business and homeowners—many of them black.

Let me interrupt myself a moment here. With social justice, criminal culpability, and "victimness" all dependent on from what racial, ethnic, or socioeconomic group a criminal or victim derives, gathering data is more difficult than it might otherwise be. With equal justice, you merely need a rulebook—hey, like the U.S. Constitution. With social justice, you need a program and a scorecard, a scale, a pencil, and, most importantly, an eraser.

When criminals proliferate, good neighborhood people are no longer free to exercise their rights to live life peacefully and walk the streets in relative safety. They can't let their kids play outside without fear some gangbanger will jack their new Nikes while they're playing tag. Or cap their children as innocent bystanders while committing a drive-by shooting. People are not able to live free of the fear that infects an area when increased criminal activity exists. This is particularly shameful when the situation exists in large part due to the political games politicians play with their constituents' lives. For many of them, the neighborhoods serve only as social engineering game boards. It's shameful when the government, established to protect the good people, acts so blatantly to the contrary. Instead, they work to protect criminals' rights.

Pursuing happiness means something different to each person. It generally signifies a person's right to direct his or her life without government interference and with its protection from harm, theft, or fraud. Let's look at some examples of how cops, even in seemingly innocuous ways, preserve people's liberty and the peace in general.

The call comes in: a woman sits in her car blocking in another driver because he "stole" her parking space. This woman has taken it upon herself to hold this person's car—and thus the person—hostage because she feels the driver's boorish, though not illegal, actions have offended her. The second driver, fearing the blocking driver may become violent, calls the police.

The officers arrive and listen to both sides. They reach a conclusion and take action. "Please move your car, ma'am," an officer says.

The first driver may have had a right to be upset that the second driver "stole" her parking spot. Lord knows how that frustrates—hell, pisses off—all of us, but the reasonable person realizes the idiocy of calling the police over something as trivial as a parking dispute. The reasonable person moves on to find another spot and allows karma to take care of the parking space villain.

In a nutshell, the officers direct the woman to move her car and to find another place to park. They may have also said a word or two about her wasting valuable police time, but I digress. In this action, the officers have served to protect the parking space thief's liberty. While he may have indeed "stolen" the space, it's just as likely he didn't see the woman waiting, or he may have actually gotten there before her. After all, it was literally a he-said/she-said proposition. Cops have to make an objective and sober decision regardless of the description of the parties involved.

But…just imagine if government social justice played into this scenario: "Okay, sir. This woman's ancestors suffered at the hands of your ancestors, so please move your 1987 Honda Civic out of that parking spot so she can park her 2016 *BMW i8*." Then, upon further investigation, the officer determines that, while the woman is only half African-American, the man says he is three-fourths Hispanic. Since institutional black slavery but not Hispanic slavery occurred in America, does her half-black "out-victim" his three-quarters Hispanic? Later still, the officers find out the black woman was raised in an affluent family and in her profession, she commands a higher salary than the Hispanic man. How will this fact affect the social justice calculations? Should cops just say "screw it" and let the drivers figure it out themselves? Now, extend this to every police call. Go ahead. You can say it. *It's stupid!*

What if the police didn't exist to resolve these conflicts and keep them from becoming violent? Without police, we'd all be on our own to defend our own interests in some Wild West free-for-all. What if the man wasn't an office geek but a buffed up, ex-con, anger management class dropout instead? The physically strong would most often prevail over the weak, and our safe communities would be effectively lost to the barbarians among us.

The man blocked within the parking space would have had few options against a bigger, stronger man. Either give up the space or remain and physically fight him for it. Or, without the cops, should he have physically attacked the woman in the BMW to "win" the parking space? Police respond to these kinds of calls all the time and even these relatively innocuous incidents aptly illustrate how cops guard our liberty every day.

Without the police, criminals would be free to prey on the weak. Law-abiding folks would be forced to fend for themselves in a brutal world where liberty had become a fairy tale. While the above parking kerfuffle was ludicrous, you can imagine how savage our society could become without police. Consider the crimes some people are willing to do even with the threat of police action. Then ask yourself what they'd be willing to do if cops didn't exist.

CHAPTER 11

RUDENESS OR OFFICER SAFETY?

O fficer Franklin is about to meet his sergeant for a cup of coffee when a beige 2013 Prius sails through a red light. Officer Franklin tails the Prius and catches up to it. He activates his emergency lights. The Prius driver pulls over to the right and stops. So far, so good.

Franklin calls in the stop over the radio and runs the plate on his computer. The information is slow to come back, and the dispatcher hasn't gotten a return either. The driver is fidgeting. Finally, the information comes back: registration current/not stolen. But that's only about the car. Time to meet the driver.

Franklin gets out of his patrol car and, palming his gun handle, begins his methodical approach. In the few seconds it takes to get to the Prius, he'll watch out for traffic, look for passengers, see if the driver is reaching for something, be mindful of the car being shifted into gear—especially reverse—and be ready in case the driver or a passenger jumps out with a weapon.

As Franklin arrives at the car, he places curled fingers under the lip of the trunk and tugs upward. *Secure.* Once at the window, he greets the driver, glancing at the man's hands while scanning the car's interior.

"Hello, sir. The reason I stopped you is you didn't stop for that red light at James Street."

"I don't know about that, Officer, but you don't have to be so rude. That was ridiculous."

"Sir, what was rude?"

"Walking up here with your hand on your gun like I'm some criminal."

"I'm sorry if you took it that way, sir. I need to be safe. I don't know who you are until I meet you. Even then, I still don't really *know* you, do I?"

The man pauses and then says, "No, I guess not. But still…I mean…come on. You think I would hurt you."

* * *

That's just it; *you* won't hurt the officer, but only you know that. The officer doesn't know that, and she's not about to bet her life on it.

* * *

Back in the police academy, instructors taught me to speak to people according to the circumstances of the encounter. For example, yelling and swearing at an elderly lady because she's illegally parked is unacceptable. Common sense says so. To the other extreme, using the Queen's English and *Emily Post's Etiquette* guide to interact with a gang member would be as unacceptable, not to mention pretty damn amusing.

A friend of mine—a newer officer at the time—got suspended for swearing at an MS-13 gang member (not for physically abusing him but for using only words). This Central American drug gang is known as one of the world's most brutal. They don't just commit crimes; they commit atrocities that would make ISIS proud.

This is what the FBI has to say about the gang: "MS-13 members engage in a wide range of criminal activity, including drug distribution, murder, and rape; prostitution, robbery, and home invasions;

immigration offenses, kidnapping, and carjacking/auto thefts. Most of these crimes have one thing in common—extreme violence."

When I viewed my friend's potty mouth incident on video, I wondered a couple of things: *He didn't seem to mind the camera was on?* and, *That wasn't so bad.* It seemed well within the street banter that happens between cops and criminals. In fact, when the officer uttered the inciting swear phrase (though admittedly vulgar) for which the department sanctioned him, I detected no animosity in his voice. Even the gangster didn't appear offended. Actually, he seemed amused.

I don't swear a lot. Never have. A testament to my mother's skill with a bar of soap. Still, I recognize the need for an officer to communicate on the suspect's level, appropriate to the officer's nature and as the suspect's behavior warrants. Each officer's manner of speech will reflect his own nature, comfort level, and the situation. Truthfully, sometimes, with some people, swearing works. If it's between saying to the six foot five, 240-pound, tatted and buffed ex-con, "Won't you please lie down on the ground, sir?" or "Get your f!@#$%ing ass on the ground before I blow your f!@#$%ing head off," from experience, I can tell you which phrase is more likely to gain the suspect's compliance.

A driver once stopped me in traffic, causing me to hold up the car behind me. The driver who stopped me could have been reporting an emergency. Within two seconds of stopping, well before the driver had the chance to tell me why he'd flagged me down, the driver behind me honked his horn—repeatedly. So much that I couldn't hear what the driver who'd stopped me was saying. I asked the driver who'd stopped me if he had an emergency. He said, "No." I said, "Wait here."

I got out of my car and walked back to the honker. He showed no distress other than impatience. I was upset because the driver who stopped me might have had a genuine emergency to report. When I got to his window, I asked him, "Do you have an emergency, or are you just being an asshole?"

This is a comment that might get applause when watching a TV cop show, but these days it could get a cop fired. On paper, the emotion taken out of it—robotized—the comment may seem inappropriate. But cops are people. They have emotions. I'd argue that the driver interfering with police business, distracting the officer with his horn, earned the response I gave him. To be honest, with job survival in mind, I don't recommend this tactic these days. Still, the encounter being so organic, the "asshole" honker never complained. Who knows? He may have realized he *was* being an asshole.

I could have cited him for improperly sounding his horn (yes, it is an infraction). Instead, I made my point in a way that got his attention without having to resort to enforcing a law against him. In today's hostile environment, I'd keep my mouth shut and write him a misuse-of-horn citation. This also follows the earlier "cite *or* lecture" admonition. I'd say calling the guy an asshole might fall within the "lecture" category. Incidentally, the first man had stopped me to ask directions.

The rudeness versus officer safety issue is a trade-off that affects cop-citizen relations as much as anything else cops do. Come to think of it, it's an issue that gives people a negative view of cops due to ignorance and, again, a lack of public education about what cops do and why.

I'm not accusing people of ignorance as necessarily negative. There's nothing shameful about ignorance borne of simply not knowing something. I'm ignorant about lots of stuff—*not wanting to know* is different. But knowing and pretending you don't is worse. Whenever a police officer stops you, you and the officer will view the contact in vastly different ways. You'll be more focused on what happened to involve the police such as, "Was I speeding?" The officer needs to assess other things quickly before he or she has the luxury of focusing on other details. The scene needs to be as safe as practical for everyone. That involves several rapid assessments.

First, after positioning the police car or motorcycle for safety, the officer must assess your threat level. Even if the officer evaluated you as being little threat within seconds, he or she would still remain aware for anything that might alter the assessment. Remember, people who wish to hurt officers will often feign good humor to get officers to lower their guards. A seventy-year-old woman can pull a trigger as easily as a twenty-two-year-old man. An eighty-year-old woman once punched an officer I know in her face.

Your size, gender, age, demeanor, and clothing can play a part in this safety assessment. Are you bigger or do you appear stronger than the officer? Are you a female who statistically pose less physical threat? Are you a twenty-six-year-old male bodybuilder who may pose more? Are you aggressive from the outset, or are you calm and cooperative? Are you drunk or high? What are you wearing? A woman wearing a bikini presents much less of a threat of concealing a weapon than a man in a winter coat. A person's demeanor can always change, but a cop has to go with what he or she confronts and stay ready to adapt and react.

Police academy instructors teach officers the first thing they must do at any incident or scene, from a traffic stop to a collision, assault, or homicide, is to assess officer safety factors. These factors include anything from how the officer positions the patrol car at a traffic collision, to how the officer stands and walks, to controlling suspicious subjects, to checking surroundings for potential threats. This is not paranoia. This is not rudeness. This is prudent police procedure.

In a 2010 roll call, we learned a Washington state trooper was lying in a hospital bed. A suspect had shot him twice, once in the head. Another trooper had made a drunk driving arrest, and the victim trooper had stayed behind to wait for the tow truck. While waiting, an unknown man suddenly approached, shot the trooper, and fled. Remarkably, the trooper survived.

This was yet another law enforcement officer shot during a "routine" traffic stop—actually, not even that, while waiting for a tow truck. At the heart of the matter is the trite comment "no traffic stop is routine." It is trite for a reason—it's true.

Authorities believed the shooting and the initial drunk driving arrest were unrelated. This illustrates how unpredictable police work can be. Unlike in a declared war where opposing sides wear distinctive uniforms, in this war, only the police wear uniforms while bad guys look like good guys. Firearms instructors teach that the officer will be the second person to find out he or she is in a gunfight. Criminals are aware of what they intend to do, but cops don't have crystal balls. Theirs is a game of preparation and reaction. You hope to God you've prepared well enough to react properly when that life-threatening moment comes.

People must learn that even though *they* may know they mean officers no harm, cops don't know that and would be foolish to take chances. Every officer has heard stories of injured and dead colleagues who underestimated "harmless" people. Officers owe it to their fellow officers, the public, and their families not to let down their guards—ever.

I remember a dashboard videotape of an officer approaching a driver during a "routine" traffic stop. At the driver's door, the driver shoved a pistol in the officer's face and pulled the trigger. This occurred within one second of contact. Somehow, like the trooper, this officer also survived.

I've had people become upset when I asked them to keep their hands out of their pockets. I've seen upset go anywhere from mild annoyance, to grievous affront, to profound outrage. What bothered me most was these were otherwise good people who refused to see things from my perspective and became upset when I was simply trying to keep both of us safe. If officers can see the person's hands, the person is less of a threat.

In the wake of the Las Vegas concert massacre in October 2017, following his eighteen-and-a-half-hour shift, a Las Vegas police officer who'd responded to the shooting wrote on Facebook, "I'm sitting there eating my much-anticipated Chipotle on my lunch break, radio broadcast…active shooter at the Mandalay Bay Hotel. For the next 11 hours, we all experienced a number of things."

Among those things were people, even in this horrifying mass casualty incident, who mistook officers' actions to protect them as affronts to them. The officer wrote, "The citizens and tourists we all swore to protect, running for their lives, hoping that we could give them a miracle. And, of course, the frustration we get when people question you...'Why do I have to leave?' 'But my hotel is that way.' 'Why are you yelling at me to put my hands up? That's not very nice.' 'Why are you pointing rifles at me? That's scary.'" What's truly scary is people resisting cops trying to keep them safe.

Balancing officer safety tactics with what someone might perceive as rudeness can be challenging, especially after the sun goes down. One night I was driving toward a bus stop. I'd glanced away from it, and when I looked back, a male was standing there. It seemed he could only have come from some bushes next to the bus stop or from behind an adjacent house. Since I wasn't sure where he'd come from, he was suspicious but not to the point of a Terry stop. It's possible the shadows had concealed him and I just couldn't see him, but I didn't think so. I decided to talk to him.

The man seemed apprehensive but calm and had a nervous habit of putting his hands in his pockets. I asked him to keep his hand out of his pockets. He didn't seem to be doing it to upset me, but I had no idea if he had a weapon. Since it was a noncustodial contact (no legal detention or arrest factors existed at the time), I asked him if I could pat his pockets for weapons. I told him that afterward he could put his hands in his pockets all he wanted. He agreed. Remember, he could have walked away at any time (although, as we discussed, cops can no longer ask this of people in Washington State).

How does this protect us both? After checking his pockets, I was sure he had no weapons in those pockets. If he reached into one of those pockets from habit, I wouldn't react as if he might retrieve a weapon, protecting us both—from *my* reaction. Now, if he reached somewhere else, that'd be a whole new realm of reaction. If I had not been allowed to ask him to take his hands out of his pockets, I would have had to seriously consider whether I should investigate him at all. As it worked out, he lived nearby, was waiting for a bus to go to a friend's house, and admitted he had to pee badly and had taken a leak in the bushes. I gave him a break.

As I discussed in chapter 6, not allowing officers to ask suspicious people to take their hands out of their pockets while they talk, without the stop becoming custodial, leads to de-policing. Should a cop stop to talk to known burglars, gangbangers, robbers, or other potential criminals loitering in a neighborhood? Yes. Should they interfere with their potential criminal activities? Of course. But how can they if cops can't use traditional, commonsense officer safety tactics? Why should they? In fact, many cops will not stop to talk to *anyone*—at least, the smart ones won't anymore.

One problem in these situations is that *you* can't imagine anyone seeing you as anything but good. Some of you take great offense at perceived disrespect. But again, *you* know you're a good person. The officer doesn't and can't until he or she has assessed you and sometimes not even then, depending on your demeanor. Put yourself in the cop's position. I can appreciate how a good person might feel anxious when around an authority figure. But you have to ask yourself how else can the officer be safe? Is it unreasonable to keep your hands out of your pockets while you're talking to a police officer? It's not unlike turning your interior dome light on when an officer stops you for a traffic infraction after dark. It's a common courtesy toward someone whose job is to serve and protect you. Help them do it.

With 24/7, 365-day video coverage not only of police activity but also of everything else, there is another related issue to discuss. As I mentioned above, a person may not mean officers harm, but cops don't know that. How could they? Cops have to be aware of their "360s" (the 360 degrees surrounding them) at all times. To survive and go home, they have to keep distractions and threats as low as practical.

I once watched a TV special with *Fox Business Network* anchor John Stossel, a libertarian. John is one of my favorite reporters and writers. He is a pioneer of extolling the benefits of limited government and common sense to a national audience, first at ABC and now on Fox. His coverage of libertarian issues is second to none. In the show, John included a segment where people had videotaped officers who weren't—how shall I put it—feeling *Hollywood* during an incident and became camera shy.

Sometimes the officers overreacted and made what appeared to be questionable arrests. However, these dubious instances contrasted with other examples that weren't questionable. In one instance, even though the woman was in her own yard, she was standing behind officers with her cellphone, recording the incident where officers were dealing with suspects. The nearest officer explained he wasn't comfortable having someone standing so closely behind him and told her to go inside her house. She refused. If someone wants to harm an officer, where better than while standing close behind the officer?

Once again, the woman may have known she meant the officer no harm, but she refused to put herself in the officer's place. She wouldn't acknowledge that the officer couldn't know she meant him no harm. In fact, the officer would have been negligent to have allowed someone to stand so closely behind him. Especially someone obviously hostile to cops.

While dealing with suspects, officers can't afford to be distracted. Suspects may look for any opportunity to escape, injure, or even kill a police officer. People should realize this. Again, that's one reason for this book. Police rarely teach this stuff to the public. Maybe it's *too* common sense for cops, and police agencies think people should just know it.

Cops arrested the woman for obstructing a police officer and rightly so. She was clearly upset to be carted off to jail. In her mind, she'd done nothing wrong. However, what community service did she think she was providing by recording the incident while standing so close to police officers? Was she hoping the cops would act badly? Was she provoking them to act badly? Would it have been unreasonable to back off to a nonthreatening distance and use the zoom function?

During the show, Stossel mentioned a videotape of an incident could show an officer acted correctly, even exonerate him, if a complaint resulted. But if you dissect this case, the officer didn't confront the woman about recording the incident. He warned her about standing too closely behind him. He didn't tell her to stop recording. He told her to go to her house where she would have been free to continue documenting the incident *without* posing a potential threat to the cops. By distracting them, the woman put police officers in danger. Distracted people are more likely to make mistakes. And a police mistake can be fatal.

Again, it goes back to putting yourself in the cop's shiny black shoes. You may want an immediate explanation at the scene of an incident, but it's not safe for an officer to divide his or her attention while trying to handle a police incident. Cops can't arrest people who video record them in public just because they don't like it. Still, how many people would enjoy someone filming them at their workplace? There isn't a cop alive who hasn't dealt with rude people. It's an occupational hazard. As far as I'm aware, they haven't outlawed rudeness. The jails would fill up quickly if they did.

CHAPTER 12

INTENT VERSUS LETTER VERSUS SPIRIT

Although admittedly nuanced, law enforcement can break a law down into three basic enforcement elements: the intent, letter, and spirit of the law. These can assist an officer from a position of reason and discretion. For a simple example of this let's take the ubiquitous stop sign. That nasty engineering device that mocks you as you try to get to work on time. The stop sign law's *intent* is for drivers to safely negotiate intersections. The *letter* of the stop sign law requires drivers come to a complete stop and then not proceed until it's safe. The intent is to enhance traffic safety. We'll get to the spirit in a moment. But how many people actually *stop* at stop signs?

For you Californians, I mean *stop* in the sense that your car's wheels actually cease moving. Do you stop, completely, even when there are no other cars? Technically, you're supposed to. Between you and me, my vehicle rarely ceases motion completely at a stop sign—even when I was in my patrol car. *Shhhhh!* But in those cases when I didn't come to a complete stop, having violated the letter of the law, did I violate the intent of the law, which is to negotiate the intersection safely? I don't believe so. I normally slow to a near stop, scan to make sure no danger exists, and then I drive on. This is where the spirit of the law comes into play.

Most people violate the letter of the stop sign law—nearly every time is a safe bet. However, as long as they've complied with the intent of the law, to proceed through the intersection safely, then the driver has complied with the spirit of the law: displaying a healthy respect for public safety generally. In this case, it was reasonable for me to show drivers leniency. Do I have the moral authority to enforce a law to a higher degree than I obey it myself—even as a cop? For instance, should any officer who routinely jaywalks routinely ticket jaywalkers?

Traffic laws are supposed to make the roads safer for motorists, cyclists, and pedestrians. However, the hyper-enforcement of these laws is not only unreasonable but can also be tyrannical. Most drivers are decent, law-abiding people harmlessly pursuing their happiness. However, if they commit an infraction that creates actual and not theoretical danger to others, that's when an officer must step in to correct the behavior because they are violating the spirit of the law. Traffic enforcement is not supposed to be a numbers competition or a government tax-raising racket. It's supposed to enhance public safety.

Generally, my traffic enforcement steps went like this:

Presence: Most people will improve their behavior upon seeing an officer, a patrol car, or police motorcycle.

Warning: Most people will modify their behavior upon a verbal or written warning. (Admit it, even a terse lecture is better than a ticket.)

Citation: The final step. Some people don't, or won't, get the message and refuse to take responsibility for their hazardous actions. A costly citation may be the only way to motivate such drivers to change their dangerous behaviors.

When I mention *theoretical* danger versus *actual* danger, these are among many factors cops consider when deciding whether to issue a warning or a ticket. The more important factors are: was the infraction intentional, did it pose an actual danger to people or property, and does the driver take responsibility?

Potential or theoretical versus actual danger means did the driver put any people or property at risk because of the violation. If a driver slows significantly and looks all ways but fails to stop at a stop sign at a wide-open intersection with clear visibility in every direction, the driver has put no one in imminent danger—not even potential danger. But theoretically, on paper (the letter), everyone who runs a stop sign commits what could be a dangerous violation. Police don't work in a theoretical world. If it's not clear by now, cops work in the real world, with real people.

What applies for the stop sign can also apply to criminal laws: misdemeanors, gross misdemeanors, and felonies. Most cops try to be fair when they commit law enforcement. A better term than *fair* might be *reasonable*, as fair may not be an option in cases involving political elements such as no-tolerance laws and mandatory arrest policies. But a reasonable action is always preferred to an arbitrary one. Sometimes, what is "fair" can be known only after an incident, following a complete investigation. If an officer is at least reasonable, there is a better chance of a fair outcome in the end.

Officers should always try to combine reason with discretion when enforcing the law. Only sometimes are things as they seem while doing police work. Surprises arise all the time. It is incumbent on officers to use common sense—not *civilian* common sense but *cop* common sense—during all phases of an investigation.

There exists the danger of emotional connections or bonding that can affect a cop's decision making. As you can see, even beyond intent, spirit, and letter, we're back to discretion. Discretion is an important responsibility that every cop should take seriously. And while it is wrong to take away officer discretion, officers must understand that to use discretion wisely, he or she must remain objective, neutral, and keep the spirit of the law in mind during any investigation. Sometimes it's harder than you think.

I've had incidents where a victim was so compelling that by the time I was headed to get the suspect's side of the story, I was ready to stamp his or her passport to jail. According to the letter of the law, I might have been authorized to make an arrest right then and there. However, my responsibility, according to the intent and spirit of the law, is to get to the truth if I can and make appropriate decisions based on facts.

In some situations, after "bonding" with the "victim," things may shift—even flip-flop. Victim becomes suspect, suspect becomes victim, they both become victims, or everyone becomes a suspect and they all go to jail.

After speaking with the apparent suspect or witnesses and putting together the evidence according to what each has told me, it may have become evident the victim was lying. Then, it might be the original victim-turned-suspect who the cops check into the Grey Bar Motel.

You see how important it is for police to stay as neutral as possible? Even though the officer may still feel those initial bonds with a person, the officer must continue to be open to adjusting as circumstances dictate. To do otherwise may foster a miscarriage of justice.

Even if an officer initially sympathizes with an apparent victim, the officer should not allow that person to know how he or she feels. False victims will pounce on this and exploit it, trying to influence an officer's final decision.

Cops need to remain neutral. I've had domestic violence cases where, after seeing the victim bleeding from an injury, I'm ready to haul the brute hubby to the pokey. Then I'm stunned by an independent witness who says the "victim's" injuries were self-inflicted.

Just because a "victim" is freaking out doesn't automatically mean he or she should be believed over the "suspect" who is calm. Demeanor can play an important role. In closing this chapter, these examples aren't all related to domestic violence, but they convey the essence of the concept of how differently humans react.

I once arrested a robbery suspect who we'd removed from a car and had lie down in the street to be taken into custody. This guy yelled and screamed like he had a hornet's nest in his pants. People were looking on with disgust as if we were torturing this guy. At one point, the two officers who'd handcuffed him stood and backed away. The suspect continued to scream "police brutality" at the top of his lungs while officers rolled their eyes.

To the contrary, I once responded to a serious assault. The victim was sitting on the sidewalk, blood dripping from his head down his face. Still, he was apologizing to police officers, firefighters, and paramedics for causing us "such a hassle." What had happened? A suspect had struck him in the head with a hatchet. The victim didn't want us to "waste" our time with him when we had "more important things to do."

I've also had wild-eyed, screaming victims and calm, contrite suspects. Dealing with people is the proverbial crapshoot.

Being a cop is hard.

CHAPTER 13

RIOT POLICE

An overcast late November day is waning; darkness comes early in Seattle this time of year. Betsy sits watching her evening programs. Her silver hair is neatly pulled up and coiled into a silky bun. Her dessert of Earl Grey tea and a Mint Milano cookie wait patiently on her TV tray. She lifts her teacup, not as steadily as she once did, then stops. There's a strange scuffling noise coming from outside the door to her mudroom. She turns down the TV, hears nothing. Turns it back up.

There it is again—louder. At first, Betsy writes it off as the local raccoon scofflaw that routinely prowls her property. But not today. Something feels different. She puts her tea down and walks into the kitchen, staring at the pantry opening. She sucks in a breath as the doorknob to the back door shifts right and then left. There is no doubt. Someone is trying to get into her house—and it's no raccoon.

Betsy thinks about calling her grandson or a neighbor, but the danger is imminent. From the feverish thumping, whoever's outside is intent on getting inside. She picks up her phone and presses three digits.

"911—all lines are currently being assisted. Please hold and an operator will assist you shortly," the robotic voice says, and the line transitions to the city's new World Music "hold" melody.

Betsy is stunned. How can this be? She's on hold with 911 while some burglar or drug addict is trying to break down her door?

The back door appears about to give way. The 911 dispatcher finally answers, "911, what is your emergency?"

Betsy says, resisting the urge to panic, "Someone is trying to break into my house."

"Right now?"

"Yes, now!" Betsy begins to panic.

"Are you at 2500 East Cherry Street, ma'am?" The dispatcher confirms the ANI/ALI (Automatic Number Identification/Automated Location Information) of the Enhanced 911 System.

"Yes, please hurry!"

"Okay, ma'am. I'll get officers started as soon as I can, but I need to let you know that because of the political demonstrations going on throughout the city there may be a significant delay."

"A delay?" A few more kicks and the person will be in her house.

"Yes, ma'am," the operator begins. "Ma'am, I need to advise you to get out of your house through another door and go to a neighbor's house. Is that possible?"

"Do I have a choice?" Betsy says. She drops the phone as the burglar smashes through the door. Betsy makes it to the front door and then safely across the street to her neighbor's house. Once safe and calmer, she and her neighbor discuss what exactly they are paying their taxes for. Betsy wonders what she'll find when she finally goes back home. She peeks out the curtain and sees shadows flickering past the windows in her house.

Betsy calls 911 from her neighbor's house and waits on hold again until she is able to give an update.

"So, you are out of the house now, ma'am?" the operator asks.

"Yes, I am."

"Is the burglar still in your house?"

"I can't see very well from here. But I think so."

"Okay. Well, don't go back there until it's safe."

Betsy says, "Okay, but how am I supposed to know if it's safe? Are the police coming?"

"No, ma'am. Since you are safely out of the house and officers are tied up with the protests, police won't respond until later."

"So, what do I do?"

"Hopefully, you can stay with your neighbors or a family member tonight," the dispatcher says. "Officers will be there to investigate later."

"Tomorrow?"

"Maybe, but within two or three days for sure."

* * *

Before we discuss this issue, rather than direct causes of de-policing, this chapter falls in the realm of public education of what police do, how, and why. However, the policies and reactions of liberal mayors that you'll read about are a part of the de-policing problem generally. On to our discussion. Does Betsy's situation sound like fiction? It isn't. This happened during Seattle's 1999 World Trade Organization riots.

Instead of using their radios, there are times when some police officers have to call 911, for example in Seattle with certain stolen vehicle investigations. The 911 system actually put me on hold a couple of times. It's a strange feeling as a cop; imagine how it feels to a victim. Violent demonstrations could also be seen as another type of de-policing, one where cops who should be patrolling neighborhoods are taken away to deal with the protestors. There are so many things people don't know about police work. Here's a short introduction to the "riot police."

Riots are dangerous for police officers for many reasons. For one thing, the standard rules of force are tossed out the window. If I were walking a foot beat and someone attacked me with a brick, rock, or Molotov cocktail, I can reply with bullets. If I were working a riot line and someone attacked me with a brick, rock, or Molotov cocktail, my bullets would be virtually useless. The sheer volume of "peaceful" people surrounding these felons who are destroying property and attacking cops helps protect them.

Riots are also dangerous for the residents of a city even if they don't live near the protests. The media covers the violence and damage caused by people who riot, such as in Baltimore, Ferguson, and Seattle. However, before we examine what "riot police" do, there is a little-discussed facet to riots rarely reported on by media. What happens when you hear that rattle at the back door, like Betsy did, when all the cops are busy with people who ignore the *peaceful* part of their right to protest?

First, what is a riot? Washington State recently revised the name of the crime of "Riot" to "Criminal Mischief" in the Revised Code of Washington (RCW). Proponents argue the new title better describes the crime. If you ask me, it downplays the crime. More liberal BS? Probably. Oh well. A riot by any other name still smells like tear gas. Curiously, the definition has not changed:

RCW 9A.84.010

(1) A person is guilty of the crime of criminal mischief [formerly riot] if, acting with three or more other persons, he or she knowingly and unlawfully uses or threatens to use force, or in any way participates in the use of such force, against any other person or against property.

So, if one person is breaking a window, and the two people with him are not, but they aren't acting to stop him, they are all engaging in a riot—oh, I mean, *criminal mischief.* Regardless of the new title, I'll still use the term *riot* to describe a riot.

People should take responsibility for participating in violent demonstrations. The truth is, they don't. That's why people like Betsy who need police services may have to wait, maybe for a long time.

As I mentioned, police will rarely if ever shoot real bullets at a violent suspect in such a crowd because it is too dangerous to "innocent" bystanders. Legally, if you choose to stay at a violent demonstration after police have issued commands to leave, you have become a part of the riot regardless of your level of participation. Cops don't have the luxury of separating "good" from "bad" in the heat of battle. In fact, the mere presence of those who are not physically violent serves to protect those who are. These "non-violent" protesters tacitly provide their comrades cover and confusion to commit violence. I saw this occur at many demonstrations.

SPD puts general unrest situations in the category of "unusual occurrences." These days, riots have become almost routine in America's big cities. Before Ferguson and Baltimore, where specific incidents sparked riots, the Occupy Wall Street (OWS) movement conducted general anti-police demonstrations. One "occupation" was in Oakland where that city's OWS-sympathetic mayor practically invited disorder. Other big city mayors tacitly did the same. Not surprisingly, violent demonstrators RSVP'd. Aside from property damage and other mayhem, their crimes included a reported rape at an illegal Occupy encampment in Seattle.

Many people don't understand how police respond to demonstrations or the far-reaching, unintended consequences these anarchic protests bring upon their communities. In Seattle, leaders of the OWS protests and encampments neglected to obtain city permits to demonstrate or march. The city issued no permits to camp on city property or to block city streets and freeways, causing horrendous traffic snarls. Yet, these folks demonstrated and marched and went virtually unchallenged by city government. Think the Tea Party would have been treated the same?

If your group (usually politically right of center, such as from the Tea Party movement) has paid for city permits to hold lawful demonstrations, you should demand refunds. Better yet, you should sue the cities for civil rights violations, unequal treatment under the law.

Think Eric Holder's DOJ would have mounted an effort to protect your right to protest?

Does anyone doubt that Seattle required Tea Party protesters to obtain permits to demonstrate and would've shut them down if they hadn't? Does anyone doubt the city will continue to require conservative groups to obtain and pay for permits in the future? Me either.

As I mentioned at the beginning of this chapter, crowd control is a strange beast. People should remember that law enforcement is necessarily reactionary. Cops don't plan demonstrations; protesters do. Cops show up because the protesters are there, not the other way around. Cops respond to the demonstrators' location and react to an individual's or the crowd's collective behavior.

This is why, in contrast to Tea Party demonstrations, the OWS protests required a large number of police officers. This staffing costs cities like Seattle tens of thousands of dollars for security (for each event) as well as trash and damage cleanup and repair. The Tea Party demonstrations, on the other hand, required minimal police presence (and that presence was often to guard against potential actions committed *against* Tea Party demonstrators). And the venues were cleaner after the Tea Partiers left than before they arrived. Leftists such as anti-WTO and Occupy folks, to the contrary, leave garbage dumps and property destruction as a "signature" of their commitment to the environment and social justice. Caught on video, one clever Occupier demonstrated his respect by defecating on a police car parked on Broadway in Seattle. His parents must be so proud.

* * *

"Hey, Steve," my wife (a firefighter always alert for cop-harassing opportunities) calls out from the living room where she's watching the news. "They've called out the *riot police* again. This time in Oakland, I think."

I stroll in and watch as the riot police engage unruly demonstrators who hurl insults along with urine-filled bags, flaming torches, rocks, and bottles at them. In response, nightsticks swing, flash-bangs burst, and fountains of pepper spray douse the anarchist horde. Fortunately, I was not at this one. Unfortunately, fellow officers were.

"Hey, hon," my wife begins with a wry lilt in her voice.

Oh, here it comes.

"Where does SPD keep their *riot police*, anyway? I mean when there are no riots?" She grins. She knows the answer. But being a fire-fighter, she can't let an opportunity to push one of my cop buttons go unpressed—not even once.

* * *

The term *riot police* is one of my pet peeves. I don't lose any sleep over it. Nonetheless, it nags at me when I hear it. First, let me dispel any misapprehensions. While police departments field highly specialized tactical teams like SWAT (Special Weapons and Tactics) and ACT (Anti-Crime Team), the so-called "riot police" aren't one of those specifically designated specialty units.

Police departments don't have warehouses where dehydrated riot cop robots are stored: *just add water and deploy.* So-called riot police come from your neighborhoods.

Allow me to explain: the next time you see an officer on a traffic stop, investigating an accident, arresting a bad guy, performing CPR, delivering a baby, or showing up to investigate your burglary, you're looking at a *riot cop.*

The WTO conference-turned-riots was the week that had the single greatest impact on me as a cop. I learned a great deal about crowd control, political interference, and being the "riot police." I got so adept at donning and doffing my gas mask I could have done it while asleep.

It's important to explain the nature of the officers deployed during large-scale riots because they include about every police officer in a department, assigned to various roles of crowd control. Often, a department will need as much manpower as possible, which means riot lines will be staffed with all available officers. Most of these officers come from the patrol division, typically a police department's largest single unit. If a department has to divert officers who should be patrolling neighborhoods and answering 911 calls to demonstrations, the community suffers.

Specialty units such as SWAT are sometimes deployed to use more sophisticated crowd control tactics and weaponry. The Mounted (horse) Patrol provides unparalleled crowd control assistance. It's difficult for a protester to push a 1,200 lb. horse out of the way. Detectives are also conscripted to staff crowd control events, sometimes on the front lines with patrol, other times for logistics and prisoner processing.

Even Harbor Patrol, which conducts waterway security, will be utilized when needed to control demonstrators on the water, near bridges, or at the shoreline. In 2015, Harbor Patrol responded when Seattle "kayaktivists" boarded their plastic kayaks and paddled to demonstrate against Shell Oil's *Polar Pioneer*. The seagoing drilling rig arrived in Seattle for maintenance before heading to Alaska. It's more than ironic that the kayaks protesters were using were made from plastic—a petroleum (oil) based material.

Many people don't recognize the distinction between the riot police and the regular police. This is important due to the practical implications. Do you expect police to arrive when you call 911? Do you expect them to come quickly? You expect them to arrive *today*, right? During WTO, some crime victims, taxpayers, had to wait several days before an officer showed up to investigate their incidents.

It's imperative for people, especially those who participate in violent demonstrations, to acknowledge the critical resources of which they are depriving their neighbors. Some might argue this is the price we pay for our constitutional rights. That's bullshit. Of course, people have a right to assemble *peaceably* to demonstrate. Is that what's happening in New York, Baltimore, Seattle, Portland, Ferguson, etc.?

When governments tolerate violence as "understandable" or even "excusable" when the political left's ordained oppressed does it, the line between civilization and anarchy blurs. Remember Baltimore's leftist mayor Stephanie Rawlings-Blake commenting that protesters needed "space to destroy." Former Oakland mayor Jean Quan was equally accommodating to OWS demonstrators. They rewarded her kindness with violence. The AP wrote:

> Quan's critics say she has struggled to formulate a coherent response to the Occupy encampment that has overtaken the plaza in front of Oakland City Hall for the past few weeks. Police raided the camp last week and fired tear gas during skirmishes with marchers before Quan allowed protesters to return a day later.

When people violate other people's rights with violence and destruction, they have renounced their right to constitutional free speech protections. Despite Rawlings-Blake's mayoral proclamation, people are not allowed a "space to destroy." Unless she wants to allow it for her own house.

Violent demonstrators deny law-abiding taxpayers the police services they have a right to and deserve. They keep police officers occupied who would otherwise be deployed to their regular duties. Perhaps "Occupy the Cops" would be a more appropriate term for this radical movement.

For example, demonstrators consciously choose to violate the law and other people's rights when they block freeways and city streets. Not only are people prevented from using the roads but also police cars, fire engines, and ambulances are delayed, exacerbating medical and other emergencies. Sometimes EMTs or paramedics are not able to get to a patient at all.

Do cities hold demonstrators accountable? With all of the social justices in charge of America's major cities, what do you think? I haven't heard of much if any accountability. As far as I know, if people are even charged during riots, cities rarely prosecute or even issue wrist-slaps. Worse, some cities have paid out settlement cash to protesters who sued cities for that dose of pepper spray they asked for. These people are not passionately dedicated to a cause; they are chronic, antisocial troublemakers. I've seen signs that have one cause written on one side and an unrelated (though still lefty) cause printed on the other side. Leftist politicians and the media give these folks far more credibility than they deserve.

Protesters, such as those paid by leftist organizations, took to the streets following Donald Trump's election as president of the United States. The demonstrators would have America believe they are just ordinary folks, upset by injustice, so they got up off their couches and took to the streets to protest. *Not!* Folks such as Antifa are comprised of perennial, professional Marxist, anarchist, social justice agitators who protest the leftist cause of the moment. In the current case, that a democratic election did not go their way. Can anyone imagine what they'd be saying if Hillary Clinton (or Bernie Sanders if the Democrats had let him try) had won and right-wing groups took to the streets? The media and left politicos would be up in arms at such an affront to our election system. Instead, with the social justices marching, the mainstream media, leftist groups, and their politicians laud the radical left's right to protest despite their violence, property destruction, and blocking of public streets and highways. This can be deadly. There are numerous news reports of ambulances, transporting critical patients, being delayed by demonstrators.

Police delays that violent protesters cause are significant in other areas. For one thing, investigative steps, including gathering evidence such as latent fingerprints, become much less fruitful over time, as does the possibility of solving the crime. Evidence gathering and other more practical investigative minutia aside, there are also the more esoteric, macrocosmic, or philosophical issues to consider. In a truly free society, people are blessed with unalienable rights, but what often goes unsaid is the just-as-important counterpart to those rights: their corresponding responsibilities.

Leftist demonstrators are selfish. *Their* perspective is the only one that matters. But if you enjoy the right to free speech, don't you have the responsibility not to infringe on another's free speech rights? If you have the right to property, you have the responsibility not to destroy, steal, or commit fraud, right? If you have the right to life, surely you have the responsibility not to commit murder. If you have a right to come and go freely, aren't you bound to allow others the same right? And if you have a right to pursue happiness, how can you interfere with another person's right to do the same?

This caution is for everyone who participates in hostile political demonstrations, especially those people who know an event likely to become violent or even intend to participate in the mayhem. People in America have the right to peaceably assemble. Unfortunately, some people choose to disregard the *peaceably* part. This is the part that contains their responsibilities. Instead they choose to place people at risk because of their political egocentrism. Is their cause more important than anyone else's cause? Because most people's "cause" is simply to live, love, work, and play. Most people make the world a better place by being decent, productive, and law-abiding.

A *peaceful* assembly, even of tens of thousands of people, requires scant police presence. Some police are always necessary if for nothing else traffic control and to keep those hoping to disrupt peaceful gatherings from doing so. You may remember the demonstration in Dallas before a vile sniper assassinated five police officers. It had been peaceful prior to the shooting thanks to Dallas police officers.

Speaking of peaceful demonstrators, remember, the late Andrew Breitbart? In 2010, he offered 100,000 dollars for evidence proving that during a peaceful anti-Obamacare protest someone from the Tea Party called Democrat Congressman John Lewis a ni**er. Despite the proliferation of cellphone videos, no one has corroborated Lewis's claim or collected the reward. Many view this as Congressman Lewis's blatant attempt to tarnish the Tea Party as racists. What a shame, especially from a civil rights icon who knows well what real institutional racism was all about.

Try this research experiment to determine whether the left or right conduct truly peaceful demonstrations: Find footage from major WTO and OWS demonstrations and then find footage from major Tea Party demonstrations. Now, compare and contrast. When it comes to disruption and violence, there's no contest. The WTO and OWS demonstrations were infamously disruptive and violent. Many in Seattle lamented WTO as the city's loss-of-innocence moment when a quirky, live-and-let-live town became a live-and-let-die (or kill) political activist city. To the contrary, Tea Party demonstrations in Seattle and across America were peaceful and devoid of violence even when the crowds were massive.

I am a veteran, in riot lines, of the entire week that saw the WTO riots in 1999 forever change Seattle. I was also privileged to have participated, as a civilian, in Seattle's first Tea Party demonstration in 2009 at Westlake Plaza in downtown.

Many will say that at WTO only a small percentage of demonstrators became violent. But with crowds in the tens of thousands, how many violent people comprise a "small percentage"? Fifty? A hundred? A thousand? Fifty violent people can wreak an awful lot of damage. Hell, five can.

The problem with the "peaceful" protesters who ignore police orders to disperse when others become violent is it makes it that much more difficult for police. Cops can't choose which person to remove and who not to remove from a street their commanders have ordered cleared—of *all* people, violent or peaceful. Even if you are not being physically violent, you are still one more body not complying with police orders because, wrapped in your holier-than-thou shroud, you're incensed that cops don't recognize you as "nonviolent." I'll repeat this: if you choose to stay in a "riot," you have chosen to become a part of it.

On the other hand, right-leaning folks held large, peaceful Tea Party demonstrations in cities such as Atlanta, and San Antonio and an enormous gathering on the National Mall in Washington, D.C. According to print reports and television video evidence, as with Seattle Tea Party events I witnessed, which is also worth repeating, Tea Partiers left the areas cleaner than before they arrived.

Tea Party demonstrators are predominantly politically right of center but also include a number of independents as well as Democrats who wonder how the socialists stole their party. When the Tea Party hits the streets, a community will barely know the event is happening because they'll experience little or no disruption to city services.

In stark contrast, leftist demonstrators almost always require police presence, keeping cops from serving you. These social justices will intentionally snarl traffic, and, being the "guardians of the environment" they claim to be, they'll leave behind dead grass, damaged plants, and mountains of trash.

During patrol roll calls when officers hear about a Tea Party demonstration, it barely elicits a reaction. Officers know these crowds are not prone to violence or even civil disobedience. The Tea Party peaceably assembles no matter how many or few show up.

Ironically, it's when cops hear about a "peace," "antiviolence," or "antiwar" demonstration that cops become concerned they'll have to don all that hot, bulky riot gear. Odd that these leftist "peace" groups are so often militant while right-wing groups, more likely to support gun ownership, the police, and the military, are most often peaceful.

The distinction between peaceful and violent assembly is not a specious one. It makes all the difference. Many liberal city leaders allow violence to thrive, somehow finding radical participants illegal actions justified because of historical abuses. When law and order collapses, so does public safety.

Although I may oppose a particular cause, I ardently support the right to demonstrate *peacefully* for or against it. But when protesters start damaging property and posing a danger to other people, they spit on the U.S. Constitution they hide behind. They wish to enjoy a convolution of what they believe are their rights while denying actual rights to others. This common social justice ends-justify-the-means strategy also leads to de-policing. Violent demonstrators are rewarded for breaking the law while the cops are punished for enforcing it.

I'm not saying there isn't a time for civil disobedience. Nevertheless, property destruction and violence are not victimless acts of civil disobedience. They are crimes with victims. But there seems to be a new type of protester these days compared with their predecessors. Back in the 1960s, during the civil rights movement, Dr. Martin Luther King and his followers engaged in acts of civil disobedience. Police arrested them. However, the demonstrators committed no property destruction or violence. What they were fighting for was important enough to nonviolently break a law and then accept the consequences of their actions. The arrested offered no resistance as cops (most of them Southern Democrats—sorry, couldn't resist) beat, set dogs on, used fire hoses against, and dragged them off to jail.

These days, protesters engage in what they claim is civil disobedience and then, rather than accept the consequences of their actions, they whine and complain when police arrest them. Officers have to use force to overcome the protesters' defiance and then the protesters cry about injuries and going to jail.

I thought that was the purpose of civil disobedience: to get attention by breaking the law and then suffering the consequences? But I guess that's old-school thinking. I would never presume to speak for Dr. King. However, based on his words, the violent and aggressive behavior of many "civil rights" demonstrators today would likely cause him shame and embarrassment. If you won't accept my word, ask Dr. Alveda King, MLK's niece. Her uncle was so upset when she physically resisted arrest during a demonstration march he'd led that he let her sit in jail rather than bail her out, for not adhering to his nonviolence restrictions.

This story is a good note on which to end this discussion. It's not all about rights; it's also about responsibility. As much as you have the right to demonstrate and exercise your free speech, you have a social responsibility to not interfere with other people's rights. Someone else's speech is not "evil" or "hate" just because you don't like it.

Your "cause" is not so important that it trumps the U.S. Constitution and the provisions it codifies to ensure American liberty. And remember, that cop you are keeping occupied (no pun intended) may be needed to respond to your mom's house when someone's trying to break in. Before you participate in a potentially violent demonstration, ask yourself if it's worth the risk of calling out the riot police?

CHAPTER 14

COPS AFFECT REAL PEOPLE'S LIVES

This is a proverbial two-way street: it's important for cops to remember they are dealing with real people, like their own friends and families. It's equally important for people to realize that cops are also real people, like their own friends and families.

For cops, there's a danger when police and political leaders focus too much on what they consider law enforcement "productivity." Some only see productivity as arrests and traffic citations. Such activities can create the potential for police conducting law enforcement as a numbers competition that ignores that cops affect *real* people with *real* lives, especially with traffic stops, the most common police-public interaction.

Police act as society's insurance policy rather than as factory workers producing widgets. While proactive policing can be effective, police also need to be available when folks need them for emergencies. Cops need to strike a balance.

Police "productivity" should also include crime prevention activities. Here's what I mean: a cop who's having a quiet day might become more "productive" by increasing patrols in high burglary, high car prowl areas. But how is this productivity measured? Some bosses only want immediate, concrete numbers such as arrests and tickets. However, increased patrols lead to decreases in crimes and a commensurate decrease in those enforcement actions. This correlation needs to be in the "productivity" equation.

Rather than number of tickets an officer writes, how about a patrol car's mileage for the shift and the time spent in high-crime areas? Or an officer might conduct traffic emphasis in a neighborhood where speeding complaints have been high. This is expected of a diligent officer. You can measure this activity by fewer neighborhood complaints in the future.

But when people wonder if a cop stopped them because of arbitrary emphasis numbers, it can reduce a community's trust in its law enforcement. Policies like this can also lead to de-policing when community complaints increase and the cop's leaders then side with the complainants over the officers. This is the height of irony since it was the leaders who ordered the specific "productivity" increase.

Police productivity is a tricky thing. For example, how can you measure how many crimes an officer prevents? Just driving past a location where a criminal was about to commit a crime but stopped when he or she saw a patrol car is valuable. While crime prevention results can be gathered through statistics in the long run, in the short, no one can know for sure the crimes officers prevent with their presence. Isn't this still productivity on the officer's part?

Cops are competitive by nature, especially newer officers. They want to get the bad guys. They're eager to commit law enforcement because the "system" hasn't slapped them down yet (and, in case you haven't noticed, the current system is in a cop-slapping mood).

Sometimes officers fall into the numbers trap where they see even good people as statistics rather than folks who have real lives that a police officer's routine decisions affect. For example, a traffic citation comes with a monetary penalty, and a driver's insurance rates might increase, affecting a family for years. This cannot help law enforcement when people complain about police who are sent on an obvious revenue-raising mission instead of a public safety one.

Officers should always be motivated by public safety and not by personal aggrandizement. Let's say I head out to my district and do several things to keep my beat safer. Aside from arresting bad guys and writing tickets, I patrol the streets and alleys vigorously to deter crime. When I write a report, I position my patrol car to discourage unsafe driving. My motivation is to keep the area safe for the good people who live there without negatively affecting their quality of life. My impetus shouldn't be to lie in wait to *get* them so I can write more tickets than Officer Smith.

Now, if I went out intent on arresting a certain number of people or issuing a certain number of citations to outdo other officers, impress supervisors, or increase the city's coffers (yeah, like I cared about that), shouldn't my "productivity" be suspect in a country that prizes individual liberty? The people I served would have seen me as a petty tyrant instead of an officer there to protect and serve—and they would have been right.

Police actions become suspect when officers enforce laws to increase city treasuries rather than decrease crime. Cops shouldn't forget they're dealing with real people—people like their own families. This brings up another cop-public issue: most of the public are *not* the cops' own families. Cops need to care about people but not overly invest themselves emotionally. Cops couldn't do their jobs properly if they felt the same way about strangers as they do about their own friends and family. It's not emotionally healthy. Officers need to be objective. Emotional attachment, positive or negative, can interfere with an officer's neutrality and objectivity.

That said, officers shouldn't let objectivity and detachment turn to indifference. It's possible to give proper police services without emotions negatively affecting police decisions. A bit of empathy is a good thing. Cops have to keep in mind real people also have their life's stressors, e.g., debt, kids, school, work, marriage, illness, deaths, and so forth. And while these issues are no excuse for committing traffic or other infractions, officers should realize that citations can affect people in significant ways. Not only their finances but also the attitude they carry forward about all cops. Cops owe it to fellow officers to be aware of their demeanor when dealing with the public. I'm not talking about handling career scumbags with Nerf gloves. I'm talking about treating normally law-abiding people respectfully, reasonably, and fairly—as most cops do.

Some people deserve citations while others deserve warnings. Most reasonable people know when an officer is treating them unfairly. If an officer focuses on getting the highest stats, he or she is more likely to issue citations to violators when warnings might have been enough. Now, I'm not saying these officers are making illegal stops to cite drivers to achieve a certain number of tickets. They're not.

Their enforcement is still legal, as the drivers have committed legitimate infractions. But some of these offenses are for what officers refer to as "chippie"—minor—offenses that often call for warnings, not citations. The good relations that warnings foster are worth more than the negatives police suffer when a petty tyrant damages a good person's faith in the police by issuing a citation when a warning was enough.

Treating people fairly is a cop's responsibility to society and to his fellow police officers. And every person has a social responsibility to treat police officers respectfully. Each good person treated unfairly by a police officer will carry that destructive sentiment, and it may stain every other cop the person deals with from then on. People who refuse to respect police officers add to the anti-cop environment that increases de-policing.

You also need to realize the cops you're dealing with are also real people with friends, families, and life problems just like you. You need to understand the officer doesn't know you, can't read your mind, and wants to go home after shift. But this is a real person just like your father, mother, brother, or sister. Think about how you'd want your friend or relative to be treated under similar circumstances.

Of course, no one is happy to get a ticket. And even some normally reasonable people turn otherwise when cited. Hell, I'm retired, and good people I know still get upset when they tell me about that ticket they got from a cop. I'm still pissed off about the one I got. So, let's just treat each other, cops and drivers, like real people and not like ticket targets or caricatures of badge heavy brutes.

CHAPTER 15

COPS AS TAX COLLECTORS

D irty Harry stops a driver for a traffic violation. The driver says to Harry something to the effect of, "What...you need to make your quota?"

Harry, glancing down through dark sunglasses, coolly replies, "Oh, haven't you heard? We don't have quotas. I can write as many tickets as I want."

* * *

Police and political administrations around the country blather on about improving relations between their police officers and the community, all while instituting policies that result in the opposite. Why do law enforcement agencies and their jurisdictions do this so often?

One day, my wife told me she was driving through a 20-mph school zone, having proceeded after a red light turned green. She was behind other vehicles that had just turned left out of the high school driveway. Police were running radar up ahead, so she was cautious about her speed. As she passed the officer, he directed her to pull over.

As he walked to the car, she could tell he recognized her. She's a firefighter in the same area. She asked why he'd pulled her over. He said for "speeding" through a school zone. She was stunned. She was careful about her speed and could see the officer the entire time, *and* she was behind other drivers who were also driving at the legal limit.

"How fast does it say I was going?" she asked, glancing at his radar gun.

He said, "Twenty-one." And then he became silent and appeared embarrassed. The speed limit is normally 30 mph, but 20 mph when kids are present, which there weren't because students had just been released and the road and crosswalk is a very long driveway from the school.

The officer told her he'd give her a break that day and let her go with a verbal warning. My wife was incensed. I gave her crap about the fact she was actually over the limit—*practically racing*. In retrospect, the comment wasn't my smartest move, but that's another story. The fact is she is a safe driver and expected more fairness from officers enforcing traffic laws. Again, this created bad feelings, and for what benefit? *Ah*, read on.

My wife and I noticed that traffic enforcement continued in that area for weeks. You couldn't pass the location in the morning or early afternoon without seeing cars police had stopped. We assumed the school had complained about speeding drivers, so police were doing an emphasis enforcement. We figured wrong.

My wife was at work at the fire station when one of her cop friends visited. She told him about the officer who'd stopped her. He rolled his eyes and told her that the increased enforcement there was so the department could justify the expenditure for another traffic unit. The unintended consequences? She now resented a police administration that would enforce the law with such a perverted motivation. It put her at odds with police officers with whom she works so often and so closely. Many drivers probably felt like that after that two-week "fund-raising" effort.

Law enforcement purely for revenue raising, i.e., tax collecting, is unethical. When police enforce laws that enhance public safety, only then is it right and ethical. It serves to keep people safe. When law enforcement's true goal is to raise revenue, individuals who get swept up in the "tax sting," who previously had a positive view of police, may change their views of police to the negative. Don't they have a point?

In Ferguson, Missouri, where, as we all know, a police officer shot and killed a robbery and assault suspect, the DOJ arrived to investigate the "racist" cops. One ancillary issue the investigation alleged was that police were targeting minorities when conducting traffic enforcement.

The liberal media and DOJ jumped to conclusions that racism had to have been the reason officers issued citations and arrested minority drivers in Ferguson. One complaint is that the police department doesn't match the demographic makeup of the city. Most Ferguson police officers are white while the community they serve is mostly black. Can police departments force black candidates to apply? Some of Ferguson's officers *are* black, so hiring does not exclude qualified black applicants from becoming police officers.

In 2014, noted conservative pundit Ben Shapiro wrote for *Breitbart.com*, "The media's favorite game is to suggest that statistical correlation implies racist causation, even when there is no hard evidence to back that position." The leftist media and the DOJ set the narrative and then chase down only the facts that fit neatly into the script.

The cops don't set the policies. Local government does through its elected and appointed officials. The edicts they issue take effect, and what is the result? It seems often the individuals penalized under these policies are minorities. So, what do those who instituted the controversial policies in the first place do? They join in allegations that the cops must be racists.

Remember, cops don't favor many of these policies, such as impounding the cars of drivers stopped who had suspended licenses. Why are the "victims" of these policies often minorities? Because they tend to live in lower income areas and are more likely to default on tickets they can't afford, which results in a suspended driver's license status. Note that before Seattle police could tow a car, a driver had to have been stopped for a traffic violation and received a previous ticket he or she had not paid, resulting in a DWLS3 status.

There are other frustrating elements that damage police-community relations. One is recognizing that there is no one-size-fits-all approach to policing. Even well-meaning conservative law and order folks have a difficult time understanding the broad and diverse nature of police work. This is another reason the quasi-federalization of local police forces through bogus consent decrees is so bad for our country.

Not long ago, 2016 Republican presidential candidate Dr. Ben Carson appeared on a TV news program and commented on the state of police-community relations in America in light of the high-profile incidents in Ferguson and Baltimore. Carson said he believed cops should be embedded (reside) within their communities. He mentioned one cop in a neighborhood who doesn't have to bring a lunch because people invite the officer to eat with them. How *sweet*.

I don't mean to be sarcastic. I am a big fan of Dr. Carson, and I'm not saying it doesn't happen—neighborhood people invited me to lunch twice during my career. I'm only saying that, depending on your jurisdiction, you cannot count on it. Also, while the sentiment is well intended, it is an *Andy Griffith Show* view of American policing. It sounds nice and feels good. Who knows? It might work in some areas. But what politicians and other law enforcement theoreticians need to understand is in the real world there are practical considerations regarding cops living where they work.

In major cities such as New York, Chicago, or Detroit, working a beat in violent areas, officers run a high risk of bumping into the gangbanger he or she arrested last week if cops must live in areas in which they work. This could be perilous, especially while with a spouse or children. This is not theoretical. This happens. While off duty, most officers, if not all, have run into criminals they've handled on the job.

I remember a gang member in Seattle's Central District threatening not only an officer but also his family. Many officers have had similar experiences. I know officers who've had criminals show up at their homes—even in an outlying suburb many miles from the city where they work. Cops never know where they'll will run into someone they've arrested. In fact, in 2004, President George W. Bush signed the Law Enforcement Officers Safety Act (LEOSA) into law to address the risks unarmed cops faced while traveling out of state. Because of this law, qualified active duty and retired police officers can carry a concealed firearm in all 50 states.

Better police integration into their communities may be laudable. However, reality and practicality must temper the notion. Fantasy and political experimentation have no place in police work. There may be smaller towns here and there where Dr. Carson's example might work, but not necessarily in major cities or even their surrounding communities. At least not while the social justices, crisis entrepreneurs, and uncivil rights activists control things. I can only say I wish Dr. Carson's vision could come true. There is nothing a cop enjoys more than community support. If cops could only get the support of their political and department leaders, de-policing might be less of a worry.

No jurisdiction should reduce the honorable profession of law enforcement to that of tax collectors on wheels. The officer's job is to promote, maintain, and enhance public safety. It's to keep Peter from harming Paul, not to take money from Peter and Paul and Pauline and Paulette to buy some new gadget or fund a program. If police can't justify the necessity of an item without abusing residents, then logic tells me the thing may not be necessary. Manufacturing a public safety crisis specifically to institute an emphasis patrol for raising revenue is unethical, and playing games with people's time and money—and liberty—is downright immoral.

CHAPTER 16

MILITARIZATION

T he dark man in a suit and tie, a brown leather briefcase in his hand, stood behind a throng of agitators. Some were dressed as sea turtles, others as various strange characters, and some others were clad all in black and wearing masks.

The man was late for a meeting at Seattle's 1999 World Trade Organization convention. The crowd was pushing him back and would not let him go to the front of the line to speak with police. At one point he made a run for it, pinballing off demonstrators, before leaping over the front rows of the crowd into police lines. Mid-hurdle, his jacket flew open, exposing a holstered pistol. Once in the police lines, officers learned he was a foreign agent assigned to a dignitary's security detail.

Here was a man, a guest in our nation, charged with the responsibility of keeping another guest safe. And what were these American demonstrators doing? They were interfering with the man's right to go where he had every right to go as a peaceful and legal guest in America.

The man who had tumbled into the police line identified himself, and the cops let him go to his assignment. During the leap, the demonstrators had stolen the agent's briefcase and refused to return it. Not only were the demonstrators demanding protection from the Constitution they were violating but also they were petty thieves and bullies. What needed protection was that man's rights, not the crowd's criminal behavior.

* * *

I stood on a skirmish line near the Four Seasons Hotel during the WTO riots. Throughout the week, I'd seen thousands of demonstrators exercising what they believed were their First Amendment rights while infringing on other's right to free movement. I'd seen foreign delegates prevented from attending conferences they had every right to attend. These people were guests in our country. Later, near my position, a demonstrator threw a brick that struck an officer in the head. Demonstrators tossed bags of urine, rocks, and Molotov cocktails at police. I also saw rioters set dumpsters ablaze adjacent occupied buildings.

After seeing what happens when a group of peaceful protesters turns into a violent mob, I understood what militarization of the police meant and why communities are better off when it happens. While standing in that police line, a captain I knew well came up from behind and tapped me on the shoulder. I'm sure he could see I was on edge because we were a line of only twenty-five or so uniformed officers facing thousands of angry demonstrators. Just before the captain tapped my shoulder, I noticed the crowd had become more docile. People had lowered their clubs and dropped their projectiles. Some walked away; others lingered—peacefully. I was about to learn why.

The captain said, "Look behind you." I turned to find hundreds of SPD officers in riot gear, SWAT officers in their armored vehicles, and swarms of National Guardsmen and their vehicles staged behind us. I can tell you that was the sweetest "militarization" *I'd* ever seen. The effect it had on the angry crowd was palpable. There's a lot of talk about de-escalation these days. Well, this de-escalated the potential for violence—big time.

* * *

Militarization—referring to tools, weapons, and vehicles obtained by police departments from federal military surplus programs—is an interesting word because it conjures images of what some people perceive to be the worst aspect of the military—the violence. Perhaps they're not even associating the word *militarization* with the American military but with a third-world despot's armed forces. Still, the stigma attaches, even for police supporters. (Good people often have a difficult time believing bad stuff can happen—cops suffer no such illusions.) Despite the military's continual high placement topping Gallup's list of most respected American institutions, when many people think of something becoming *militarized*, often it connotes negative images. It's as if something peaceful and wholesome has suddenly become violent and evil.

To understand it, it's best to consider the word *militarize* and its implications on a personal level. For example, if you practice martial arts or buy pepper spray, a Taser, or a firearm for protection, haven't you *militarized* yourself? When cops militarize, they are acting to protect the public and themselves, often based upon incidents that demonstrate the need.

Still, the tools should fit the law enforcement circumstances. An equipped, surplus U.S. Army Humvee wouldn't be necessary for a traffic stop on an unarmed eighty-year-old woman. However, it would be a great tool to deploy when facing an SUV load of armed bank robbers, skinheads, or Black Panthers.

The problem with utilizing the word *militarism,* as opposed to something like *police-ism*, is that the police are already a para*military* organization. They employ military tactics and command structures, use weapons, and wear body armor. When people complain about police departments becoming militarized, they forget that police *are* de facto militarized. The problem is some folks live in a la-la land where they believe police will never confront situations that demand increased militarization.

Here's a basic example of a community's need for "militarization." In the mid-1990s, a Seattle police officer was working a uniformed off-duty job, providing security for a North Seattle bank. A man robbed the bank, fled, and the officer pursued the suspect on foot. The officer carried a department-issued revolver. The suspect had a semiautomatic pistol. That's six rounds for the cop versus the robber's up to fifteen or more rounds. And the bad guy's semiauto is easier to reload than a revolver.

Following this incident, under Police Chief Norm Stamper, most Seattle police officers transitioned from revolvers to semiautomatic sidearms. Some argue this change "militarized" the SPD, while police supporters and cops argued this improvement enhanced both officer and public safety. With the increased firepower, critics argued that cops would get into more shootings and masses of innocents would fall in a hail of gunfire. The Wild West scenarios the social justices warned about never happened.

Remember the North Hollywood, California, shootout in 1997? Bank robbers donned body armor and shot at police with automatic weapons. During a nearly forty-five-minute gun battle, the duo had cops outgunned, firing over 1,100 rounds. These guys avoided or absorbed the cops' bullets and kept coming. Talk about fighting zombies. This was a horror movie come to life for responding officers.

At the time, some police departments, even larger agencies, were still issuing six-shot revolvers to their officers. Officers could carry additional rounds, but reloading a revolver, even with speed loaders, can be a time-consuming, clumsy task. And even for officers who were armed with semiautomatic pistols, trying to face down rifle-wielding criminals is more than daunting.

Because of this incident on that crazy February day back in 1997, the Los Angeles Police Department (LAPD) and other agencies nationwide, including the SPD, implemented rifle programs. The programs trained officers to use the AR-15 semiautomatic rifle during high-intensity incident responses. I'm sure the officers involved in the North Hollywood incident would have welcomed all the "militarization" they could have gotten on that unforgettable day. The Hollywood shootout is an example of an incident that led to cops becoming militarized. Who would oppose such an increase to enhance public safety?

The argument shouldn't be that police departments are becoming more militarized. The argument should be that, generally, there isn't anything wrong with acquiring improved technologies. After all, isn't that what militarization is?

People need to view these issues in their proper context. To have Barney Fife patrol Mayberry in an armored vehicle armed with a Glock Model 22 on his hip and an AR-15 slung over his shoulder might be overkill. Still, incidents requiring those tools happen even in Mayberry.

In 2014, Alton Nolen, a knife-wielding Islamist terrorist, decapitated a woman at the Vaughan Foods distribution center in Moore, Oklahoma. Another employee, an armed—*militarized*—off-duty reserve deputy sheriff, shot the suspect before the lone terrorist could injure or kill anyone else. Good guys with guns stop bad guys with guns.

An agency must engage in a balancing act dependent upon the frequency or likelihood of such highly violent incidents. Officers in larger cities are much more likely to experience such incidents. Most see these high-risk, low-frequency events as prudent reasons to increase their military capabilities. Larger cities are only prudent to deploy these tools closer to the front lines rather than holding them in reserve. On the other hand, Mayberry might be sensible to have higher capacity tools ready but to hold them in reserve, yet easily available, in case the unthinkable happens.

Here is a personal anecdote about so-called militarization. I live in a small town eight or so miles north of the Seattle city limits. Many years ago, an incident occurred that helped me appreciate how people might react negatively to police militarization. When my youngest son was twelve years old, he and his friends were in the woods that run behind our houses playing "army," with fatigues, helmets, and their paintball guns. We live in a quiet, typical American, semirural/suburban neighborhood of one- and two-story, single-family homes.

One of the neighbors saw them and called the police. Apparently she thought some nascent, diminutive militia was conducting black ops in the woods. My wife happened to look out the window and saw a patrol car from our small-town police department appear at the end of the street. An officer exited his patrol car armed with an AR-15 (military-style rifle) slung over his shoulder, suspended over his chest.

I can see why any reasonable person might see this as overkill, considering the "suspects" were only kids playing in the woods. But any reasonable cop understands that a responding officer doesn't know for sure that it's kids playing. With no backup officers arrived yet, the officer was not going to bet his life on it being kids playing.

While kids playing is the likely scenario, the officer has to consider other possibilities and must be prepared, just in case. Adjacent to the woods is a middle school. Is it unheard of to have a heavily armed suspect assault a small-town grade school? It is rare but it happens. The cops may hope for the probable, but they have to be prepared for the possible—even the seemingly impossible.

Some argue that militarization alone amounts to the police department's provocation of the community. I have a hard time wrapping my mind around this concept. I'll concede it's possible for police to intentionally or unintentionally provoke a crowd or person to hostility. However, this is the exception and not the rule. Everyone should remember that cops are not psychics—at least, I don't remember being issued tarot cards with my badge and gun. Cops go where they are dispatched. Generally, a crowd's behavior precipitates the level of police response. When the crowd shows signs people are about to commit property damage or other violence, police will increase or intensify their level of response. Again, the key word here is *response*. The cops are primarily reactionary, responding to where they are needed.

If a cop posted on a riot line lashes out and strikes a peaceful but mouthy demonstrator, this can legitimately provoke a crowd to violence. In my two-plus decades of coppin' in one of the most protest-prone capitals in America, I have never seen or even heard of an officer intentionally provoking a crowd to hostility. This doesn't mean it doesn't or hasn't happened. But it seems rare, considering the number of demonstrations I've worked and have discussed with other officers.

On the contrary, I've seen hundreds of protesters taunt officers and attempt to turn innocuous actions into provocations. I remember a demonstrator yelling at an officer for lowering his helmet's face shield. He seemed to view this prudent officer safety precaution a "provocation."

Look, it's only prudent that police arrive at violent demonstrations already clad in riot gear, riding in surplus military vehicles, ready to deploy gas and other nonlethal crowd-control measures. Cops don't have phone booths in which to make a five-second change of clothing. If some people see this police response to a riot or potential riot as provocation, it's obvious they were intent on committing violence from the outset and needed an excuse.

Such a show of force might offend the uninitiated and ignorant. However, it's another thing to be offended by a police response that matches the threat and violence potential. A massive show of force can be a potent deterrent that de-escalates and prevents violence. It doesn't cause it. And when police and city leaders refuse to use cops properly to stop violence and property damage, criminal morale increases as police officer morale plummets. Not to mention, de-policing also increases (okay, so I mentioned it).

FEDERALIZATION

Although we've discussed social justice versus equal justice, I mentioned previously we'd go into more detail in chapter 17 because social justice is the Trojan horse within which liberal federal, state, and local governments have conducted the quasi-federalization of local police. So, welcome to chapter 17. The insidiousness of social justice, as defined by leftists, is that liberal government uses it to insinuate itself where it does not belong. One of those places is local law enforcement training and policy.

I should mention that even though there now appears to be a pro–law enforcement federal administration in power, the damage done in the past should still be discussed. Many state and local governments remain politically left and continue to exhibit anti-police tendencies.

First, federalization and federalism, though they sound similar, are two distinct concepts. Seth P. Waxman put forth the definition of federalism in a lecture he gave at the University of Kansas School of Law:

> *"Federalism" refers, of course, to the principle that sovereign power should not vest in a single potentate or government, but rather should be dispersed across all levels of government. "[S]plit[ting] the*

atom of sovereignty," as Justice Kennedy aptly put it, is perhaps the most innovative contribution our Founding Fathers made to the principles of democratic governance.

Federalization, on the other hand, would mean transferring local law enforcement authority to the federal government. Lance Eldrige, writing on PoliceOne.com, discussed federalization. While he doesn't believe federalization would be done quickly in America, he wrote about the Obama administration's attempts to incrementally "federalize" local departments. "He [Obama] said that we—where the meaning of 'we' is <u>federal officials</u>—should work with 'local law enforcement to improve policing techniques to eliminate bias.' Remarks from Attorney General Eric Holder regarding Arizona's new immigration control law reflect the Administration's belief that local law enforcement officers routinely violate federal civil rights standards with little regard for ethics or the Constitution."

Today's liberals oppose federalism and embrace federalization because they need a strong central government to pursue their big government agendas. It cannot be emphasized enough how the federalization of local police departments has also led to de-policing. With its disparaging of excellent police departments and the work their officers do, how could it not?

Our founders feared a too powerful federal government. Thus, they created a system whereby the states and the people retained the freedom necessary to conduct their daily activities without unwarranted federal government intrusion. The U.S. Constitution gave the federal government limited authority primarily to provide security from foreign threats and to preserve Americans' individual liberty. In fact, as an insurance policy, they included the Tenth Amendment, which gave powers not specifically delegated to the federal government to the states or the people, respectively. Over the last seventy-five years, the federal government, with the help of liberal Supreme Courts, has corrupted the letter, intent, and spirit of that amendment. Evidence of the increasing federal government intrusion into the everyday lives of Americans is pervasive. Can you say Obamacare?

Ever since the states ratified the Constitution, the federal government has grown—especially after the nineteenth century—and it continues to grow. Hopefully, the new administration can stanch that trend. Our government has insinuated itself into all aspects of Americans' lives, into places our founders neither intended nor imagined. Thanks to the policies of the Obama administration and its politicizing of the DOJ, the federal government was exerting more influence over local law enforcement than ever. The feds committed financial extortion by making cities spend precious financial resources trying to comply with federal consent decrees.

Once embedded within a police agency, the feds pressure cities to engage in political indoctrination dressed up as law enforcement training (not that Seattle needed much pressure). They threaten to withhold federal funds if police departments fail to comply with federal edicts. I once had to go through two identical hazmat [hazardous material] training sessions over two consecutive days. That was the only way the city could comply with federal requirements to receive funding. The training was worthwhile—*once*. What isn't worthwhile is the waste of time and money to qualify for federal funds. I should have been back patrolling my beat instead of attending a duplicate class.

These nonsensical regulations and fraudulent consent decrees demonstrate the federal government's attempt to federalize local law enforcement. Rather than overtly take them over, they covertly coerce local jurisdictions to comply by attaching strings to funding and threatening its loss for noncompliance. This is another example of the liberal ends-justify-the-means rule followed in Washington, D.C.

* * *

It is one thing for liberal city leaders to overtly push politically skewed law enforcement training. It is another thing when local governments attempt to covertly indoctrinate their police officers with political ideology disguised as police training.

Think I'm exaggerating? Consider Seattle. As I mentioned, for the past several years, the city has forced its cops to attend supposed police "training." During these classes, instructors use only leftist sources for "educational" materials. They emphasize such traditional "law enforcement" themes as *white privilege* and *social justice*: both ideological left catchphrases. If this were to happen in reverse, the left would never tolerate it.

After learning in class that your city government officials believe you are a racist, even unconsciously, and that your police actions are racially biased, how willing would you be to enforce the law against minority offenders? Even conservative black cops are taught they are racist—against their own race! But that's the point, isn't it? Sowing division is a hallmark of the new left. This is de-policing.

Today, cops across America confront dangers they never imagined back when someone special pinned those gleaming badges onto their crisp, new uniforms. These unimagined perils do not come from the thugs on the streets. Cops expect human tragedy and criminal mayhem. The fisticuffs, pursuits, car crashes, and even the rare gunfights are among a cop's occupational hazards. Political indoctrination is not.

Ironically, the real danger comes from liberal bullies at city hall and police headquarters. Leaders issue leftist-inspired policies that put their police officers at unnecessary mental and physical risk. Remember, when leftist politicians want to enforce their social justice policies and laws against the public, they will need the cops to do it. How will liberal governments attempt to get conservative cops to do their dirty work? In part, by federalizing them.

When my wife pinned my badge onto my uniform twenty-five-years ago, I imagined the things I might confront. But in all my mental wanderings, I never imagined that one day a mayor or police chief would order me to submit to partisan, political indoctrination. I also never imagined they'd use their official powers to abridge police officers' First Amendment free speech rights. But they did and they do.

Often, police officers who espouse other than the leftist party line are told to shut up, surreptitiously retaliated against, and forced to go to political "re-education" classes. Meanwhile, police officers on what the left considers the "correct" side of issues even get away with wearing their uniforms and using department equipment to demonstrate that support. Many years ago, I rode a police bike during Seattle's Gay Pride Parade as part of a protection detail for Chief Norm Stamper. The parade was saturated with signs promoting all manner of left-wing causes and Democrat political candidates. Anyone think the chief would have participated in an equally right-wing event? I certainly didn't see any chiefs at any Seattle Tea Party gatherings.

Local government spreads the social justice infection. First, liberal bureaucrats, administrators, and politicians contaminate the police department's lexicon with leftist terminology. Through notices, directives, and training bulletins they insert terms like the seemingly innocuous *social justice*. In classes they spout liberal notions such as *white privilege*. And what about the ridiculous memos proclaiming terms such as *brown bag*, more recently, and *Wite-Out*, back in the '90s, as racist? I'll explain in chapter 25. And then the federal government comes in, declares cops racists, and capitalizes on the fabricated public outrage.

As I mentioned before, but it bears repeating, this omnipresent term "social justice" may sound like a noble pursuit. But when government uses it, it is the proverbial wolf in sheep's clothing. It creeps in carefully and waits for an opportunity to pounce.

Although the concept of social justice is now pervasive in the public discourse, again, it's often difficult to discuss because there's no universal definition. For example, an SPD's Media Relations Unit sergeant once challenged me. He argued that even Catholicism promotes social justice. This is true; after all, as mentioned in chapter 2, a Catholic priest coined the term. But again, the Catholic Church cannot use the force of law to compel a person to do something to advance their version of social justice, but government can. This is a profound distinction.

How is social justice connected to federalization? The left's quest for social justice attempts to use a liberal federal government hammer to bludgeon cities into submission. I repeat, social justice and equal justice are incompatible. The social justices move ahead with policies as if the Constitution's guarantee of equal justice can be muted, suspended, or ignored.

In my *Guardian* articles, I repeatedly asked for anyone in Seattle's ivory tower to explain how social justice, as leftist government defines it, can share space with equal justice as the Constitution defines it. Not one official has ever even attempted to answer. Why not? It's obvious. The two forms of justice are, pardon the pun, not equal. While social justice deals with people as members of groups, equal justice is about the individual. Consider these sources:

- The *Fourteenth Amendment*, Section 1, equal protection clause:

  "*...nor shall any state deny to any **person** within its jurisdiction the equal protection of the laws.*"

- *Black's Law Dictionary* definition of Equal Protection of the Laws:

  "***Individual's*** *right of access to courts equal treatment under the law.*"

- Also from *Black's Law Dictionary*:

  What is an INDIVIDUAL?
  "*As a noun, this term denotes a single **person** as distinguished from a group or class...*"

Equal justice for every individual, every "single person," should be the guiding principle in any criminal or civil legal matter. The Declaration of Independence ideal that "all men are created equal" espouses this. The Fourteenth Amendment's equal protection clause further augments this American paradigm. The problem is those on the left not only feel some groups suffered discrimination but also that those groups should enjoy special (unequal) treatment under the law to make up for historical transgressions. It's beyond a doubt some groups suffered under past governmental policies. But liberals feel these wrongs can be mitigated by treating individuals within those groups differently *today* based on the group's "oppression credentials" and regardless of an individual's personal history.

Let's say we suspended equal protection and we all agreed that specific groups should receive special treatment. Who decides when a group has achieved restitution, restoration—revenge? How far back in history should we go? How do we correlate a person's DNA percentages of race and ethnicity proportions with worthiness for benefits? As we discussed in an earlier chapter, how do we judge a person who is 50 percent white European and 50 percent black African? What if the 50 percent black individual comes from an area where slaves were never transported to America or from black ancestors who actually sold other blacks into slavery? What about those who may look partly black (or think they do) but aren't black at all? (Can you say Rachel Dolezal?) What about the black descendants of *black* slave owners? Blew your mind, right? Pardon the pun, which I think was inevitable, but discussions on race are not all black and white (there, I said it). I'd encourage everyone to read David Barton's eye-opening *American History in Black & White*. It doesn't diminish one whit the horrors that happened to black slaves, but it'll have you wondering what the heck teachers have been teaching—or not teaching. He places racial history in a much needed social and historical context.

Assessing racial percentages sounds silly, right? Yeah...that's because it is. Not what some people's ancestors suffered but how the left exploits it. Since equal justice for all is the ultimate aim for conservatives and libertarians—as it is, or used to be, ostensibly, for the liberals—let's attempt making what's possible better and leave creating a Utopia to God.

CHAPTER 18

LIBERTY COP

This topic needs a preface because, as with some other chapters, it doesn't deal directly with de-policing. However, it does deal with a method of policing that, if done, would make de-policing less likely. Rather than the current leftist contamination of police departments, law enforcement should be done with a more libertarian/conservative focus. This is my view of how law enforcement should be conducted—you know, if I were God. I noticed over the course of my career that most times when there was contention between cops and their leaders, it was due to some kind of liberal BS. So, instead of liberal let's try libertarian. This chapter's mission is to convey how a more libertarian view of law enforcement can reduce the tensions between cops and their communities.

The recent BLM, cop-hating sentiment aside, there are legitimate issues ordinary people have with cops. Many times these arise when government takes too heavy a hand and uses cops to enforce unfair laws or laws unfairly. For example, it's true the Ferguson "hands up, don't shoot" scenario never happened. But reports of complaints by Ferguson residents of local government using police to raise revenue through strict traffic enforcement seems to have merit. This policy drives a wedge between a community and its law enforcement.

When law enforcement follows a libertarian philosophy, using cops for revenue raising is anathema. A cop's rightful duty is to protect people and their property from those who would harm, steal from, or defraud them. Cops wouldn't be playing mommy and daddy, citing people for not wearing helmets or seat belts, smoking within twenty-five feet of a store's doorway, holding a cellphone to their ear while driving, or not having litter bags in their cars. These laws have cops enforcing laws against people who are harming no one. A more libertarian police department would better facilitate people freely pursuing their happiness.

So, what is libertarianism? Like social justice, it seems to have multiple definitions. However, there are some constants. One is a strict adherence to limited government and individual liberty. Let's take a look.

* * *

The man thunders into the parking lot on his gleaming, black-and-chrome Harley-Davidson. He glides through a parking space onto the sidewalk. He rolls to a stop near the meeting hall's front entrance. He kills the motor, sets his kickstand, and leans the bike to rest. He dismounts and scans the lot. He doffs his helmet and places it on a rearview mirror. He saunters toward the open front door.

Inside the modest room a confident-looking woman stands at a long table, arranging the coffee urn, cups, and cookie trays. She turns toward the entrance where the leather-jacketed man's silhouette dominates the doorway. The placard on the refreshments table reads "Eastside Libertarian Club." The woman smiles. And before turning back to her work, she says, "Welcome. Please, take a seat."

The man hesitates a moment. Then he walks toward the rows of neatly arranged folding chairs. Before sitting, he turns to the woman, grins, and says, "Don't tell me what to do."

* * *

I love telling this old libertarian joke. Oh, and don't think the irony is lost on me that I'd end up making my living as a cop, *tell-*

ing folks what to do. As a libertarian cop, I may have thought more about certain law enforcement tasks than officers who were strictly Republican, Democrat, independent, or even apolitical. For example, enforcing politically motivated, nanny-state laws concerned me. Fortunately, I often could use my discretion so as not to compromise my integrity when forced to confront such violations. I arrived at a formula that worked, and I stuck with it during my daily patrol activities.

This was the general formula I used for traffic enforcement:

> Was the violation intentional or inadvertent?
> Was the violation inherently dangerous?
> Was the violator contrite?
> Did the violator accept responsibility for the infraction?

Depending on the various factors (officers have to decide for themselves regarding the violator's sincerity), I'd decide on the level of enforcement:

> The violation was minor, inadvertent, and put no one at imminent risk. The driver was contrite and accepted responsibility. *This driver likely deserved a warning.*
>
> The violation was intentional but put no one at imminent risk. The driver was contrite and accepted responsibility. *I may or may not have cited.*
>
> The violation was intentional and not imminently dangerous. The driver was not contrite and was an irresponsible jerk. *Welcome to ticket-ville.*
>
> The violation was intentional and unsafe. *Yes, he'd also be welcomed to our little citation village.*
>
> A driver commits an inadvertent, unintentional, but inherently dangerous violation. *The driver may be contrite, but the act was too dangerous to not have it enforced by citation.*

None of this is written in stone. Every officer establishes his or her own formula. As with other aspects of law enforcement, circumstances can change as quickly as Seattle's weather. Officers must deal with the situation and the facts at hand.

For libertarian cops—all cops, application of constitutional principles is not theoretical. Cops have to apply them daily—in the real world. Sometimes they have to compromise where and when they can when laws infringe on liberty. For example, I don't support nanny-state laws such as those mandating helmet and seat belt use. I don't oppose their use, just their *required* use. I mean, come on, my mother stopped dressing me when I was six. I used my discretion and tended not to cite for such infractions. After stopping drivers for moving violations who also wore no seat belt, following the appropriate enforcement for the moving violations, I'd warn them they could not count on getting similar discretion from other officers for not buckling up.

However, I wouldn't hesitate to back an officer who chose to enforce such "soft tyranny" violations because the onus is on the people to change nanny laws—if they want to. While such laws go against the spirit of our Declaration and Constitution, they're not against the letter of these two documents because localities may pass their own laws. States and local governments may enact such laws so long as people don't mind another link welded into the chain of soft oppression. It's sad when governments shackle Americans with soft tyrannical laws, but it's pathetic when Americans vote for their own bondage.

Sometimes the violations on people's liberty are more blatant. Before his unsuccessful reelection bid, former Seattle mayor Greg Nickels pronounced what amounted to yet another "royal edict," attempting to ban firearms from city parks and community centers. This is so blatantly unconstitutional it would be comical if he and his fellow social justices hadn't been so serious. Some infringements on liberty are nuanced. However, there can be no compromise with transparently unconstitutional acts such as a mayor abridging gun rights. It would be the same as prohibiting a protester from carrying a sign in a public place because the mayor doesn't like the cause. Federal and state constitutions must always be upheld. Officers must not cross the line into enforcing explicitly unconstitutional laws, whether violating the First or Second, or any, amendment, and must be prepared to deal with that decision before the situation arises.

Local liberal governments are learning well the lessons of Barack Obama and his penchant for ruling by executive order when things didn't go his way in Congress or the courts. Aside from the former Seattle mayor's antigun attempt, Washington governor Jay Inslee decided to suspend capital punishment by executive fiat. *Abracadabra!* It's like magic. The will of the people be damned. I guess Governor Inslee doesn't trust Washingtonians to vote his way, so he just leaves them out of a decision that is rightly theirs.

It's true that America has just voted for a populist Republican to lead our national government. This seems to be a good thing for law enforcement so far. I suspect it will continue. Nevertheless, Washington and other states and local communities still have to contend with the accomplished social justices their liberal voters have reelected locally. By unilaterally suspending the state's duly legislated death penalty (sometimes imposed on cop killers), the governor demonstrated the Democrats' contempt for laws they don't like.

This is similar to the contempt the left seems to have for police officers. The left doesn't grasp what it's like for officers on the streets, so they condemn the work cops do. When the average person reviews a high-profile, use of force incident, they mentally play out the violent scenarios. But in their minds, the pieces fit neatly in place and situations always work out for the best. They can't imagine how an officer could have acted in "*that*way." How easy it all went—well, only after the fact and in the mind's eye. Police officers live out incidents in stark reality, with all the unexpected distractions and nuances that come crashing down on them. Rarely does any police incident involve exactly what a dispatcher initially broadcasted.

Another facet of police work is cops often deal with the same people, repeatedly. I once had car prowls in my district increase to over fifty in one week—from only three the week before—following the release from jail of a prolific auto prowler. One criminal can commit an awful lot of crime. He was the first suspect who'd ever run from me. Problem was, I didn't know why he ran. I was a rookie, newly on patrol, when he darted across a park road in front of my car, glanced at me, and then took off like an urban jackalope. Police were always chasing him but rarely catching him because every time he saw a cop, he ran like he'd just stolen something, which he probably had. Later, I learned what an extraordinary thief this guy was. He was from a family of "frequent fliers." They were always calling 911 to solve their problems, switching places between victim and suspect on each call, expecting the government to *fix it*. Which brings up another libertarian point: government dependence. Libertarianism rejects institutionalized, individual dependence on government.

People dependent on government grow accustomed to calling upon it to remedy even minor problems. If they have a stomachache, they call the fire department. If their kids won't do the dishes, turn off the lights, or finish their meals, they call the police. (Yes, this happens.) A political philosophy that conditions people to summon the government for their every need is insidious. This is because liberals can't give people stuff (in exchange for votes) unless they can convince people they need stuff and aren't able to get it for themselves. It's the good liberal's job to convince people they are needy, that only the government can fill that need, and to keep them that way.

It doesn't help when local governments order their police to respond to non-police calls. It encourages people to call 911 for frivolous reasons. You remember the woman in Florida who called the police because McDonald's ran out of Chicken McNuggets? I have many personal examples I could use, but this one comes directly from a screenshot of my patrol car's computer terminal I saved. In my call queue from December 2011 was the following, verbatim: "C COMP IN DISPUTE W/13 YR OLD DAUGHTER. SHE IS REFUSING

TO GET INTO HER CAR. DAUGHTER IS IN THE HOUSE."
Yes, I really got dispatched to this call. *People*...this is not a police
matter! Police should never have been dispatched.

When I was a kid, after my father abandoned our family, we
were what most would consider poor, at least on paper. Mom did
a good job of not letting us realize how poor we actually were. And
though she temporarily received public assistance, things like gov-
ernment-surplus food before the days of food stamps, she never got
the government dependency mindset. Born in Paris at the beginning of World War II, she gained an early appreciation for self-reliance, growing up in a postwar, devastated but rebuilding, Europe.
Children often had to pitch in by getting jobs to contribute to household incomes.

My friends' American parents seemed to be of a similar nature,
perhaps because they were the children of Depression-era parents.
In my lower working class, white but ethnically diverse neighborhood, calling the police or fire department was rare. Police and fire
departments were for *real* emergencies. People handled most crises
themselves. I'm not saying that's always right; it's just the way it was.

One time, our neighbor in the apartment next door called the
police after a rare burglary. My mother also called the police only
one time I can remember. She heard a noise in the kitchen closet.
Something or someone was dragging paper bags stored there into a
hole in the floor. Mom thought someone was trying to break in from
the cellar.

The officer arrived, investigated, and determined the burglar was
a rat. Those are my only two childhood memories of police responses
to my neighborhood. Well, other than to chase us little hoodlums
around for our mostly benign mischief making. But I don't think
anyone called the cops for that; it was just a part of their fun, too.

The reality is we have to safeguard our liberty and fight for the
freedoms we've lost, but let's keep our feet planted firmly on the
ground. A libertarian view of law enforcement, where police protect
people from criminals and not from their own adult decisions, would

enhance police-community relations. Police must not be misused for political social engineering. Liberals need to figure out that they are setting cops up as the bad guys in situations where it is not necessary. Maybe they have figured it out and don't care. If the social justices keep on with their social engineering, bad relations between cops and their communities will thrive, and the environment for de-policing will forever plague American society. Or worse, the only people willing to become cops will be those that don't mind being used as tools of an oppressive government.

CHAPTER 19

GOOD IDEAS VERSUS GOOD LAWS

My grandmother was fond of this expression: "There should be a law!" She'd shout this after witnessing an offense either on TV or in real life. My once-formidable grandmother, who'd raised three children during the Nazi occupation of Paris, died at ninety-four years old. A lucid mind hadn't followed her healthy body into old age. But that lament remained in her arsenal to the end.

One time, she saw kids skateboarding on the sidewalk near a grocery store. After casting them a sneer intended to knock them off their skateboards, she scowled and said, "Those things are too dangerous. There should be a law."

My grandmother often equated a "good idea" with a good law, as if one naturally led to the other. Too many Americans renounce their liberty, their birthright, when they share the viewpoint that a "good" idea is de facto a good law.

What "good" comprises a good law is often subjective. Rather than good, perhaps "appropriate" would be more accurate. Whether a law is appropriate is objective. Is a law appropriate for the situation it deals with? People shouldn't murder other people, so there is a law against it—appropriate. However, you've heard about government officials wishing to outlaw certain foods. Among others, two targets are the trans fats and salt used in restaurants. Former New York City mayor Mike Bloomberg led this crusade. He also turned the large soft drink into a controlled substance. The audacity of government paternalism is mind blowing. Is it appropriate for one adult to tell another adult, or another adult's children, what or how much of a legal food to eat or drink? If you feel it is, maybe you need to reevaluate your feelings about liberty versus big government intrusion into personal decisions.

In a TV spot I saw, a margarine company cites a new law in Denmark similarly prohibiting trans fats. Beautiful, happy, and healthy Danes frolic about in their social-democratic Utopia. The announcer then comments on how Denmark's new anti-trans fat law is "good." Perhaps, eating foods without trans fats is good, but a law prohibiting it offends individual liberty. It's certainly not pro-choice. I thought the left was all about *choice*? I thought a woman's body was her own? When aborting a baby, yes, but I guess not when guzzling a 32-ounce soda pop.

It's a pathetic argument that Americans should do anything just because another country does it. I can hear my grandmother now: "*If the Danes jumped off a bridge, would you do it?*" The Danes may be a wonderful people, but they are Danes, not Americans. Danes derive from an ethnicity; Americans derive from an idea. (I recommend watching U2 singer Bono's comments during a Georgetown University speech regarding America as an idea on YouTube.) Although we are allies and friends and share many cultural traits with the Danes, they've evolved into a highly taxed European society of less than six million (about the population of Wisconsin) somewhat homogeneous, people. This does not describe America.

Some folks acknowledge no difference between a good idea and a good law. Like my grandmother, they believe the two notions are interchangeable. If something's a good idea, why not make it a law? Well, only if the social justices think it's good. Many Americans believe it's a good idea not to have an abortion—even many so-called pro-choice people believe this now that science is catching up to the issue. But do many progressives feel outlawing abortion would be a good law? I bet they don't.

It may be a good idea to restrict trans fats from your diet. Hell, it may be a great idea. But who is best suited to make that decision for you, government or you? This is where the crux of the argument lies. As Ronald Reagan said, "When government expands, liberty contracts." Too many laws are born of liberal folks wanting other folks to live life as the liberals think is proper, even if by government force.

Every time a "good idea" law takes effect, government expands and your liberty shrinks. You are less free with every stroke of a social justice's pen. As previously mentioned, these laws include bicycle and motorcycle helmet laws, seat belt laws, many anti-smoking laws, as well as trans fat and other food and drink bans. People may feel these mandates and bans are "good ideas," but is mandating or prohibiting something that has long been legal—for someone's own *good*—a "good" law? I don't just say no. I say, HELL NO!

As for antismoking laws proliferating across our country, I'm one of those who personally benefit from the law. I don't like the smoke stench clinging to my clothes and hair when I come home after a night out. However, how can any liberty-loving American support government dictating to business owners what legal activity they can allow within their own establishments? To be intellectually honest and consistent, you can't.

Smoking tobacco products is legal in America—so far, anyway. Business owners should be free to allow it if that's what their customers want. I may choose not to go there, but that's my problem—and the owners', not government's. Adam Smith's invisible hand will take care of this in the marketplace. If enough people stop patronizing a business because it's choking with cigarette smoke, the owners will likely change their policies. Cash flow creates a significant motivation.

The most common retort from social justices on the smoking issue seems to be, "I have a right not to breathe in secondhand smoke." Well, you do, within reason. But who put a gun to your head and forced you into a smoke-fogged restaurant? People seem to forget something: no one is forced to patronize that establishment. The social engineers breeze past this fact. Logic and reason offends their sensibilities as much as the cigarette smoke. The marketplace is the best—and fairest—regulator.

I should mention that employees of establishments where people are allowed to smoke would have the strongest argument against working in such an environment. But, even in those cases, those people chose to work at that bar or restaurant. And, they choose whether to remain.

America is a nation where individual liberty and limited government are culturally preeminent. America has a population of well over three hundred million diverse people. America's experiment with self-government and individual liberty has propelled it to become the greatest world power—militarily, economically, and culturally—in human history. America, today, is the sole superpower on earth. What, in 1999, French foreign minister Hubert Vedrine elevated to a "hyperpower."

Part of how America got here was by focusing on appropriate laws, protecting people from criminal harm, and then letting people decide for themselves what is or is not a good idea. Although, sometimes the two overlap. As I mentioned earlier, a law against murder is appropriate, but it also happens to be a good idea. So, while all good, appropriate, laws are also good ideas, not all good ideas are good laws. Let's think critically when these issues come up, keeping each in its proper place. Subjectively "good ideas" becoming law, when they infringe on individual liberty, are not good laws. Adhering to a more libertarian policing concept would help to keep laws appropriate for a truly free society. This would also reduce the circumstances that lead to de-policing.

CHAPTER 20

WHY COPS HATE HATE CRIMES

"If I'm stabbing or shooting someone, for whatever reason, I certainly don't love 'em," said one of the best cops I've ever known about hate crimes.

* * *

T he above statement is how this officer—now a retired sergeant—responded to the subject of Washington State's hate crimes legislation when it came up in roll call several years ago. In my experience, police officers tend to oppose such laws. As I mentioned earlier, officers need discretion to do their jobs properly. Hate crimes are akin to no-tolerance and domestic violence laws. They are a part of the social justice scourge, and they usurp officer discretion. They force officers to treat some victims differently—better—than others. To paraphrase George Orwell's *Animal Farm*, all people are equal, but some people are more equal than others. Today's lefties couldn't have said it better. Talk about something that is adding to the de-policing phenomenon.

Hate crimes have government picking winners and losers among victims and suspects. If you belong to one or more government-sanctioned victim group, you're golden. If not, you're up the creek looking for a paddle. If you're in the right group, a violent crime committed against you is more consequential than one committed against someone without a "historical victim" stamp. One person cracks someone's skull because he or she is a(n) [enter authorized victim class here], then throw the book at 'em! If that same person cracks your head open, but you're not black, Hispanic, gay, Muslim, or some other approved grievance class, your attacker will not suffer the same penalties for having committed the same crime against you.

Assaulting anyone is an act of hate. The motive behind the act, an aspect of mens rea (guilty mind), should only matter in the courts for proving the defendant committed the act, not for some arbitrary enhancement during charging and sentencing.

Think about it. If I'm walking down the street and I haul off and slug someone "just 'cause"—not too hard—but he gets a sore jaw, I may get hauled off to jail and may get charged with misdemeanor assault—or, I may not. However, if I'm walking down that same street and I do the same thing but before I clobber the dude, I shout, "This is what you get for being a(n) [enter preferred victim class here]," suddenly I've propelled myself into a realm of special jurisprudence.

This is what happens if you commit a crime against a person whom government deems more valuable than another due to perceived and real historical abuses. Not as an individual but as a member of a class or group because of the victim's race, ethnicity, religion, sexual orientation, and so on. Social justices have fought for years against what they assert is a biased criminal justice system. Now, the left seems content with a biased system, as long as the bias is aimed in the right direction. In the past, while the criminal justice system has certainly been biased against certain groups, the ultimate standard remained to be fair and treat everyone equally under the law. Shouldn't that still be the goal?

Unfortunately, it appears the goal has changed. Now the left wishes to remedy past wrongs by bestowing upon certain groups special victim status, setting one group above or below another to achieve some amorphous restitution. A sort of "see how they like it" version of criminal justice. Believe me, the part of me that hates the schoolyard bully sympathizes with this motive. Revenge (some would call it justice or social justice) might feel good. But as a reasonable adult, I know that the social justice behind this retribution and American equal justice cannot occupy the same space in the criminal justice system. Again, who decides when things are "fixed"?

The worst thing about hate crimes is if you take the emotion out of the issue and stop to think about it objectively, they also punish thoughts rather than actions alone. The difference in the assaults I described above isn't the degree of injury. It was the same. The difference is only in the assailant's particular motives and the protected class the victim falls into. Where does a criminal's motivations come from? Their thoughts, of course. If a person assaults me because he's angry, he suffers a lesser punishment. If he assaults me because I'm gay, black, or Hindu, he suffers a greater penalty. Does this sound like the American way of justice?

The American legal system is supposed to punish people's actions not their thoughts. The First Amendment covers this pretty well. You can stand on the sidewalk and proclaim your biases and prejudices to the heavens as long as you don't violate anybody's rights. However, if you follow your speech with violence, then society should penalize you for your actions but not the thoughts behind them.

This warped legal concept goes even further when government picks and chooses which types of thoughts are elevated to hate crimes. If I smack someone wearing a New York Yankees ball cap because I hate Yankees fans (this is purely hypothetical, of course, and the fact I'm a Red Sox fan has no bearing on this example), government doesn't consider that a hate crime. Why not? Because Yankees fans are not a historical victim group. Well, being from Massachusetts, I can tell you there's plenty of historical bias against Yankees fans. Hell, that's even true in Seattle and, come to think about it, in most baseball cities. And what if I assault a woman because she's got kids and no husband. I do it because I hate single mothers. Though despicable, this is not a hate crime. Why not?

What if an OWS, so-called ninety-nine-percenter, assaults a one-percenter businesswoman because of a bias against the wealthy? Or how about this one: what if you smack an off-duty police officer because you know he's a cop, and you hate cops? Now, this has got to be a hate crime, right?

Nope—remember Animal Farm. According to the left's crooked notions of justice, cops who protect society don't merit special protections, but others who don't risk their lives daily do. This is yet another thing that adds to de-policing. I'm not arguing cops—or Yankees fans—should be tagged as a hate crime-protected class. Remember, I reject the premise. But if those who act as the swords and shields of civil society don't have special protections as individuals against harm and "hate," is it right that anyone should? Even some conservatives and traditionalists jump on board the hate crimes bandwagon, if they agree on the victim group: bikers, cops, military, etc. I think they forget the liberty-damaging context of the notion itself.

On The O'Reilly Factor, Bill O'Reilly reported that on Election Day several black men assaulted a white man because they believed he'd just voted for Donald Trump. Bill said he felt such a crime should be made a "hate" crime. I understand his intentions but disagree with his goal. I do believe if someone assaults another person because of whom he or she voted for, there should be increased sanctions. Not because of what social class the victim is in but because of the victim's actions at the time. They assaulted the man because of an action, because he was voting. Assaulting someone specifically for exercising a civil right should be in a special class. This crime is right up there with physically preventing someone from voting or threatening them to vote a certain way. Actually, that's precisely what this is. Ex post facto voter intimidation.

Not to be outdone by the state and local arms of the American legal system, federal social justices have gotten into the act with federal hate crimes legislation. This is another attempt at federalization, this time of state and municipal judiciaries. The advent of hate crime laws has another insidious aspect. They place people opposing such laws in an awkward position.

Leftists accuse you of being racist, homophobic, Islamophobic, Scooby-doobyphobic, and so on, if you oppose any hate crime legislation they propose. Just because you don't support particular categories for crimes against "special" victim classes doesn't mean you're against prosecuting criminals who harm those victims. The conflation is absurd, but the left does it all the time.

I'm not arguing against increased penalties for violent crimes. Hell, to the left, it doesn't even matter if I support enhancing sentences for all violent crimes against any person. If I don't express my particular outrage because a criminal targeted a person for a narrow, social justice-approved reason, then I'm deemed a racist, bigot, sexist, or heartless. ("And why don't you care about black/Hispanic/Muslim/LGBTQ...people?") And what about hate crimes applying to your political affiliation? I can just imagine it: Republicans and conservatives would be exempt because, for the left, you probably can't commit a hate crime against a "hater."

Domestic violence is another area of law similar to hate crimes that usurps officer discretion. The only time in my career I felt I'd arrested people who didn't deserve to go to jail was during domestic violence incidents. Typically, Washington State's Domestic Violence Protection Act (DVPA) mandates if a victim makes a "credible" report of physical violence, the suspect must be arrested. "Credible," meaning a "victim" asserts the "suspect" assaulted him or her, and, despite the absence of physical evidence or corroborating witnesses, cops must take the suspect into custody.

The DVPA establishes ever-expanding "qualifying" relationships. Basically, DV law involves people over a certain age and in specific relationships perpetrating crimes: spouses, domestic partners, dating relationships, parent-child, siblings, and those who've lived together—at any time—ever.

One case I investigated involved a man and his son—a close relationship, right? A family member called police to report the son had assaulted his father. Domestic violence. No one reported any injuries. In fact, neither the father nor the son reported the incident. Another family member who feared the situation would escalate called 911. The situation had calmed so she called to cancel police. Many agencies dictate police can't cancel because once reported; they are required to respond and assess DV-related calls.

On arrival, we separated the suspect, victim, and witnesses and investigated the incident. All parties agreed that the father and son were arguing. At one point, they had inadvertently bumped into each other. The son had then pushed his father away, causing the father to bump against a wall.

The facts confirmed the son had pushed the father. Since this was a DV-related incident and offensive physical contact was made, we had to arrest the son for DV-Assault. The only reason we arrested the son was because he'd "assaulted" his biological parent. Also, the fact the dad, the "victim," didn't want his son arrested (and said he wouldn't cooperate with any prosecution) didn't matter.

Now, as the late, great Paul Harvey used to say, "here's the rest of the story." Although the parties were biologically father and son, until that day the two had never met. If the same thing had happened minus the blood relationship, after the victim had said he didn't want to press charges, we would've been down the road headed for coffee. In fact, since it wouldn't have triggered the DVPA, we likely wouldn't have shown up in the first place after the complainant had called to cancel.

Here you have a classic case of the social justices' "good intentions" gone awry. In attempting to protect "more valuable" members of society—toying with people's humanity—the left makes other people less valuable under the law and, thus, more vulnerable.

No-tolerance policies, hate crimes, and DV laws take discretion away from the officer on the scene and places it with those sitting behind desks. These social justices write catchall laws and then pat themselves on the back, thinking they're solving problems. In the realm of the social justices, the leftist-revered "ends justifying the means" rules the day.

Anything that takes away officer discretion adds to de-policing.

CHAPTER 21

So Many Laws, Too Little Time

T oo many laws is another area in which cops and their communities are negatively affected. Community activists and politicians work to pass unnecessary and intrusive laws that cops are expected to enforce. Then people get angry at police officers, anti-police sentiment rises, people complain, and, inevitably, departments punish cops. Remember, cops do not make the laws; you do—through your elected representatives. The problem isn't with law, generally. The problem is with too many bad laws. The societal impact of bad laws is bad feelings toward cops. And what does this lead to? De-policing.

Does it seem strange for a cop to grouse about too many laws? More laws = job security, right? Well, maybe, but that shouldn't matter in a nation based on individual liberty. Besides, there's always enough good ol' fashioned crime—theft, robbery, murder, and so forth—to keep cops busy. When society has too many laws, the good laws, the laws that protect Peter from Paul, get mixed in with frivolous "do something" political laws—laws that protect Peter from himself or those that place social justice above equal justice, thus having cops treat people unequally.

On another John Stossel Fox News Channel TV special, John spoke with (now former) Washington, D.C., city councilman Michael Brown about the lax taxicab laws in D.C. compared with other major U.S. cities. Brown was pushing for increased oversight of taxi businesses and touted having passed many new laws since entering office. Then John asked him how many laws he'd repealed. Brown said, "None."

Incidentally, according to a *Washington Post* report in May 2014, Brown was convicted of accepting bribes and sentenced to three-plus years in federal prison. Brown admitted to being caught up in a "culture of corruption running rampant in our city." Politicians don't make influential friends—or money—if they repeal instead of enact laws.

This shows you the mentality of some who hold public office. Simply "doing something" does not necessarily mean fixing real problems. Doing something too often means passing new laws—sometimes unnecessary and redundant laws, to feign doing something. Many times, these laws affect the law abiding much more than criminals.

In the aftermath of the Las Vegas massacre, anti-gun nuts were on a tear to enact "do-something" gun laws despite two things: no one on the left can seem to come up with what new law, short of repealing the Second Amendment and confiscating people's guns, would have prevented the crime—and, even then, probably not. Also, many liberal jurisdictions refuse to enforce gun laws currently on the books. Social justice prevents prosecutors in liberal cities from charging many armed criminals as they deserve to be. Why? Because it's society's fault they commit crime, of course.

Today, from tax and environmental to administrative and criminal, U.S. laws are so onerous and invasive that I challenge anyone to go a single day without breaking a law.

"Just stay in bed and do nothing all day," you might say. I'll bet I might even find a law you were breaking while staying in bed at home. (You haven't removed your mattress tag, have you?) Isn't it sad that even in our ostensibly liberty-loving country, staying home in bed might be the only way to go through a day without becoming a scofflaw?

Across the nation, aside from new gun laws, people are debating "talking on a cellphone while driving" laws. Some are calling it Driving Under the Influence of Electronics. This is an excellent example of unnecessary and redundant laws. Washington State passed a law in 2009 making it a secondary offense to speak on a handheld phone while driving. Police could only cite you if they first stopped you for a primary offense such as speeding or running a stop sign.

Once again, as with seat belt laws, the nanny statists lied. They always do. Talking on a cellphone while driving is now a primary law. And such is the insidiousness of the nanny state. Social justices introduce laws as secondary to garner initial support. They promise they're not interested in making it a primary law. But once the secondary law is passed, the left *always* eventually advocates for making it a primary offense. Of course, this has come to be expected of these intrepid social justices always in need of a new crisis. And good people keep falling for this ruse. The left often rebuffs the right's "slippery slope" argument but then work to slicken the slope.

Now a primary offense, this means police may stop a driver simply for speaking on a cellphone regardless that the motorist displayed no behaviors dangerous to anyone on the road. And if you think you'll get a hands-free device, well think again. There is another movement in the country that has targeted not the devices but conversation itself as the dangerous activity. Last I heard, they were debating this law in, of all places, Alaska.

There are a couple of issues here: first, police shouldn't have the right to pull any American over for "nothing" because that's what speaking on a phone while driving absent any public safety issues is. Second, regardless that a statute is bad law, it's also redundant and unnecessary—that's why it's a bad law. Every jurisdiction in America has an infraction similar to the one Seattle calls Inattention to Driving. Police can already stop people they observe driving dangerously while talking on a cellphone, eating a hot dog, or performing downward dog. This law is sensible and already exists.

The Inattention statutes allow police officers to stop distracted drivers and issue a warning or citation. For example, if an officer observes a person speaking on a cellphone while driving, but there's nothing to indicate they're a danger to other motorists, that officer should not be allowed to stop the driver. However, if officers observe drivers talking on cellphones while also failing to signal turns, rolling through stop signs, or swerving over the centerline, these actions are inherently dangerous, and police need to pull these drivers over for a little chat.

For example, driving while texting. Unlike talking, drivers can't look at their phones while texting and watch the road at the same time. Texting drivers aren't dangerous because they're simply using a cellphone while driving. They're dangerous because of what unsafe actions are happening while they're using the cellphone. A driver's full attention is drawn from the road while texting or reading texts.

Prohibitions regarding talking on a cellphone while driving are examples of typical nanny statist "do something" laws. In the long run, this is something that helps create an environment where de-policing thrives. The do-something disease afflicts many people, especially those on the left (although they exist on the right too). They find some emotional issue, sensationalize it, and then exploit it. Then supporters of the proposed law inflame people by whipping up a frenzy, citing outrageous examples that obfuscate reasoned debate. The fact that a law is unnecessary seems inconsequential.

I'm fond of closing my missives to my political representatives with the admonition, "The least you can do for me is the most I want you to do for me." As a retired cop, when I mention to nannycrat lefties that cellphone bans are unnecessary, I receive blank stares, which are inevitably followed by a change of subject. I've yet to get any reply of more substance than, "Well, *something* had to be done," or "It's still a good idea." No, it is not a good idea—or a good law! Didn't we cover that?

Think about what happens when you expand item-specific prohibitions out to their logical conclusions. You'd have to create a separate law for every distinct thing you could do that could be considered distracting while driving. Otherwise, you run the risk of someone getting away with a dangerous violation because that action wasn't specifically prohibited by law. Like the guy I stopped for eating a breakfast burrito while driving. Oh, did I mention the driver was using a fork? And the food was on a plate—on the front passenger's seat.

You'd have to enact laws against applying makeup while driving, as well as reading a map, shaving, eating a cheeseburger with fries, practicing yoga, etc. There would be a virtual Napoleonic Code of distracted driving statutes. And if the no-cellphone-use-at-all, not-even-hands-free, nanny statists get their way, the next "logical" step would be no more conversations with passengers while driving, and you certainly couldn't listen to that distracting radio the auto manufacturer conveniently installed. What about your GPS? *Yikes!* And what about all the billboards and other signs like the ones federal, state, or local Departments of Transportation (DOT) install. These signs flash and twinkle, and shine, sparkle, and shimmer as you cruise down the roadway? Of course, those pesky traffic signs would all have to go. Well, they're distracting, damn it. And besides, *there should be a law!*

Crossing the centerline while distracted on a cellphone is inherently dangerous, not just theoretically, and would require enforcement action. It directly and immediately jeopardizes public safety. However, the sanction would be the same if the driver committed the violation while reading a map, changing the radio station, or daydreaming. This specific-item prohibition could keep government nannies in business for decades, as they go down the checklist of possible activities to prohibit while driving.

Free societies must deal with people's actions and not the physical objects they happen to be using. It's not the pencil; it's the person writing the threatening note. It's not the car; it's the guy driving away from the robbery. It's not the gun; it's the criminal robbing or shooting someone. And it's not the cellphone; it's the driver running the stop sign.

In researching our culture of too many laws, I counted the number of parking infractions on the "cheat sheet" some officers carry. The sheet lists the various infractions, their code numbers, and associated fines.

In mine, I counted over one hundred parking infractions in Seattle available for your violating pleasure. In addition to parking violations, traffic laws numbered well over three hundred. Even all those statutes weren't inclusive of every traffic-related law and statute. I again challenge anyone to not break some law while driving or even parking in Seattle. And I did that count many years ago. I don't have the intestinal fortitude to count again. In my experience, like the associated fine amounts, laws tend to increase and rarely decrease.

A few years ago I went out to a club on Broadway to celebrate my daughter's birthday. We parked our cars a couple blocks away because finding parking in Seattle is as rare as discovering a diamond (not to mention as expensive). When I returned to my car and my daughter to hers, we'd both received parking tickets. We were confused because we both bought parking permits from one of the city's—new at the time—parking permit machines.

So, what was the problem? Well, it seems we hadn't affixed the parking permit to the correct window. Yes, really! We stuck them to the driver's side window rather than the front passenger's side window. And we were penalized the same amount as if we hadn't bought a permit at all. For all of you lefties concerned with government fairness, does this strike you as fair? I suppose we could have read the fine print more carefully, but we were on our way to celebrate a birthday, so…*Happy Birthday, Sweetie* from the City of Seattle.

Many years ago, one particularly inspired Washington State legislator got a law passed making it illegal to fail to keep a trash bag in your car. The thinking was that drivers would not litter if their cars had trash bags. Penalize people who throw trash out of their cars, sure, but for not having a trash bag? Answer this question: if the driver is predisposed to being a litterbug, what do you think he's going to do with the bag once it's full?

Hey, politicians! Stop making cops the bad guys!

When redundant or frivolous laws are enacted which infringe on individual liberty, the public's general respect for all laws suffers. What will the driver think of the police officer who pulls her over because she answered a call from the babysitter to verify the amount of medication she's supposed to give baby Sally? Some will say the driver should pull over to take the call. Be serious. In the real world, this is not always practical, and it may not even be safer than remaining in traffic. What will happen to community respect for police officers when an officer cites the woman for taking this call? And, uh oh, what if she doesn't have a trash bag?

Wouldn't she feel the government had mistreated her—that the police officer had? Wouldn't you? How friendly do you think she's going to be to police officers in general after this interaction—not to mention the $100+ fine? This adds to the general anti-policing attitude that contributes to de-policing when even ordinary people join the cop critics.

Years ago, a Washington state trooper stopped me for allegedly violating the state's motorcycle helmet law. I *was* wearing a motorcycle helmet. Nevertheless, the trooper saw our group of bikes riding on a state highway at the posted 60 mph as he passed us, going in the opposite direction. He suddenly turned around as if we were Osama bin Laden and his terrorist entourage and charged after us. To make a long story short, he cited two of us even though he lacked any legal authority to stop any of us in the first place.

No one can make a determination, neither officially nor technically, that a helmet is or is not "legal" simply by glancing at it while passing a group of motorcyclists at highway speeds. An officer can only have a suspicion—a guess. In America, that's not supposed to be enough. There need to be objective facts that rise to probable cause that a traffic offense has been committed. The trooper could've physically inspected the helmet *after* he'd stopped me, but he hadn't accused me of having done anything else "wrong" to initially warrant a legal stop. He just *assumed* my helmet was illegal.

Interestingly, even during the stop he never asked to inspect my helmet. He never even touched it, though I'd taken it off and placed it on my handlebars. So, even if he suspected my helmet was illegal, he conducted no investigation to prove his allegation. Regardless, he cited me for a helmet law violation.

At the time, enforcement of Washington's helmet law was deeply flawed. But don't take my word for it. Think about this. Let's say you're a cop and you observe a driver drinking from a sports drink container, but you *think* it contains beer. You may be right, you may not be. Either way, you need probable cause to believe there is alcohol in that lemon-flavored Gatorade container before you can stop the driver for that violation. You would need evidence no matter how much you believe it. To prove the point, if a driver were drinking from a Bud Light can, you'd have probable cause to stop the driver. Now, if the driver actually had lemon Gatorade in the beer can (I don't know why anyone would, either; just humor me), you could not take any legal action. However, your stop would still be legal because you had evidence of the violation.

Now, let's say you want to stop a motorcyclist for wearing an "illegal" helmet. Even if it were illegal, how could you know by looking at it while traveling at 60 mph, and the rider with the helmet is traveling equally fast in the opposite direction? I'm not talking about a biker wearing a baseball cap backward or some oddly constructed cardboard contraption. I'm talking about a helmet that looks the same as so many other motorcycle riders wear.

In my case, I was wearing a helmet with a chinstrap and a hard, shiny black surface that covered my head down to my ears. How could any officer determine this helmet is illegal solely by looking at it? The officer would at least have to physically inspect it. That's the problem. They can't legally make that stop. In court, the trooper offered as visual "evidence" that my helmet was illegal because it was not "thick enough." Well, the relevant statute didn't provide a minimum thickness requirement. The helmet was supposed to contain text imprinted within the interior lining—it did. My helmet had the required text verbatim. In general, the helmet law was vague and basically unenforceable. But some officers and judges don't care.

It's a law that anti-biker zealots and well-meaning social justice cops who presume to care for your noggin tend to enforce. However, it's still a law that doesn't protect Peter from Paul. It attempts to protect Peter from his own adult decisions. I'm not sure about you, but, as I said earlier, my mother stopped dressing me when I was a little kid. I don't need government dressing me as an adult.

Take the above as an example of how a person, even when he's a cop himself, may view cops after being stopped for something that posed no harm to any other person. For many years, I bristled whenever I saw a trooper when I should have seen them as brothers and sisters in law enforcement. I understood that was irrational because he was only one cop out of thousands in Washington and hundreds of thousands in America, but that's how I felt as a tax-paying citizen of Washington and the United States—not to mention, as a human being.

Most troopers I related the incident to said their fellow trooper's behavior embarrassed them. To be honest, many expressed their embarrassment that a cop would write another cop a ticket at all for such a minor infraction. I later learned this trooper was so unpopular with motorcyclists that the local Harley shop sold helmet decals with the Troopers name preceded by a nasty invective beginning with the letter F.

So, what should you do? Pay attention to these types of laws. Try to take the emotion out of the discussion and think critically about whether they are good or bad laws. Decide whether or not you can support them. If not, then work to prevent them or repeal those already enacted.

Again, as government grows, liberty shrinks. You may not immediately feel the weight of a helmet law because you don't mind wearing them or you don't ride a motorcycle or bicycle and don't have to wear one daily. Or maybe you don't drive a car and don't have to worry about wearing a seat belt or talking on a cellphone while driving. Just remember, it's not only the laws themselves but also the political zealotry used to institute them that should concern us all. It's the attitude and paradigm shifts necessary to gain support for future social justice laws that you should worry about. What is becoming the "new normal" is what's insidious. If government infringes on anyone's liberty, it infringes on everyone's liberty.

And liberals seem strangely indifferent to how these types of laws and their expensive citations affect low-income drivers. My father-in-law was a cop for thirty-six years in Massachusetts. When he'd hear about yet another driver mandate, he'd say, "They're driving the poor man off the roads." And that was back in the 1980s.

The advocates' primary defense of social justice laws is that they are protecting the people's tax money when the state has to redistribute funds to the uninsured after their injuries are more severe in a collision than they supposedly might have been had they been wearing a helmet or seat belt. The problem with this equation isn't that people aren't wearing helmets or seat belts. The problem is that government punishes you by transferring wealth from you to uninsured people for their medical care and then passes liberty-infringing laws that punish you all over again.

Thinking about the issue dispassionately, why should government pay for any person's medical care in the first place? It doesn't pay for other bills like for car or motorcycle repairs, which are also essential to a family's financial well-being (although, I know some social justices would argue government should pay for those things too).

Why not at least send a bill to anyone who has incurred medical expenses but can't or won't pay the bill? Some will pay, some may not, but individual responsibility would be inscribed on society rather than government dependence. I'd rather a person pay a dollar a week, three dollars a month, or even ten dollars a year than have their debts summarily transferred to me. Even this minimal payment preserves a person's self-respect and gives them a true stake in their own welfare as well as that of their nation.

Before I go further, I should thank you for your patience and remind you that the reason this issue ties into a book about de-policing is because it's the cops the social justices use to advance their liberal agendas. Every time I write *government*, read *cops* because it's the cops who enforce what legislatures pass and courts rule on. Thus, police officers become more unpopular with the public they serve, which leads to de-policing.

Now, back to my insightful digression.

So, government creates the so-called "public burden," where Peter is forced to pay for a helmet- or seat belt–less Paul's medical bills if he can't pay for himself for legitimate or illegitimate reasons or simply won't pay. Then government sets out to limit both Peter's and Paul's individual liberty to ostensibly safeguard Peter's tax money that is going to pay Paul's medical bills. *Brilliant!* The social justices have set up a system where government can claim to be helping people when what they're really doing is usurping rights, transferring wealth to gain votes, thus perpetuating a socialistic government dependency.

Philip K. Howard wrote an article that appeared on *nydailynews. com* titled, "Drowning in Law: A flood of statutes, rules and regulations is killing the American spirit." Howard looks at laws affecting the economic health of America. He writes:

> *The sheer volume of law suffocates innovative instincts, while distrust of lawsuits discourages ordinary human choices. Why take a chance on the eager young person applying for a job when, if it doesn't work out, you might get sued for discrimination? Why take the risk of expanding production in another state when that requires duplicating legal risks and overhead? Why bother to start a business at all?*

And when government gives officers the authority to stop people for not wearing seat belts while driving cars or helmets while riding motorcycles or bicycles, they set the officer up as a bully, which is damaging to law enforcement, generally. *Why bother to enforce these types of laws at all?* Cops are stopping people for something that should be none of the government's business. They're stopping people for *no good reason*. And sometimes these stops go awry, and cops end up disciplined, or cities dole out settlements, stemming from something that shouldn't be a law in the first place. Cops are supposed to protect people from other people who put them in danger, not from their own safety decisions.

To reiterate, a driver not wearing a seat belt or rider not wearing a helmet puts no one else in danger. Government is overstepping its constitutional duties by attempting to pass "good" ideas rather than focusing on good laws. The only thing cops are protecting when enforcing nanny laws is progressive government's version of social justice and their penchant for changing the essence of the American experiment in individual liberty. When governments force cops to engage in soft tyranny, the only question is how far behind is hard tyranny?

CHAPTER 22

No-Tolerance Policies

T he impulse behind so-called "no-tolerance" policies is to control a specific, perceived negative behavior. I say *perceived* because many people disagree on what constitutes negative behavior. For example, antigun zealots think anything related to the dreaded gun is negative. We'll get to that in a moment.

No-tolerance policies can lend themselves to lazy leadership. These policies can create an environment where individuals who are supposed to use their discretion to make decisions are no longer required or even allowed to. They can rinse the matter from their hands and defer to policy. ("*Blame the policy, not me.*")

This is why I always tried to use active instead of passive language when I enforced the law. If I issued a driver a traffic citation, I didn't say, "You're being issued..." I'd say, "I'm issuing you..." And rather than, "You're being arrested for..." I'd tell them, "I'm arresting you for..." I was not only taking symbolic but also literal responsibility for my actions. With misdemeanors or infractions, I couldn't blame my boss, the law, or the policy when I was the one with the discretion (except for domestic violence, of course).

No-tolerance policies can lead to inequitable and sometimes ludicrous results. I read about school officials lambasting a young boy for possessing a Lego gun. Yes, the colorful plastic building block toys you use to create a Lego version of any object in the known universe. Well, the manufacturer also provides accessories, including tiny plastic toy guns with which the builder can arm his or her intergalactic warriors. This "gun" was the size of two quarters side by side. What's that? Two inches?

The previously mentioned Philip K. Howard wrote a marvelous book titled *The Death of Common Sense* (Random House, 1994). In it, he documents the inane policies institutions adopt, many governmental, that defy—well—common sense. The Lego incident merits inclusion in Howard's book. So much current lunacy does.

The school's no-tolerance policy blindsided the unsuspecting Lego-wielding whelp and his parents. It doesn't matter that his parents told him he'd done nothing wrong. No matter how innocent his actions, he'll carry residue of his "transgression" against political correctness for a long time. All due to an adult's gross overreaction when enforcing a no-tolerance policy. Seems they have no tolerance for common sense.

Similar to squelching free speech, this action causes a proverbial chilling effect on other parents and students. Since conservative folk respect law and order and tend to follow laws—even if they don't like them, this chill will cause many of them also to replace their common sense by bowing to politically correct nonsense. After all, they want to keep their kids in school—and getting good grades.

Many school districts no longer allow teachers and administrators to use their common sense in such matters. Teachers could be disciplined or even fired if they don't follow no-tolerance policies. And since so many American school boards, administrators, and teachers align with the social justices, their antigun biases are likely to burn red hot during such occasions. They're more than happy to clamp down on the plastic toy arms race.

And don't forget the foreboding Gun-Free Zone signs plastered all over our children's schools. These no-tolerance gun policies imprint on students the notion that guns are bad, even evil, in and of themselves. These policies are so ridiculous many schools apply them even if a child draws a picture of a gun or pantomimes a "gun" using a hand gesture.

In another instance, school officials suspended a little boy for tossing an invisible grenade during recess to save his buddies. The seven-year-old, Alex Evans, said, "I was trying to save people and I just can't believe I got *dispended*." The second-grader explained further, "It's [the game] called, rescue the world." Suspended? *Are you kidding me?*

School authorities sanctioned another child for biting a Pop-Tart into the shape of a pistol. In our brave new world, a two-dimensional crayon drawing of a gun or a partially eaten pastry pistol qualifies as firearms possession? For five-, six-, and seven-year-olds? This is lunacy.

Rather than teach children that guns are evil, we should teach them how guns work, why they can be dangerous, and what to do if they find one. When they're old enough, we should make them familiar with basic gun safety. This not only helps gun owners' children learn gun safety at home but also what to do if Jenny or Jermaine encounters a gun in another child's house or finds one in the bushes. Do you know if guns are kept in homes where your kids play? Are the child's parents responsible gun owners? Does that child know gun safety? Does yours?

Gun safety education should be universal. When I was a young teenager in the '70s, even in liberal Massachusetts, the local state Fish & Wildlife officer taught a gun safety course for kids. Believe me, you never know when or where your child might come across a firearm. Fire departments teach kids to Stop-Drop-Roll if their clothes catch fire. Parents teach kids not to talk to strangers. High schools teach kids driver's education and sex education (hopefully, not at the same time). It's an abdication of responsibility not to teach kids basic firearms safety rules.

A man once flagged me down to turn in a gun he'd found behind a dumpster. Nearby were many apartment buildings and a playground. Aside from being happy the guy didn't shoot me, it thrilled me that a child didn't find it first. The gun he'd handed to me was loaded.

Back in the '90s, I served on the East Precinct Community Police Team (CPT). CPT officers did not normally handle 911 calls and were free to deal with chronic neighborhood nuisances and crime problems. Shortly after taking the position, I was looking through a storage area in the precinct basement parking garage. Several boxes of public service items for CPT to distribute had accumulated. I discovered some boxes filled with Eddie Eagle booklets, which the National Rifle Association (NRA) publishes to help educate children about gun safety. No matter what you think of the NRA, gun safety and education has been their area of expertise since 1871. Full disclosure, I am an NRA Life Member.

The NRA's aim is to teach children, pre-kindergarten through third grade, the proper response when they encounter a gun:

> *Stop!*
> *Don't touch.*
> *Run away.*
> *Tell an adult.*

This doesn't sound too radical, does it? Perhaps liberals should think of it as a prophylactic. In other words, it's perfectly fine for school officials to distribute condoms and birth control pills at school to prevent disease and unwanted pregnancies but not to teach children about firearm safety. In 2010, officials at Seattle's Ballard High School provided a fifteen-year-old student transportation to a clinic for an abortion without notifying her parents. But they wouldn't dream of teaching her gun safety even at the request of her parents.

I guess it's too much to ask to give kids a booklet that could prevent accidental shootings. Liberals expect conservatives to suck it up when schools dispense birth control to our children "for a child's own good." But somehow gun safety *for a child's own good* is taboo? Where is the logic? Don't look too hard. You won't find it.

The liberal powers that be think guns are so evil you can't talk to kids about them even if it might save a child's life. Liberals are fond of saying, "It's for the children" and "If it only saves one life..." But apparently for liberals there's a caveat: only if the idea is liberal.

When I asked people at work why CPT hadn't distributed the booklets, I got either more blank stares, laughter, or answers like, "Yeah, right. Gun safety education—in zero-tolerance *Seattle*?" The issue wasn't up for discussion, even by gun education supporters. The proverbial writing was on the concrete walls of liberal intolerance. What a shame. The left has adopted a philosophy akin to the scared child who closes his eyes believing the danger will not get him. If he can't see it, it can't hurt him.

As with any inanimate object, a gun has no intrinsic evil. It has only the qualities you assign it, depending on how you use it. When I was growing up, my mother had this huge Bible she kept on a table in the living room. You could kill someone with that thing it was so big. Well, that is if you could manage to lift it and then hurl it at someone's head. Would killing someone with the Bible make the Bible evil? Guns and Bibles are inanimate objects. Bibles don't kill people; people kill people.

And how should cops feel? How can schools teach kids that guns are evil without tainting everyone who carries them, legally and illegally, as also evil, including cops? Schools should not disparage as bad a police officer's most important tangible work tool. No one should. Leftists should be aware of the negative they may be conveying to children about police officers because they carry guns—perhaps, some are aware but don't care. And what about drugs? (Insert ominous music here.)

Again, to the schools. Even middle and high school kids have gotten into serious trouble for possessing such horrendous drugs as...yes...wait for it...*aspirin* (music gets even more ominous here).

According to *Eagleforum.org*'s education reporter,

Several states are reconsidering "zero-tolerance" policies, the draconian regulations affecting many public-school children since the 1990s. Even in Colorado, where the 1999 Columbine school shooting catalyzed a huge increase in zero-tolerance legislation nationwide, legislators have been reconsidering the policies. "We tried to add a little common sense," said Colorado state Sen. Kevin Lundberg (R-15th District).

There are too many examples of no-tolerance madness. I'm sure you've heard or read about them in various media. Here are just a few:

- Police arrested and a school suspended a seventeen-year-old girl in North Carolina for "weapons possession." She'd accidentally brought her father's lunchbox to school. The lunchbox contained a small paring knife he planned to use for an apple he'd packed.
- Police handcuffed, then took an eleven-year-old Florida boy to jail and charged him with a felony for bringing a butter knife to school.
- In California, police arrested a six-year-old boy and charged him with sexual assault for "inappropriately" touching his best friend on the playground. The boy's father said the boys were playing tag when the incident occurred.

The list could go on and on. A kid has a headache and pops a Bayer aspirin. Teacher reports it; kid's suspended. A student gives two aspirins to a classmate with a headache. Teacher reports it; school administration suspends both students, gives teacher drug prevention award.

Now, I'm not saying schools shouldn't have policies on the dispensing of medications at school, even aspirin. I mean it's not asking too much for a student to get pain relievers from the school nurse. However, kids bringing and taking medications at school that they can legally purchase at a grocery store should have each case judged on its merits, not by inflexible no-tolerance policies.

Occasionally, police agencies adopt no-tolerance policies. In my book *Officer*, I wrote about a classic no-tolerance case. One evening, I was riding my motorcycle home from work. A few blocks from my neighborhood a motorcycle cop buddy of mine was on a traffic stop. The woman he'd stopped was sitting in her car crying. He signaled me to park and wait. After the stop, he came over and said he'd conducted a community meeting the night before to discuss neighborhood complaints about speeding traffic. During the meeting, the neighbors agreed to a "no-tolerance" policy for speeding.

The neighbors voted to have police stop and cite any driver clocked at six miles per hour or greater above the 25 mph speed limit. No warnings, no exceptions, no tolerance. The next day, my buddy and his radar gun set up in the neighborhood to monitor drivers' speeds.

My buddy turned away and glanced at the driver he'd stopped. Tears running down her cheeks, she was staring, as if in disbelief, at her copy of the speeding ticket.

"Yeah," my buddy looked back at me. "She's the block watch captain. The meeting was at her house."

No-tolerance policies are good ideas until they're not. Cops know better than anyone the real-life nuances that can occur to make discretion the preferred option. Individuals should be responsible for their behavior and decisions. That's how rights work: you have a God-given right to life, liberty, and property. Therefore, you have a God-given responsibility not to harm others or take or break their stuff.

Here's another tricky no-tolerance policy issue: sex offenses. People who peddle child pornography and commit child molestation are some distance below the lowest scum on earth. They don't deserve your understanding. They deserve your contempt—or worse.

Is there anything worse than taking a child's innocence in such an evil, despicable way? The consequences for the child, physical and emotional, from these vile criminals' wicked actions do not end after the assault. The children these monsters victimize will suffer for the rest of their lives.

Having said this, look at how sexual offense no-tolerance policies can damage people and society and reduce their effectiveness on truly sexually deviant criminals. There's the case of nineteen-year-old Georgia high school honors student and football player Marcus Dixon. Convicted of statutory rape, the court sentenced him to a mandatory—*no-tolerance*—ten years in prison for having consensual sex with a girl at a party. She was fifteen and he was eighteen at the time. Both were high school students.

According to the *New York Daily News*, juror Kathy Tibitz said, "I thought to myself, 'Oh my God, what have we done?' The law was written to tie our hands."

Dixon's charges were eventually reduced. He went on to play pro football in the NFL and later in the CFL. Regardless of your feelings about the age difference, the consensus is that the punishment did not fit the crime and was intended for different circumstances.

In another ludicrous instance of a no-tolerance policy, police arrested a fifteen-year-old New Jersey girl for "distributing kiddie porn." So, what "child pornography" did she distribute? She sent nude photos she'd taken with her cellphone to her boyfriend—of *herself*. Smart on her part? Not remotely, but criminal? Hardly.

The other side of the issue should be mentioned: judges doling out lenient sentences and engaging in political activism from the bench. These mockeries of justice are often where no-tolerance policies are born. In fact, this next case resulted in beefed-up laws. I'm not saying stronger laws are necessarily bad. Tossing sex offenders in the pokey and throwing away the key is fine with me. But if judges and cops want to keep their discretion, they need to use it appropriately.

The sexual assault case of Stanford swimmer Brock Turner is a good example of warped jurisprudence that can lead to no-tolerance policies. At trial's end, the judge, Aaron Persky, sentenced the swimmer to only six months in jail. The judge cited Turner's youth and clean record (yeah, he wasn't a rapist...until he was). Some believe his swimming career, a possible Olympic contender, also played a role in the judge's decision. Turner was released after serving only three months—for good behavior.

What did Turner do? Only rape a fellow student's sister behind a frat house dumpster. Oh, did I mention the young woman was unconscious at the time? *Six months!* What was that judge thinking? What if that poor girl lying on the ground unconscious near trash dumpsters, that piece of garbage on top of her, had been *his* daughter?

Turner barely took any responsibility, mostly blaming the incident on alcohol despite being underage. Regardless, drunkenness is not a legal excuse unless the intoxication was involuntary, which it was not.

You can see how inconsistency can drive no-tolerance policies. A guy like Marcus Dixon incurs a penalty excessive of his crime while Brock Turner's sentence falls well short. People need to be aware of who they are electing to the bench and hold them accountable for poor decisions at either end of the justice spectrum.

Sexual assault crimes when committed and interpreted as the law intended are serious felonies. But by charging people whose actions don't fit with the intent or spirit of the law, the consequences for real sex crimes and true criminals are diluted. These cases serve as distractions from the serious business of prosecuting real criminals. Let's get back to when common sense was more common.

CHAPTER 23

THE LINE COPS SHOULD NEVER CROSS

"Okay, quiet down—ROLL CALL!" the silver-haired sergeant barks. His hash marks, marking his long career, stretch like diagonal piano keys on his left sleeve from his wrist up to his sergeant stripes. Officers joke that Sarge's hash marks need a hinge at his elbow so he can bend his arm.

"Well, the mayor's given us another doozy today," the sergeant says, clearing his throat and pursing his lips, as if he'd sipped a bitter IPA. "Seems our gun-hating potentate has decreed that people cannot carry guns, open or even concealed with a permit, into parks and onto other city property."

Like collapsing dominoes, one by one, officers roll their eyes. Then the groans start, signaling the imminent cynical cop comments sure to gush forth, but the wily sergeant intercedes. "Hold on. I know…I know…but before you go all Patrick Henry on me, listen…" The sergeant scans the room full of officers, from rookies to patrol veterans. "This is blatantly unconstitutional, and I would not enforce it." There is another slight hesitation before he adds, "Roll call's over."

Officers begin the post-roll call free-for-all he'd expected but, now, he doesn't have to preside over. Officers nod at their patriotic sergeant, who'd effectively preempted their building fury. Now, they'd have to be content to unleash on each other. They hash out their frustration with their liberal city government over yet another attempt to stomp on people's liberty and then expecting to use cops—*them*—to enforce it.

* * *

Other sergeants might have handled it differently, but I don't think many. Another sergeant, thinking more about his career and not rankling the social justices above, might have supported the edict. However, a law or rule that infringes on people's constitutional rights is different from a minor policy change. Abridging any of the Bill of Rights is a serious affair. Anyway, the sergeant didn't tell the officers not to enforce the law; he just said that *he* wouldn't enforce it, leaving the decision up to his officers' discretion.

The above vignette is an amalgamated description based on my and other officers' observations related to me of patrol roll call reactions throughout the department to Mayor McGinn's antigun diktat. I used a composite—quasi-fictional—sergeant to protect the patriotic. But the gist of the roll call I sat in is accurate. I am proud of that sergeant. I also never heard of any rank-and-file support for McGinn's folly.

Getting back to the mayor's antigun decree, it was disconcerting when supervisors told officers the SPD chain of command had *signed off on it*. I don't want to point fingers or embarrass individuals, but I hope that broaching the subject will cause police leaders who'd succumbed to political strong-arming some retrospective soul searching. Whatever the case, the department didn't disseminate the mayor's decree to officers in the usual open manner. Instead, a photocopy of a draft of the signed memo suddenly appeared in the precinct. It was as if the command staff knew the mayor had overstepped, but they didn't have the courage of their sergeants to stand up for the

Constitution. Makes you wonder how far they'd go to keep their masters happy.

Everyone's heard about the infamous symbolic barrier called the Thin Blue Line: America's law enforcement officers standing between civil society and criminals. Taleeb Starkes writes of the Thin Blue Line, "[It] has become a tightrope that all officers are walking." It's the few who keep anarchy from swallowing society whole. Think about that concept. It's critical because there are only about eight hundred thousand cops to police a nation of over three hundred million. Seattle's population alone nearly equals the total number of police officers in America. Today, many police departments devote 50 percent or more of their resources to units that do not work the streets answering 911 calls. Communities are lucky if they have one officer per one thousand residents.

There's also a more notorious and precarious phrase: the Blue Wall of Silence. This refers to that rare "wall" or barrier that rises when cops go silent to protect one another. When agencies fail to protect their officers, officers need to protect each other. This is not a matter of lying or refusing to cooperate to protect a fellow officer. It's a matter of knowing that police officers working the streets see things differently than civilians—and some of their bosses, especially those involved in liberal politics and the media.

There is another line, just as important as the thin blue one, that police officers shouldn't cross. I call it the Fraying Constitutional Line. As with Mayor McGinn's political gun edict in Seattle, this line appears when superiors ask or order officers to violate the People's constitutional rights. Too many social justices have little respect for the U.S. Constitution as a whole. They see much of America's law of the land as an impediment to achieving their radical political and social goals.

Remember this? President Obama referred to the Constitution as "a charter of negative liberties," which "says what the states can't do to you [and] what the federal government can't do to you, but doesn't say what the federal government or state government must do on your behalf." President Obama, supposedly a constitutional scholar, doesn't seem to *get* that document at all. Or he gets it; he just doesn't respect it or like the parts he finds politically inconvenient. Conservative scholars speak reverently of our founding document while acknowledging its flaws and recognizing the measures the framers included to correct them. Conservatives don't tend to pick and choose which rights to respect like liberals so often do. Liberals love the First Amendment, though not necessarily where it pertains to religion or what they consider "hate speech" (i.e., speech with which they disagree), but they thoroughly hate the Second Amendment. Conservatives respect and revere both.

And remember what I said about former House Speaker Nancy Pelosi. When a reporter asked her where Congress got the authority to pass the Obamacare mandate, she mocked him, asking repeatedly, "Are you serious?" Does Speaker Pelosi have a clue as to what the Constitution says on the matter of forcing Americans to buy a product, or does she not care? Which would be worse?

Clearly, she rejects the concept that Congress gets its limited authority from the Constitution. How sad is that, coming from a Speaker of the House? From the woman who said, about the Obamacare legislation, "We have to pass the bill so you can find out what is in it." Kind of like a lawyer advising a client to sign a contract before reading it, so the person affected by it can find out what it says. Speaker Pelosi later said, "When people see what is in the bill, they will like it." Oh, well then, what were we all worried about?

Seattle elected a mayor, Mike McGinn, in November 2009. If anyone wondered about his position on outgoing Mayor Nickels' gun law, McGinn's response to the judge's striking down the law clears up any confusion.

Mayor McGinn told *King 5 News*, "I am disappointed in today's [Friday's] ruling. Cities should have the right to restrict guns in playgrounds, pools and community centers where children are present... It's time for the state legislature to change that law." Scary? You bet.

Either this man doesn't understand constitutional law, or worse, doesn't agree with it despite having sworn an oath to uphold it.

I'd wager McGinn agrees Seattleites have the right to self-defense, but apparently, he opposes a right to acquire the most practical means to exercise it. Is it just me, or is this like people having a right to travel but not a right to choose the most efficient mode?

Michael Medved, whose popular national show is broadcast from Seattle on KTTH 770 AM, called Mayor McGinn "the worst elected official in the United States of America." After his defeat, Mayor McSchwinn, as some called him due to his penchant for wrecking Seattle's roads with a convoluted system of bike lanes, rode his bicycle off into the political sunset, but liberals need not worry. Someone would step up to fill the void. Enter Ed Murray. (McGinn attempted to run for mayor again in 2017. He didn't even come close in the primary.)

Not to be outdone, the Murray administration imposed a new Draconian tax on the sales of guns and ammunition. This is nothing but backdoor gun control and yet another example of Seattle stabbing business owners whose products they disapprove. How would they react to a conservative administration treating pot shops this way? I can guess. Some Seattle gun dealers moved their stores beyond the clutches of the city's liberal loving claws to cities friendlier to guns and ammo businesses and to the Constitution. Seattle's liberal bullies will eventually get what they wanted—no more gun shops. The "you must live like us or else" mentality prevails in liberal la-la land.

Even if gun owners eventually succeed in court, it may be too late. And what gun shop owner in his or her right mind will ever want to do business in Seattle again? Be careful, conservatives and libertarians. The liberals have time on their side. Stand up against tyranny early when you can still fight it more effectively or liberty will be a casualty.

A blog post I wrote in 2016 tells the story:

DRUG DEALERS GET MORE RESPECT
THAN GUN DEALERS IN SEATTLE

- *First victim of Seattle's gun tax flees city tyranny*

  According to Richard D. Oxley, MyNorthwest.com, Seattle government has notched its first victim of the city's new Draconian gun tax. Precise Shooter has stopped selling firearms and ammunition and will soon move its business out of Seattle and King County to Lynnwood in Snohomish County.

- *How can a constitutional right qualify as a sin tax?*

  The Seattle City Council compared the guns and ammo tax to the added taxes on cigarettes and alcohol—so-called "sin" taxes. Well, a law-abiding person owning a gun isn't a sin, and the last time I checked, the U.S. Constitution did not guarantee an American's right to keep and bear cigarettes and alcohol.

- *City getting exactly what it wants*

  City Council Member Tim Burgess argues, "the gun tax money will go toward research and other means to fight gun violence in the city." Call me a cynic, but by moving out of the city, Precise Shooter is giving the city exactly what it wants. No gun shops in Seattle.

- *Not the gun-shop owner's fault*

  I am not criticizing Precise Shooter. In the article, the owner, Sergey Solyanik, explains how his business cannot remain profitable with the tax because his shop focuses primarily on selling guns and ammo. I assume this is unlike other stores where firearms and ammunition are only a part of the business.

- *Seattle has more respect for illegal drug dealers than for legal gun dealers*

  Well, another job well done by Seattle's progressive bullies. Mr. Solyanik may as well have been a drug dealer on a

Downtown corner—oh, wait. Even illegal drug dealers get more respect from Seattle government than legal gun dealers do.

* * *

With Seattle's antigun fervor switched to full wacko, the social justices are looking for backdoor ways to violate our Second Amendment rights. In the recent past, Seattle has tried to do this at least twice. Fortunately, a King County Superior Court judge struck down Seattle's (McGinn's) gun law I mentioned earlier, as violating state preemption. (A local jurisdiction may not create a law more restrictive than the state law.) A good way to reiterate what occurred in this case is to reprint another article I wrote, which appeared in the January 2010 issue of the *Guardian*.

If anyone doubts how radical today's leftist political leaders are, it's time to pull your head out of your—um—*ass*umptions. Now, the article, which is chock-full of causes of de-policing, written by an active duty police officer at the time—me:

* * *

Drawing a Constitutional Line
The *Guardian*, January 2010

I originally intended this article for the November 2009 *Guardian*, but, as we know far too well, society suffered a horrendous loss when vermin slaughtered five [Western Washington] police officers within a month's time on October 31 and November 29, 2009, two dates now seared into the heart of law enforcement (another area police officer was ambushed and slain in December).

The *Guardian* rightfully dedicated the last two issues to these five exemplary officers who, along with their families, will forever stay in our thoughts and prayers. Those monstrous criminal acts demonstrated all too clearly the physical dangers officers face. Other dangers officers face, are subtler, but they can also be hazardous. When politicians ignore constitutional limits in exchange for ideological fiat when enacting municipal statutes, they can put their officers in legal peril. Let's hope our new city administration quashes this appalling act.

The previous administration's most recent attempt at a gun prohibition "Rule" puts its police officers in a precarious position, unnecessarily and perhaps callously. For one thing, the state legislature didn't enact this edict; a municipal government executive did so by virtual royal decree, consciously flouting state preemption. For our purposes, state preemption restricts local jurisdictions from enacting firearms laws more restrictive than state laws.

The City contends this is a moral quest to make city property "safer" for children. This ploy is the refuge of political scoundrels: It's for the children. Well, that argument is so ridiculous on its face, I recoil at addressing it at all. I mean, who honestly thinks a gun ban will keep criminals from toting guns onto any city property—oh wait a minute—that's right, the gun ban isn't aimed at criminals, it's aimed at law abiding Americans.

There are myriad unsettling issues surrounding this "Rule." Leading up to its launch, the city and police administrations had little, if any, communication with the officers expected to enforce it. For example, many East Precinct officers weren't briefed until Thursday, October 15th, during roll call, by a city attorney who informed them that the gun ban—oh, sorry—criminal trespass by quasi-associated gun possession—would go into effect the following day, October 16th, at three preliminary locations.

The briefing consisted of an informal talk/discussion supposedly bolstered by an unsigned written policy, reportedly "signed off" by the police department's chain of command, which we were directed to refer to, and which was marked: "Draft." A draft of a policy to enforce a "Rule" surely to be deemed unconstitutional, and officers are expected to believe the city will stand behind them if—when—something goes sideways should some poor officer choose to enforce this city diktat against a prepared Second Amendment advocate, thus propelling the officer to federal court complete with time in the commensurate national spotlight as the Second Amendment-hating cop who violated the plaintiff's constitutional rights.

It is unconscionable for any city to deliberately place its police officers at such legal risk and its citizens in such financial jeopardy on some ideological whim. While the plaintiff would sue the City (deep pockets) for any constitutional violation, it's the poor officer who suffers the indignities of Federal Court. Ask any officer who's been sued in Federal Court how much fun that ride is. And Seattle's taxpayers can ask the plaintiff—just how many zeros on the check?

There's a paramilitary concept that civilian leaders may fail to consider: It's a long-established legal tenet that a soldier/police officer may refuse to carry out an unlawful order. In fact, not only does an officer have no duty to follow an illegal order; an officer has a duty not to.

An earlier, and similar, but more direct, city "gun" ban died an ignoble death—and rightly so. Reading the applicable federal and state laws on a citizen's right to keep and bear arms, and taking into consideration Washington State Attorney General Rob McKenna's opinion on this "Rule," an officer would be reasonable, or even be expected, to conclude this city's anti-gun "Rule" is transparently unconstitutional.

Cops should need no refresher on an American's gun rights, but please indulge me for a moment in deference to those civilian city leaders who may be somewhat—oh, thin—on their understanding of the constitutional rights so many brave men and women fought and died to provide and keep for us.

Our Founders knew our right to keep and bear arms was so important they listed it second in the Bill of Rights. And closer to home, the authors of our own Washington State Constitution placed the right to bear arms in Article One, and it's even more explicit than its federal counterpart: "The right of the individual citizen to bear arms in defense of himself, or the state, shall not be impaired..."

In an October 8, 2009, *Boston.com* article, Second Amendment Foundation founder Alan Gottlieb accurately described Seattle's convoluted enforcement mechanism as "disingenuous." Rather than enforcing the "Rule" forthrightly, its sponsors have fabricated a back-door approach wherein the City's not enforcing a firearms violation per se, but an ostensible criminal trespass violation for possessing a firearm while on the premises.

Gottlieb describes the "Rule's" creator as intending to be "clever" by designating the head of the parks department as the "homeowner" authorized to eject a specific undesirable, in this case a person on the premises in possession of a firearm, from his "home" (city property). Perhaps someone could fill the City in on the wide chasm that exists between public and private property. There is a fine line between clever and devious.

The city would never ban political signs, even those including graphic war or abortion photos, but what would be the difference between such a ban and the gun ban? The City's view, apparently, is one would abridge the revered First Amendment while the other abridges the reviled Second Amendment.

We in law enforcement have to ask ourselves where the line is that we won't cross. There will always be laws and rules enacted with which individual officers may disagree, but will enforce as necessary. But when the law or rule blatantly abridges a constitutional right, isn't it the time to draw a line and then not tread beyond it?

If an officer wouldn't enforce a rule that blatantly abridges the First, Fourth, Fifth, or Eighth

Amendments, would it be right for an officer to enforce a "Rule" abridging the Second Amendment?

For those in law enforcement who support this rule—hopefully they are few—what Samuel Adams said a couple centuries ago, still captures the essence of the moral violation: "If ye love wealth greater than liberty, the tranquility of servitude greater than the animating contest for freedom, go home from us in peace. We seek not your counsel, nor your arms. Crouch down and lick the hand that feeds you; May your chains set lightly upon you, and may posterity forget that ye were our countrymen."

For those who think I'm overly dramatic, ask yourselves how oppression starts. Do jack-booted government thugs appear one day to usurp rights, impose edicts, and kick in citizen's doors and confiscate their guns? History says no. Logic dictates the oppressors start subtly with soft tyranny, beginning with simple decrees such as Seattle's gun ban attempt, to see what they can get away with without the overt use of force. In any case, 9/11 should have taught us that the unimaginable can and does happen—even in America.

To those for whom this is a bitter pill to swallow, but have decided to do so for expediency, reluctantly supporting the enforcement of this "Rule," but privately gagging, they might consider our Founder's sacrifices. George, Tom, Old Sam and his cousin John, and the other Founders literally risked their careers, fortunes, and lives to attain the ability to frame these cherished rights—all of them—including those contained in the Second Amendment, to pass on to us, their posterity, and for which we were entrusted to maintain and then expected to pass on to ours.

Have we arrived at the day when, while our Founders were willing to lose their fortunes and lay down their lives to guarantee these rights, we won't risk our careers, or even our upward mobility, to keep them? Officers have a tiny U.S. Constitution behind their badges, which includes the Bill of Rights—all ten of them. The Second Amendment is a prime target of would-be oppressors and was intended as our last line of defense against a tyrannical government; stand up for it!

* * *

Again, there is an enforcement line police officers shouldn't cross, but where is it? It's the line officers stand on that protects your liberty from those who would infringe on it. Not only common criminals but also common statists, bureaucrats, and politicians—the social justices.

One problem cops have always faced is the influence of partisan politics interfering in law enforcement's mission. Some say politics in law enforcement is unavoidable. That may be true, but it doesn't mean cops should lie down and allow politics to crush them. Police officers are commissioned public officeholders. They swear oaths to carry out their official duties according to federal, state, and local laws. They are not like privates in an army who simply follow orders.

While most sheriffs are elected, politicians appoint police chiefs. This can put chiefs in a position where they feel they must reflect the politician's liberal views, which tend to contrast with the more conservative officers he or she will lead. Chiefs also may feel beholden to their political benefactors, which may skew their law enforcement decisions.

So, when liberal politicians appoint a social justice (police chief) to lead a department of equal justices (cops), the community experiences a collision between matter and antimatter. It is the unique and rare leader who can bridge this gap, but they do exist. Former Sheriff David Clarke of Milwaukee County, Wisconsin, is a fine example. But like I said, he's elected. And while a city could do worse than Seattle's current police chief Kathleen O'Toole, if Seattle had a law enforcement leader like Sheriff Clarke, I might still be on the job. And he's a Democrat!

Most sheriffs are accountable to the people. Police chiefs are accountable to a town or city administration. Of course, regardless of how a law enforcement leader is selected, he or she can be corrupt or honorable. However, it seems that to be honorable today, a chief would need to resign or be fired rather than follow the leftist's law enforcement–damaging policies. Adhering to the federal and state constitutions, whether appointed or elected, is the best way police chiefs and sheriffs can maintain integrity.

Some law enforcement leaders choose the liberal way, ignoring the Constitution, not to mention common sense, when it suits them. Just look at former San Francisco sheriff Ross Mirkarimi and his culpability in the Kate Steinle murder. The sheriff first requested the five-time deported Juan Francisco Lopez-Sanchez be transferred from federal custody where he was incarcerated on a forty-six-month sentence to San Francisco County. Then the sheriff released Lopez-Sanchez. Four months later he reportedly shot and killed Ms. Steinle while she was taking a stroll with her father. Ignoring a responsibility to cooperate with federal law enforcement can have tragic consequences. Now, the entire state of California has seceded from commonsense, becoming the first sanctuary state. *What could possibly go wrong?*

As a libertarian, I revere the Constitution from, "We the People..." in the Preamble, to Article VII, to the Bill of Rights. The rights the Constitution enshrine are an American treasure as well as an example for freedom-loving peoples around the world.

While it's true this great document began with hard compromises relevant to the times, many concerned and prudent framers were brilliant enough to glimpse the future and anticipate it. They made certain the document contained provisions for amending it where and when necessary, though not easily. They incorporated methods to eventually modify the unavoidable-at-the-time concessions to evil, which, after its ratification, continued to restrict the liberty of some Americans, including indentured servants, black slaves, Indians, and women.

Don't allow presentism to warp your understanding of history. And since *perfect* is unattainable, the goal was and is to create a "more perfect" union, not a "perfect" progressive Utopia. There's still work to do, but what remarkable progress America has made.

CHAPTER 24

COPS MUST SPEAK OUT, BUT CAREFULLY

P lease, don't take this as legal advice; *it's not—not even close.* I'm not a lawyer, and I've never played one on TV. My opinions are based on over two decades of experience, what I gathered after having studied the pertinent issues, investigated crime, testified in court, and having gone through my own city's political meat grinder. And there's my having come face to face with the reality of de-policing.

While police officers should never cross the constitutional line I mentioned, cops speaking out on important issues has become necessary. For example, after the Freddie Gray incident—Gray died following a spinal injury suffered during transport after his arrest—Baltimore city cops appeared on cable news programs.

Why were these police officers speaking out? Because their leaders weren't speaking to support them. Why did they have to do so anonymously? Because police officers suffer retaliation if they speak out against liberal orthodoxy. I know; it happened to me.

Police officers are not comfortable exercising their freedom of speech because of a legitimate fear their employers will retaliate even to the point of firing them. Liberal government leaders have this weird habit of treating officer speech they like by allowing it and treating officer speech they don't like by infringing on it.

This illustrates the minefield cops negotiate while trying to navigate their free speech rights while working in leftist enclaves. But if the cops' bosses won't back them, they have little choice but to defend themselves and each other. Does it seem fair to anyone that a mayor, city council member, or police chief can get as political as they want, on and off the job, and exercise their free speech (as long they espouse leftist ideology), but for police officers who risk life and limb daily, these same people make free speech as difficult as possible?

Everyone in America has a constitutionally protected right to free speech, it seems, except for police officers. Of course, even freedom of speech has its limitations. The proverbial not being free to yell "fire" in a crowded theater comes to mind. But sometimes the line seems more obscure for cops. Regardless, officers should feel free to exercise all of their rights just like any other citizen—just as their bosses do.

Beware the costs, though. The right to speak one's mind doesn't imply that speech comes without consequences. Your free speech rights are protected against governmental infringement. You must prepare yourself for how much the oh-so-tolerant left isn't interested in your point of view. And, more importantly, your expressing it.

As much as the left claims fealty to the First Amendment, the social justices curtail the free exchange of ideas every chance they get. Today's mainstream left is not only not interested in what conservatives have to say but also, they're not interested in anyone else hearing it either. It bothers liberals to no end that compared with conservatives their radio and television programs garner such small audiences.

Their lament: "If only people heard our message, they'd understand how evil conservatives are." Yet, people still flock to media such as Fox News and Rush Limbaugh, but eschew MSNBC and, well... almost any liberal commentator. Although, to be fair, in an ironic twist, a few liberal hosts such as Rachel Maddow and Stephen Colbert are experiencing bolstered viewership built on their deranged disdain for President Donald J. Trump. I hope they at least add him to their Christmas card list—oh, wait…I should probably say holiday card list. Still, there are reports their ratings are beginning to slip again.

If you work for a private company and you publicly lambast your boss, don't be surprised if you lose your job. You won't get tossed in prison. You are free to say it, but you are not free of the consequences of your words. As a private company, owners can fire workers who refuse to respect the boss's business goals. Even government employees enjoy free speech only when speaking as a private citizen. Makes sense, right? But, it's supposed to be different when government attacks the free speech of a person speaking as a private citizen.

If you exercise your free speech as a cop, even speaking as a private citizen, you have more consequences to weigh than the average person. By law, your government employer *must* respect your free speech rights as an individual. But sometimes they don't. As a police officer, you have serious considerations. You work for a paramilitary organization. Order and discipline are essential to keeping an organization functioning properly. However, if your department is asking you to compromise your values, your ethics, or to attend political indoctrination disguised as police training, by all means, speak out—*loudly*.

Law enforcement agencies give new police officers a cursory introduction to department policies and local, state, and federal laws. They don't immerse the cops in them. There's not enough time. Laws and policies keep changing anyway. In fact, academy staff taught my class that department policies are only guidelines because they can't possibly account for every scenario a cop may face.

How times have changed. Today, if an officer violates a policy the administration doesn't care about, the policy is treated as a guideline for which the officer is allowed discretion. But if an officer violates a policy that is important to the administration for political reasons, then the accused officer is condemned as if he or she violated a policy carved in granite.

On a side note, there's another similar phenomenon cops experience. A certain activity will be mandated as critical to the mission and safety of officers. For example, assigning two officers per patrol car might be deemed critical for officer safety. Then, strangely, when the funds for the "critical" activity runs dry, somehow the activity is no longer critical or even an officer safety concern. Officer safety is always a valid topic for cops to speak out on.

In Washington State, officers have access to a wonderful resource called the *Law Enforcement Digest*. The Washington State Criminal Justice Commission, the folks who run the police academy in this state, publishes it monthly. It contains condensed versions of court decisions from around the state and nation, informing officers of changes—and at times of the liberal lunacy some justices emit. I encourage all officers to keep up with the changing laws and policies before and not after they find themselves in the political churn. In addition to keeping fresh on legal changes, there are some other important items cops who speak out should consider.

As an officer speaking as a private citizen about police-related subjects, you must make it even more clear than with non-police issues that you are not speaking as a representative of your department, your city, your chief, or your mayor. You can express yourself by writing or speaking, but make sure it is clear that your expression is yours alone.

Not to belabor the subject, I want to stress how important it is for you to explicitly establish your independence from your agency. Don't trust that because you're speaking out *against* something the city or department has done that they won't challenge you, saying you're attempting to speak for the department. Saying something like, "These are my words, not my employer's," or "I am speaking only for myself"—anything like that will do. This is important. If you don't do it, your agency might attempt to use it against you later like mine did with me.

Don't speak out politically while on duty or in uniform. Both of these could imply you are representing the city, the department, or the chief. Be confident that you're speaking out on an issue of public importance. For example, it might not be protected speech if you publicly rant about how you don't like how your captain dresses for church on Sunday, you saw him leaving a strip club, or you don't like his speech impediment. Those things are probably not of legitimate public concern. However, if you speak out about—*oh* I don't know—the city failing to enforce a law equitably because of leftist doofusness, this is of public concern, and cops should address it.

The case upon which many people base their view of police (public employee) free speech rights is *Garcetti v. Ceballos*, 547 U.S. 410 (2006). Briefly, Richard Ceballos, a court staffer in Los Angeles, found legitimate flaws in a warrant the sheriff's office requested from a judge and then served. Ceballos brought the warrant's flaws to the attention of the defense counsel. Though the information about the flawed warrant may have been legitimate, the U.S. Supreme Court held the First Amendment does not protect a public employee while conducting official duties. It only protects the person when speaking as a private individual.

In this instance, Richard Ceballos acted in his official capacity on an active case with which he was associated. When he sued for a violation of his free speech rights, the courts ruled that his employers were within their authority to sanction him because he'd acted on an active case within the scope of his official governmental duties.

Other consequences to be aware of are the possibilities for subtle retaliation. Being declined for advancement, special or favored assignments, or training opportunities are among the most common "quiet" retaliations against police officers who dare to express contrary, often conservative, views. It's tough to prove you're being declined something specifically due to things you've written or said. All the officer knows is he or she applied and was denied.

Some time ago, I had let my watch commander review a column I was about to submit to the *Guardian*. I admired and trusted this lieutenant. Although I'd written complimentary things about him in the article, others didn't fare so well. He told me if I was concerned about my career and wanted to go anywhere in the department, I should not publish the article. He added that I shouldn't write such articles in the future. Incidentally, several years later he would serve as an interim police chief. Though I lost a little respect, I still think he's a good guy—he was looking out for me.

After his comments, I did two things: I submitted the article and resigned myself that if I were going to continue writing commentary about things that negatively affected patrol officers, I'd climbed as high as I was going to in my SPD career. I made peace with my decision and never looked back.

Now that you've determined you will speak for yourself, while off duty and not in uniform, not about any current official cases in which you are involved, and about something of public interest, perhaps it's time to give it a shot. Of course, this relative "safety" is no guarantee your employer won't come after you anyway—in liberal jurisdictions they very likely may. But at least you'll have done your homework and will have built a firm foundation. As cops know too well, doing your duty rarely comes without risk. Standing up for the Constitution and against social justice tyranny is worth it.

This reminiscing, reminds me of the very first article I wrote that the *Guardian* published. The *Guardian* article that caused me to write my first piece was about guns. The officer, a lieutenant now, last I heard, who wrote the article is a great guy. But he wrote a column that implied that merely having a gun in one's home increased the odds of a household member committing suicide. Now, I could have read it like everyone else, dismissed it, and then gone about my day as a rookie (maybe should have). But *noooo!* The column struck this rookie as anti-Second Amendment and antigun. It bothered me it was written by a police officer, who should know better. I had to speak out.

In the article, I disagreed, respectfully, with this veteran officer's contention. It was a ridiculous premise that merely having a gun in a house increases the likelihood someone would commit suicide. If the officer had argued that having a gun in the house might increase the chances that an *already* suicidal person would use a gun to commit suicide rather than another method, at least that would have made sense.

An old TV show illustrates the point of that article and why I felt I needed to respond.

* * *

The ultraconservative TV character Archie Bunker and his liberal daughter, Gloria, were having a conversation. They were debating the gun issue.

Gloria says, "Do you know that sixty percent of all deaths in America are caused by guns?"

Archie replies, "Would it make you feel any better, little girl, if they were pushed out of windows?"

* * *

All in the Family never shied away from hot-button, non-politically correct politics. In fact, it embraced discussion and debate. And though created by über-liberal, genius Norman Lear, it was intellectually honest with its ideas and use of language, not like today's mind-numbing and cowardly PC culture.

Is the method really to blame for someone's suicide? Liberals don't scream about outlawing sleeping pills, ropes, plastic bags, or even knives when used to commit suicide. What about bridges?

The point is if you get that impulse to speak out on an issue, take in what was written or said and digest it. Think about it critically. Don't run to the nearest TV or radio station, write a letter to the editor, or blast the chief or mayor with a thoughtless blog. Critical thinking is lacking in our society. It doesn't help your cause to write some knee-jerk, scathing, bridge-burning column that'll have people scratching you off their Christmas card lists. Listen to your intuition. Think carefully about the issue; study it. Then, if you conclude you must speak out, do it thoughtfully, intelligently, and respectfully.

You'll know if you've got something to say when you don't care what anyone else thinks or says about your opinions. You *have* to say it. It's similar to that strange, *un-conservative* urge to show up to a public demonstration to support or oppose an issue. You need others to know that not everyone agrees with a particular leftist political view. You'll know if the issue is vital when you don't care if a single other person shows up. You believe the issue is so important, you'll stand alone to make your point.

I tried to adhere to four ground rules when I wrote my *Guardian* columns:

- *Remain civil.*
- *Don't make it personal.*
- *Stick to issues.*
- *Use a person's position, not name, when the focus is negative.*

Incidentally, I still try to adhere to these rules when I write—I said, I *try*.

I've made exceptions to Rule 4 for high officials such as chiefs of police and official social justices such as city attorneys and mayors on whose desks the proverbial buck stops.

Don't let those who cause de-policing to also cause de-participating in political speech. Police joining in political speech can make the difference between an increase or decrease in future de-policing. I fear we haven't seen the worst of this anti-cop phenomenon yet. In a related side note, as I write this chapter, in Arizona last night, a black man intentionally ran down three white Phoenix police officers. Two of the officers were injured and luckily all survived.

All in all, if you feel compelled to speak, then speak. It is curious that some brave cops don't hesitate to face down society's worst criminals but are reluctant to express views about policies that offend their strongly held values.

Your free expression doesn't have to wind up on the evening news, in the morning paper, or even in a police union newspaper.

Just stating your opinions when discussing issues with your fellow officers can go a long way, as long as you show respect for them stating their opinions in return.

Don't allow career goals to subordinate your virtue and compromise your character. By speaking honestly, you'll not only do your fellow officers a favor by standing against liberal tyranny but also you will be doing your future self a favor. You'll be able to sit, relaxing in your retirement rocker, sippin' four fingers of Jameson's or a nice, cool lemonade, watchin' the grandkids playin' in the yard, feelin' proud you didn't compromise your values.

CHAPTER 25

HOW DE-POLICING
AFFECTED ME

D
e-policing should scare the hell out of every American. Especially at this critical time when our enemies, ISIS, and other Islamist terrorists—not to mention our own criminals—are, in the truest sense of the phrase, *hunting Americans in the streets*. As I sit at my desk this morning, the news led with attacks overnight in three states. Terrorists used bombs in New York and New Jersey and a knife in Minnesota. And, a couple months later, while back editing this chapter, an Islamist radical drove a rental truck for a mile along a New York City bike path, killing eight and injuring a dozen more. Why would the left engage in something so suicidal as marginalizing police officers at a time like this? Because ideology and politics trump all. I know. I experienced it, and it had a profound effect on me and how I viewed my career.

I didn't tell anyone other than those I had to inform of the exact day I would retire, and I asked them to respect my privacy. Fellow officers knew the day was coming and wanted to get together with me to celebrate on my last day. I appreciated the sentiment more than I can say, and, honestly, sometimes I've regretted not joining them. After all, they were not the reason I was leaving. In fact, leaving them was the only thing that caused me any hesitation. However,

I did have a small get-together with members of my squad a week or so after I'd retired.

I also declined to attend the city's official retirement ceremony. I wasn't about to "play nice" with people responsible for my leaving the department prematurely—especially accepting a plaque and shaking the hand of a mayor who'd publicly said, about me, there was no room in this city for cops opposing race and justice programs. I wasn't interested in participating in any pretend civility. Though very proud of my career, my retirement was nothing I felt like celebrating. Interestingly, people I knew in the personnel department told me I was far from the only retiring officer who declined to participate in the official ceremony, for reasons similar to mine.

De-policing happens in different ways, and engaging in it is not a frivolous, conscious decision cops make to "punish" their agencies and community critics. Cops refraining from proactive patrol results when officers don't feel their leaders will back them if an incident goes wrong. Even more, that their leaders will actively side with the perennial police haters against officers.

Some police officers purposely decide to back off proactivity after they become involved in an incident where they have done as they were taught, but their departments still won't support them (remember the cases of Seattle police officers Adley Shepherd and Cynthia Whitlatch). In fact, these days, it seems some departments are more likely to assist with prosecuting officers rather than defending them. Even in the most mundane of incidents cops have to wonder, *What will happen to me if a call goes sideways?*

A white male cop sees a known black male burglar loitering in the doorway of a closed business. Should the officer contact the man to see if he has legitimate business there? Sure, but the officer knows if the suspicious person becomes uncooperative and the incident escalates to a use of force, he could easily get jammed up for "violating the man's civil rights." There was a day when checking on any suspicious man—or woman—in a closed shop's doorway was called "good police work." That day is not today.

Every cop affected by de-policing has a unique story. With some, it's what happened to them directly. With others, it's what happened to fellow officers. With some others, it's a response to the national trend of animosity and disrespect toward police officers in general. As I write this, three more officers, this time in California, were shot and two were killed. Nearly every day there are new stories of cops injured or killed. As I complete the final edits for this book, this news story came across my desk: a 19-year-old student shot and killed a Texas Tech police officer. *Enough!*

Yet, cops are still on the political chopping block. Just look at things like former president Obama and the Democratic Party routinely criticizing police. President Obama, with very few facts, told the American people that the Cambridge Police "acted stupidly" in a 2009 incident involving the arrest of Harvard professor Henry Louis Gates, Jr. And what are cops supposed to think about the Democrats' official support for cop-hating groups such as Black Lives Matter? In my case, de-policing infected me due to all of the above. I didn't want to change my approach to police work; the anti-police collective forced me to change the way I conducted patrol, out of self-preservation.

I struggled with whether I should include my personal story in this book. For one thing, it shows I do have an axe to grind. After reading my story in the upcoming series of articles, I think you'll agree the axe needed grinding. I can't possibly detail all the officers whose experiences have led them to a form of de-policing, but I can provide one—mine.

Although some may label me disgruntled, *disappointed* is the most apt description. I love the Seattle Police Department and its employees, sworn and civilian. I'm proud of the service I provided to the Seattle community during my career. I only wish the liberal establishment had allowed me to continue doing my job the way it should be done. When I was in the academy, officers questioned instructors about inadvertently getting into trouble while trying to do the job correctly. Instructors always said, "Don't worry. If you do your job right, you won't get into trouble." As a rookie, I took comfort from this advice. This is obviously nowhere near the case today.

My de-policing odyssey started with the liberal insanity that began infecting the department in the late 1990s. After fifteen years as Seattle's police chief, Patrick Fitzsimons, a former NYPD assistant chief, stepped down. Like him or not, he was a real chief; cops knew who ran the department—and it wasn't the politicians.

The next regime, headed by a nice man named Norm Stamper, arrived from San Diego, bringing a strange new brew to town. It came in the form of the politically correct insanity the left has become known for. Here's a couple quick examples out of many.

At the dawn of the Stamper administration, an edict trickled down from on high directing officers not to use the term *wite-out* when referring to an office product called... *Wite-Out* because someone in the leadership with a twisted thought process determined the name could be perceived as racist. Okay, I'm dating myself, but for younger folk out there, we used to complete police reports and forms with a contraption known as a typewriter. If you made an error, you'd use Wite-Out, a small container of thick, fast-drying white fluid, to correct it. With the small applicator brush connected to the screw top, you'd paint over your error, wait for it to dry (blowing on it and sometimes smearing it), and then type over it. Who knew an office product could be racist?

The edict directed officers to refrain from using the term *wite-out* because someone might perceive it as racist. No. I'm not kidding. This was not a *Saturday Night Live* skit. We were to replace the product's name, Wite-Out, with the term *correction fluid*. Oh, and the liberals also targeted *straight talk*. I don't believe I have any gay friends who believe this term is offensive. To the new administration, apparently, homosexuals found the term offensive and demeaning. Perhaps straight liberals should let gay people decide what offends them. *Wow!* I've heard of micro-aggressions, but this sounds like a nano-aggression. You'd think I suddenly swerved into writing fiction with this nonsense.

So, has the quest for political correctness improved in Seattle with subsequent city and department administrations? Are you kidding me? In 2013, the city issued a memo outlawing the terms *brown bag* (as in, brown bag lunch) and *citizen* as racist. I won't dignify this lunacy with an attempt at an explanation. My head hurts just mentioning it. I'll just say, evidently, brown bag is offensive to black people and citizen could offend—wait for it—illegal immigrants.

But if you're desperate for an explanation, look up Alasdair Baverstock's article that appeared in the *Telegraph* in the United Kingdom, "Seattle bans words 'citizen' and 'brown bag.'" Yes, Seattle's liberal lunacy has gone worldwide.

These incidents show the would-be-funny-if-they-weren't-so-serious side of the political correctness portion of liberal indoctrination. But those were only two examples of the social justice disease. The full-blown infection began in earnest after the 1999 WTO riots when a magnificent police department response, with dangerously few resources (cops), saved Seattle from the muck-ups (to be polite) occupying its highest offices. Oh, yes. I still remember sleeping on the Seahawks logo in the Kingdome, using my police jacket as a blanket.

My personal descent into de-policing story began with a meeting I had with a watch commander (lieutenant) in the mid-2000s. I liked telling people the truth when they asked me why it took so long to respond to their calls. I'd briefly described the 911 priority criteria to complainants:

Precedence (P) 0 through 3.

- P0: *Help the officer*
- P1: *Serious crime in progress, e.g., DV, assault, rape, robbery, etc.*
- P2: *Incident stable but could escalate quickly*
- P3 *low priority, e.g., suspicious person but no crime reported, after the fact investigations, i.e., paper calls such as burglaries, thefts, etc.*

This is what the department preferred that officers tell people and stop there. But I didn't stop. People deserved more. They deserved the truth. I'd also explain the serious lack of patrol officers. I told them the Seattle Police Department had about the same number of sworn officers that day as in 1979 despite a population increase of about 490,000 to 680,000 people.

I'd go on to explain that with all of the specialty units created to address political priorities, more and more officers were being appropriated from patrol. After the DOJ's arrival and the instituting of a bogus federal consent decree, patrol depletion got even worse. Each time the DOJ implemented a "settlement agreements" with a city, they mandate departments staff "compliance" and other support units such as Force Investigation Teams (FIT), as they did in Seattle. To put it bluntly, they remove from the streets patrol officers who are supposed to respond to your 911 calls and reassign them to superfluous units that partisan politics has created.

Apparently, one of the citizens—*Oops!* I meant *people*—to whom I'd explained response times and lack of officers used my name when calling to complain about staffing to the department. My lieutenant called me into his office. He said, "[unofficially] You're doing a great job. Keep doing what you're doing, but I *have* to tell you this: [officially] IIS/OPA [Internal Investigation Section/Office of Professional Accountability] wants you to stop telling people that SPD has insufficient staffing in patrol. They want you to explain the 911 system's priority call structure and leave it at that. Okay?"

"*Okay*," I said with a rising intonation and a smirk.

The lieutenant replied with his own smirk and said, "Now, get back to work."

Here's one example of why cops don't trust their leaders. If they're willing to have us lie or intentionally omit information to the public, how can cops trust their leaders to tell them the truth? This also provokes de-policing. For example, when the department trained officers to use the in-car video system (dash cam), instructors taught about the things that the police administration said it would never do. They said they wouldn't go on "fishing" expeditions to search through an officer's video footage for petty violations. They also assured officers the camera system only records when an officer activates it manually or automatically by turning on emergency equipment. Why would they tell cops this when they knew reviewers can go back to any video because the system is always recording? Why wouldn't they tell officers the truth?

Today, officers are routinely called to account for petty policy violations found on video review even of minor calls where officers played little or no role—even during incidents where officers took no enforcement action at all. Remember I said I was also affected by what happened to other officers? One of my squad mates saw a driver commit a sudden and dangerous traffic violation. As she whipped the car around, intending to stop the driver, she aborted. Why? Because after she'd activated her lights to make a U-turn she said, speaking to herself in the "privacy" of her patrol car, "That asshole." She realized her microphone had switched on with the camera when she turned on her overhead lights. Now, video reviewers could file a complaint for her "foul language." Also, if the violator fought the ticket, the defense could review the video and claim the officer had bias against the driver prior to making the stop due to her "abusive" language toward him.

Another officer told me he got into trouble on a call he'd started to respond to but had been called off. He never even arrived. Video reviewers found he'd passed cars on the right at a congested intersection. Passing on the right is generally a no-no, but the officer is the one there, and you remember what I said about department policies being guidelines because not every situation can be anticipated.

This veteran officer made a conscious decision to defy the letter of a policy to assure he'd arrive in time to assist other officers. If you're the officer waiting for backup, you appreciate this—so might the crime victim.

Another example of the department's sleight of hand is playing with the staffing numbers sent to headquarters each day. I saw these "manpower" sheets nearly every shift before roll call. The front desk officer is required to fill out daily staffing levels of patrol officers available for dispatched calls in each precinct and send them to Operations. Unfortunately, the actual staffing rarely reflected reality. They create an illusion of more staffing than exists. These sheets routinely included officers who were not available for 911 responses. For example, the sheet might reflect twenty officers available for 911 calls, when the more accurate number is twelve (I chose these numbers arbitrarily).

So, how does this affect patrol and the community? Well let's say the current minimum staffing is a combined number of officers for the three East Precinct sectors (minimum staffing changes depending on the day of the week—e.g., increases on Fridays and Saturdays). Each sector is assigned a certain number of officers at full staff, which rarely occurs due to vacations, temporary assignments, sickness, and injuries. When I came on in 1992, SPD had more than double the officers per sector, and minimum staffing for a watch was about twice the number compared to when I retired (and what officers tell me is still the case today). So, while Operations got a staffing report of a certain number of officers available to respond to 911 calls, the actual number was routinely closer to half that and often fewer.

As I mentioned earlier, about myself, it's likely every veteran officer can recount a shift where he or she was the only officer available in a sector with three districts. In my case, that was an area roughly ten square miles, populated with tens of thousands of people. I know; I was the sole officer responding to calls in my sector several times during my career. And this was the department's smallest precinct by geographical area.

During one period, the precinct commander ordered sergeants to staff neighborhood traffic radar displays to address neighborhood speeding complaints. This is perfectly fine when there are enough officers to provide basic patrol services but not when there aren't even enough cops to handle 911 calls. The same thing happened with other "special" assignments, stripping officers from their squads and communities of their officers.

When I told my wife about the day I was the only patrol officer in my squad, she became upset. I was the only officer in my sector to handle calls because the other officers had been diverted to that traffic detail. This is a major officer safety lapse. Concerned about officer safety (she kind of liked it when I came home after my shift), she suggested that as a long-time precinct veteran I had an obligation to bring my concerns to my superiors.

I reported my apprehensions, based upon my many years in patrol at the East Precinct, in a respectful memo. I gave it to my sergeant and left it up to him to decide if it should go further up the chain of command. I said I felt I'd done my part in alerting him to the problem. He reviewed it and then chose to forward it to his superiors. Was the result respect for my officer safety comments? Hah! Was it a simple blow-off (which I expected) that they'd take my comments under consideration? No! It was, *How dare he bring up a safety concern? This officer must be punished!*

Mid-shift, the watch commander called me into his office and said, "The captain read your memo. You're being transferred to George Sector immediately." (A summary transfer is extremely rare in the SPD.) They didn't even wait until the next shift.

Later, I met with the captain, an affable and charming guy who'd probably be great to hang out with if he weren't your boss. I explained my sincere safety concerns and assured him I'd intended no disrespect. He said, "Well, maybe I didn't read your memo correctly." Nevertheless, the captain declined to have the transfer reversed.

I wrote another memo up the chain, suggesting my transfer was retaliatory after bringing up a legitimate officer safety concern. I met with the captain once again after claiming his actions amounted to retaliation. He replied that I'd been transferred for routine "staffing" reasons, not retaliation. (A sudden, permanent transfer, in the middle of a shift, without notice, immediately after he read my memo? *Right!*) Then, after having said he may have read my memo incorrectly, he looked me in the eye and said, "I never even *read* your memo."

After some back and forth with some chiefs, and after the captain ignored orders to transfer me back to my squad, and after eighty-one days, he finally transferred me back to my original assignment, coincidentally, just after learning a deputy chief wanted to meet with me about it.

In the end, what was the penalty for a captain not only disobeying a chief's order but lying to and retaliating against a patrol officer for bringing up an officer safety concern? He became the police chief (now retired) of a department in another state. And the world turns.

Since my superior retaliated against me for bringing up a legitimate employee safety concern, I looked into Seattle's whistle-blower statutes. Amazingly, the employee's department head was responsible for investigating the complaint. For me, former chief of police R. Gil Kerlikowske "investigated" the allegations. This "investigation" included only one component: the chief spoke with the captain and took his word that the action was not retaliatory. *It was only a matter of resource allocation, the timing of submitting my officer safety memo a mere coincidence.*

The chief did not interview me, my sergeant, or even the lieutenant whom the captain had ordered to transfer me, before arriving at his conclusions. The chief then sent me a terse memo informing me of his findings. The letter sounded more like a reprimand than an honest finding of fact. I can tell you that officers are held to a much higher standard as to how to conduct a proper investigation.

How much policing do you think I felt safe doing after this incident? How much confidence do you think I had that my leaders would support me if I were involved in a questionable incident? De-policing is a result of bad policies and poor leadership. It's not an officer's choice. It's an officer's natural distrust. Still, this was nothing compared with what happened a few years later.

Now, I'll let the articles I wrote from April to December 2010 speak to what happened that forced me to further adopt a so-called de facto de-policing approach and eventually feel forced to retire. These articles reflect my perspective at the time and provide a window into the environment confronting Seattle's police officers at that time.

A s an example of what little things an officer can do to influence his or her colleagues and contribute to the sociopolitical debate, what follows is the series of four articles I wrote and referenced within this book that were critical of Seattle's social justice indoctrination of police officers. They appeared throughout 2010 in four issues of *The Guardian*. Following these articles is the 2011 article I wrote detailing the city's and department's actions after I dared to speak out against social justice and liberal tyranny.

These articles contain the crux of the issues that originally prompted this book even before *de-policing* became the ubiquitous term it is today. The push for government-sponsored social justice is in large part what has led to the de-police—anti-cop—state we see today. I hadn't realized that the liberal reaction to these articles would be so malicious. It was just a simple, opposing political opinion. Ironically, intolerance defines today's self-described oh-so-tolerant left. Just as fascism defines the leftist group known as Anti-Fascism (Antifa). Well, it's easy when the left characterizes opposing speech as delivered by white supremacists and Hitler acolytes.

There's one last thing before you read these articles: please remember that the mayor and city councilmembers all have access to *The Guardian*. The police guild distributes it to them at city hall. *The Guardian* published the first article in the series in April 2010 and the last in December 2010. The manufactured reaction from city government leaders was shock and dismay, but it didn't come until 2011 *after* a left-wing newspaper, the *Stranger*, published an article, responding negatively to the last of the four articles. Seems city hall doesn't read its police union newspaper, but it reads Seattle's most radical leftist newspaper. This alone says a lot.

ANTI-SOCIAL IN-JUSTICE
The Guardian, April 2010 (#1)

Imagine my surprise while, back in early March, sorting through (read: rapid-deleting 99% of) my colossal number of daily work emails, coming across one congratulating the Seattle Police Department for its selection as one of five government agencies or individuals nominated for, "Government Agency of the Year!"

Neither the Seattle PD nomination, nor the fact we didn't win, surprised me. What surprised me was the "From" line: "SPD Race and Social Justice Change Team." SPD? Social Justice? Change? (What happened to Hope?) Team? One officer commented to me, "Change? From what to what?"

Should the Seattle Police Department be even remotely associated with such a highly partisan leftist political term as "Social Justice," even employing it in a unit, or "team" name? I contacted the SPD Race and Social Justice Change Team and they told me the team exists to support the City of Seattle's Race and Social Justice Initiative (RSJI). A senior SPD civilian employee and an SPD Captain lead the team. As far as the City's using the term, I don't concern myself. After all, elections have consequences, but the SPD…?

Social Justice may sound like an innocuous term, but it isn't. It's a leftist political euphemism widely used by socialist and communist organizations worldwide. When used by religious institutions for garnering support for their own endeavors, it might be laudable, as their charity is real and voluntary, but when used by government to compel a "false charity" by redistributing wealth, placing radical eco-restrictions on private property, or "leveling" some sort of amorphous, socioeconomic playfield, individual liberty is removed from the equation and the endeavor becomes corrupt. For example, the [socialist] Green Party lists Social Justice as one of its Four Pillars.

Loyola University's (New Orleans) Walter Block, the Harold E. Wirth Eminent Scholar Chair in Economics, states, "[Social Justice] is typically associated with left-wing or socialist analyses, policies and prescriptions." Professor Block, with regard to Social Justice in university policies and studies, adds, "Should an institution of higher learning demand of its faculty that they support Social Justice in the substantive left-wing sense, it would at one fell swoop lose all academic credibility. For it would in effect be demanding that its professors espouse socialism."

I couldn't help but read this passage, replacing "institution of higher learning" with police department, and "faculty" with police department employees. While it's not a precise comparison, it seems far too apt for comfort. Is the SPD compromising its credibility by associating with such a term?

Thomas Sowell, Scholar in Residence at the Hoover Institution, Stanford University, in his excellent book *Intellectuals and Society*, in which he politically dissects the intellectual left, cites Social Justice no less than fifteen times when describing the American political left's stated government goals.

A quick internet surf for "Social Justice" brings some interesting finds. In fact, I defy you to take longer than two minutes to find a socialist or communist icon such as the Soviet sickle and hammer or photos of such "liberty lovers" as Che Guevara, Karl Marx, or good ol' Vlad Lenin.

Okay, I'll even help ya out. Since we're talking about "Social Justice," just take a cruise over to *www.sojust.net*, which exclaims: "A Document History of Social Justice." On the website, you'll find a link to Socialjusticenews.com "Justice: The People's News." They've morphed the "J" in *justice* into a Soviet Union–style sickle and hammer. Their catchphrase: human rights/*social justice*/eco-justice.

A Jesuit priest is credited with coining the term Social Justice, back in the mid-19th Century. Since then prominent theologians, philosophers, and politicians, predominantly on the political left, have taken the notion and run with it.

Regardless of any individual's definition of the term, socialist, progressive, and communist groups have pretty much cornered the Social Justice market. Anyone who remembers WTO and other Seattle protests, past and recent, will attest to signs espousing this ubiquitous slogan. A socialist slogan, I'd argue, shouldn't be associated with the Seattle Police Department.

I believe words are important and that they have specific meanings and those meanings have implications. Social Justice is most often associated with issues related to various wealth redistribution, affirmative action, and other left-wing political schemes. To the contrary, I believe in individual liberty as America's Founders intended, as I believe most of my colleagues in the Seattle Police Department do. I don't know about you, but I feel uncomfortable—at the very least—with our fine department having any association with a term espousing a system of government responsible for, at best Fabian socialist misery and at worst Marxist tyranny.

Hasn't it been hammered into SPD employees that it's improper for us to engage in any form of political advocacy or opposition while on duty? It's a good rule. Police officers should be seen as independent arbiters of law enforcement and not be promoting social justice, or for that matter, the NRA, while on duty.

Oh, and by the way, have you seen our SPD website lately? Right now, there is a logo for a link to "Seattle Climate Action-NOW-Our Commitment." That's not left-wing, now, is it? Perhaps, to be balanced, they should put a Tea Party link there, too. Why not? Wait a sec. On second thought—don't get me started—again.

ARBITRARY LAW VERSUS THE RULE
OF LAW—NO CONTEST.
The Guardian, August 2010 (#2)

This is an interesting time to be living and, most particularly, working in Seattle—especially within the criminal justice system, or should I say the criminal social justice system? Apparently, in an ongoing attempt to replace an equal justice system with a social justice regime, we're seeing laws, and sentencing and filing guidelines, twisted about as a means to facilitate political ends.

For example, in an obvious attempt to protect criminal illegal aliens (I know, redundant) from deportation, the city attorney's office supports reducing the gross misdemeanor sentence by one day thus avoiding the trigger requiring the city notify Immigration and Customs Enforcement (ICE).

The social injustice continues: Now the city attorney's office has decided that officers issuing Driving While License Suspended-3rd Degree citations (DWLS-3, usually resulting from a failure to pay a previous citation) have apparently been "unfair," stating folks in the minority community, those who can least afford to pay the fines, are disproportionately targeted.

I suppose driving safely in the first place, and then not driving if your license is suspended, is seen by the City as too challenging for some folks. Driving while your license is suspended is a choice. Why not take the light rail instead—there's certainly plenty of room on board.

Some suspended drivers choose not to drive, as is right, while others ignore their suspensions and drive anyway—why reward those who do wrong? With this policy, why should any suspended driver stop driving?

It's not a judgment call when an officer issues a citation for DWLS-3, with the officer interpreting his observations, i.e., did the person stop at the stop sign, red light, or did the person disobey the speed limit? In the case of DWLS-3, if your license is suspended, it's suspended—period!

Currently, police issue a criminal citation, basically charging a defendant with the crime of DWLS-3, give them a copy with detailed instructions, and then send the court the original citation for processing: court dates, etc. But according to an article at publicola.net, The Law Disproportionately Targets Poor People, by Morning Fizz, Thursday, July 1, 2010, things are about to change.

In an effort to reduce DWLS-3 prosecutions by 90%, "Assistant city attorney Darby Ducomb said yesterday [June 30] that the city attorney's office would ask the police department to send DWLS-3 cases to them instead of straight to municipal court, and the city attorneys would decide which cases merited punishment. 'They're just a waste of money in our criminal justice system,' Ducomb said."

The city attorneys would decide which cases merited punishment? Based upon what criteria? I suppose since the prosecutor's office is primarily citing that minorities are receiving a disproportionate number of these citations, then it would only be consistent to conclude who "merits punishment" will be determined, at least in part, according to the defendant's skin color.

Some might argue prosecutors determine which cases will be charged and to what degree all the time. However, DWLS-3 is an administrative DOL status; the charge and degree have already been determined.

On July 7, 2010, Publicola.com's Erica C. Barnett conducted a video interview with the Seattle City Attorney. In answering a question as to why he was looking to reduce DWLS-3 prosecutions by 90%, the City Attorney responded very directly stating twice that his motivation lay in a commitment to "social justice."

The City Attorney justified the decision citing statistics showing officers issue a high percentage of DWLS-3 citations to black drivers. He referred to DWLS-3 as more of a "debt collection problem," and not a "public safety issue." This, of course, ignores that police had issued drivers who manage to attain DWLS-3, a traffic citation in the first place leading to the suspension. Traffic violations most often are public safety issues.

Further, in most instances, in order to be cited for DWLS-3, an officer would have to stop the driver for yet another driving infraction or crime. So, that makes the initial infraction the driver failed to pay, the determination of DWLS-3 driving status, and then the present driving offense which brings the driver's suspension to the officer's attention. Not to mention their auto insurance is likely to be compromised due to their suspended status, if they had it in the first place. So much for the "not a public safety issue" argument.

The city administration supports transparency in government, right? Well, let's see if they will be consistent with this policy. Will the City apprise officers of which drivers they cite for DWLS-3, that the prosecutor's office has subsequently determined do not "merit punishment," and most importantly, why?

If not, why not? Shouldn't officers be entitled to know whom they shouldn't be stopping or citing in the first place, so they don't waste their time? Oh, and for anyone still wondering what exactly is the definition of social justice, this policy is a clear demonstration of it—and wherever it's tried, this disease kills individual liberty.

Sometimes we officers wonder who it is passing and amending these laws in the first place, because the animus is often directed at the police who do not write the laws, but are charged with their enforcement for the city's benefit.

For example, several years ago an edict came down that officers would "mandatorily" impound a DWLS driver's car. Most officers I know opposed this law because it took discretion away from the person who is at the scene and best suited to make that decision—the officer.

However, as is so often the case, city leaders soon determined that minorities seemed to garner the most DWLS citations and impoundments. So, after inferring the police were racially profiling, the program was basically nullified and the police basically vilified.

Well, once again, it wasn't police officers who decided a status of DWLS-3 would be implemented for failure to pay a traffic citation; the lawmakers did that. Officers were simply expected to enforce the law. Now, with another implication of police racism, the city is interceding between the enforcer and the violator, to the benefit of only certain "deserving" violators, and to the officer's detriment, as they'd apparently been wasting their time issuing the citation at all.

I contacted the City Attorney's office and the chief of staff informed me that the office is currently "working through a number of issues" before implementing the new program, and did not answer the question as to whether or not officers would be notified of DWLS-3 declines to charge.

It sure looks like, at least in Seattle, Lady Justice is lifting her blindfold just a bit to take a peek at race and bank accounts, while her left drooping scales are in desperate need of calibration. This policy exchanges the rule of law for one of arbitrary prosecution: This person has adequate income and is of a certain race, therefore she "merits punishment." However, that person is irresponsible, doesn't pay his traffic fines, and continues to drive despite a suspended license—oh, but is of the "correct" race and economic status, therefore he doesn't "merit punishment."

So let it be written...so let it be done!

Trust me on this, folks. Take the City's use of Social Justice terminology and implementation of policy seriously and oppose it in every legal way possible because if we don't, we can expect a whole lot more of this arbitrary justice, and arbitrary justice is justice corrupted. This is something that should embarrass every liberty-loving, limited government–desiring, U.S. Constitution–defending Seattleite and American.

CITY SPONSORED RACIAL PROFILING?
The Guardian, October 2010 (#3)

Officers have responded to me enthusiastically regarding this year's Guardian columns pertaining to Seattle government's radical drive to replace equal justice with social justice. The many police officers I've heard from have had visceral responses to those in Seattle who want to institute socialistic initiatives and policies in the community they serve and protect.

After all, a police officer's overarching responsibility is to protect Americans' liberty and to make society as safe as practicable in a free society so the people can peacefully pursue their happiness—as they see fit.

Recently, while on a break from slogging through my most recent BAC recert (with apologies to the instructor, who is quite interesting and an excellent teacher but tasked with teaching some less than captivating stuff), an officer made an insightful comment to me. We were chatting about some of the hot air I emit every so many months in these pages, when the discussion came around to my social justice columns.

Specifically, we were discussing the most recent column (Arbitrary Law vs. the Rule of Law—No Contest, the Guardian, August 2010) regarding the City Attorney considering a new DWLS-3 policy, by which officers would submit their citations to the City Attorney's Office rather than directly to the court, where their attorneys would review the citations and then determine which drivers "merited punishment." According to the City Attorney's Office this determination would be made, largely, based upon an individual's race.

The officer pointed out, "Isn't that racial profiling?" At that moment three things occurred to me: Yes, it is, why didn't I talk to you before I wrote that last article, and lastly, why the hell didn't I think of it? Seems obvious, but perhaps we're being so inundated with this extremist, progressive agenda, nationally and locally, sometimes we miss the obvious.

Yes, by Jove, it is racial profiling, indeed—and in fact. Don't you love the irony? After many years of the City and community activist groups unsuccessfully attempting to prove that Seattle police officers are guilty of racially profiling its citizens (and non-citizens), the City offers proof that it's the one racially profiling, and further, it even wants to pass laws and implement policies to support it. Amazing!

So, now we have to ask ourselves, is it okay to racially profile as long as an individual (I know, individual is a bad word in the social justice vernacular—collectivists please bear with me) benefits by virtue of his or her inclusion in a specific racial, ethnic, or other "victim" group?

Reasonable people say, of course not. After all, the primary argument used to attack racial profiling is that the racial profiler is not treating one person the same as another person under similar circumstances due to a person's race. Opponents argue racial profiling violates the 14th Amendment's Equal Protection Clause, which states each state must provide all American citizens equal protection under the law. I agree, and by this logic, social justice similarly violates the 14th Amendment.

So, now that we've found some common ground—that racial profiling is wrong—how do we reconcile our City government's engaging in a form of institutional racial profiling called social justice?

If the goal is to end or prevent racial profiling by assuring everyone is treated equally, then how can we as police officers, guardians of liberty, tolerate the City instituting a program, Seattle's Race and Social Justice Initiative (RSJI), which includes it's embarrassingly inappropriate SPD Race and Social Justice Change Team?

Through this initiative the City seeks to implement policy and spend taxpayer money, specifically to treat some Seattleites differently than other Seattleites, based upon their race, ethnicity, and socioeconomic status.

The answer is obvious: we can't tolerate it—no respectable, Constitution-loving American could, and no American should. When Seattle's government says racial profiling is evil because it treats one citizen differently than another, in contravention of equal protection for all, they are 100% correct. The cops agree. That's why we don't do it.

So then, how can the City argue that its social justice agenda, which it proudly states exists to single out groups of citizens for special treatment over other groups of citizens—in contravention of constitutional equal protection provisions, I might add—isn't evil too?

Is it because they have good intentions? Well, other than paving material for a road to somewhere hot—and I sure don't mean Maui—the ends, in this case unequal protection, certainly do not justify the means, in this case unequal treatment.

As the great 18th Century British statesman and American Revolution supporter Edmund Burke once said, "Those who attempt to level never equalize. In all societies some description must be uppermost. The levelers, therefore, only change and pervert the natural order of things; they load the edifice of society by setting up in the air what the solidity of the structure requires to be on the ground."

It's ironic that in essence those who favor social justice's benign racial profiling, an attempt to level, if you will, violate the 14th Amendment, at the very least in spirit, if not in letter. And this is beyond ironic considering the 14th Amendment was instituted because southern Democrats refused to recognize that emancipated slaves, and even free blacks, were now fully American citizens and were entitled to constitutional rights and protections.

Once again, we are in a position to reiterate that America stands for equal justice, not social justice. Let's call for Seattle government to abandon its misguided push for social justice as they define it, and most certainly to divorce the SPD from any association with this highly politically partisan effort.

Again, I invite you, not to believe me, after all this is my opinion, albeit based in fact, to do your own research. It won't take you long to discover the truth about social justice as today's leftists practice it. And don't go to "conservative-friendly sites." Go to the authentic sources: social justice sites. Start with this one: www.sojust.net.

When you see the Soviet Hammer & Sickle and photos of Karl Marx and Che Guevara, you'll know you've arrived at the correct site.

JUST SHUT UP AND
BE A GOOD LITTLE SOCIALIST
The Guardian, December 2010 (#4)

The city, using its Race and Social Justice Initiative (RSJI), continues its assault on traditional and constitutional American values such as self-reliance, equal justice, and individual liberty. But more to our immediate concern, the city is inflicting its socialist policies directly on the Seattle Police Department.

I once wrote, *elections have consequences*. This is true, and Seattle voters will get what they deserve. However, the city has extended its leftist political agenda to the police department, which should remain as apolitical as possible. The police department is not a laboratory and its cops are not guinea pigs.

Social justice is a socialist scheme that judges people not as individuals, but by their race, ethnicity, and socioeconomic status. Again, please research it yourself. The groups touting social justice all tend toward the political left, including socialist and communist groups.

Remember when communism and socialism used to be considered bad in America? You know, for little things like slaughtering a hundred million people during the 20th Century? Even in its least aggressive forms, socialism is responsible for wrecking economies, restricting liberty, and stifling human innovation and achievement worldwide.

I'm not conflating Seattle's quaint socialist cabal with the brutal tyrants of the last century. However, any student of history knows totalitarianism begins with small bites. In 21st Century America, political repression comes in the form of what Europeans call Fabian or Democratic Socialism, which we Americans know as progressivism.

By this method, if we aren't careful, we will literally vote ourselves into tyranny. Some think we came pretty damn close to it in 2008. Thank God for the November [2010] slap down ordinary Americans gave their overreaching government.

Socialist oppression may start with the "best" of intentions by people who feel they have the right to run other people's lives. And while they may not intend oppression, this is to where socialism always—*always*—leads, to one degree or another.

In cities, it begins like this: Mayors present social justice policies to city departments. Department heads carry out the policies without much dissent, not wanting to jeopardize their jobs. Before they know it, they're complicit in implementing socialism...*Lives, fortunes, and sacred honor*...what a charming, archaic notion.

These initial policies always seem benign. The city compels its employees to participate in RSJI classes, and they conduct ostensibly innocuous surveys advancing an unquestionably leftist political agenda. They attempt to make us feel comfortable with socialist and progressive terminology through repetition and saturation. The Race and Social Justice Initiative, SPD Race and Social Justice Change Team, and Race and Social Justice Survey. I'm waiting for the Race and Social Justice Torchlight Parade and the Race and Social Justice 10K Race for Social Justice. On and on it goes until, they hope, the term no longer riles us.

Most of us refuse to believe "real" socialism will ever take hold in Seattle—in America. We know city leaders aren't going to change *our* minds. We'll always be patriotic, anti-socialist Americans. Really? Well, at what point do we say, "Hell no!" to the indoctrination? In its early, weaker stages, or later when the infection has spread and the disease is harder to cure?

Perhaps there should be no participation at all in anything involving Social Justice? At what point does our commitment to American liberty and opposition to socialism compel us to disengage from something we find so abhorrent to our nature? I don't know the precise answer to this, but don't we need to at least think about it?

Anyone think that back in 1776, Thomas Jefferson, Sam Adams, or Ben Franklin would have participated in a King's Royal Justice Initiative (KRJI?)? Complete a survey for ol' King George III? America was exceptional then, and we must remain exceptional now. And what makes America exceptional is our commitment to equal justice and individual liberty, not social justice and emulating Europe's failures.

I've given some thought to my own RSJI participation to date. The "Perspectives in Profiling" class (or as one officer put it, one of our "de-policing classes") served as a good way to learn what the enemy is up to. (Yes, enemy. A liberal after my money in taxes may be my opponent, but a socialist attacking the Constitution and my liberty is my enemy.)

The RSJI survey was an opportunity to let the city know exactly how I feel about its institutional racial profiling policy. It was another opportunity to give them my opinions on the city practicing arbitrary justice over equal justice. To let them know that I'm not okay with blatantly violating the 14th Amendment.

What happens the next time they order us to take the survey or to otherwise actively participate in promoting RSJI? Many of us have already let them know what we think about their socialist policies. (I would pay handsomely to be in the room when they read some officer's surveys.) The next time would simply mark our participation in the RSJI effort as a whole, regardless of how we answer. Would we be surrendering to their attempts to indoctrinate SPD in social justice culture? Perhaps, if some new policy doesn't force it sooner, that'll mark the line drawn in the sand.

Speaking of the survey, our precinct command staff recently carried out an order forcing all SPD employees, sworn and civilian, to complete a six-page *hard copy* of the RSJI Survey. Seems we were less than enthusiastic about voluntarily completing the *paperless* online survey. Imagine that. Compliance didn't work, so the city resorted to compulsion. How delightfully socialist of them.

There is also an ancillary issue, which is truly ironic: regarding Seattle's supposed "green" commitment to going paperless. Since all city departments are supposed to participate in the RSJI survey, and the city employs thousands, with about 2,000 in the SPD alone, I have to wonder how much paper the city wasted to print out this worthless survey.

I'll leave you with this refresher: employing the RSJI, the City of Seattle is deciding on which people do or do not "merit punishment" for a crime, based upon their race, ethnic heritage, and/or socioeconomic status. So far this only applies to DWLS-3, but one has to ask, what's next? They're also deciding purchases and the issuing of city contractsbased upon similar criteria. This is social justice, folks, and socialism has no place in Seattle, and positively no place in the Seattle Police Department.

This article tells the story of what actions the city and department took against me regarding the previous articles, after the investigation concluded, and I was once again allowed to speak:

MUZZLED OR SPEECHLESS IN SEATTLE
(From 2011)

Seattle Police Department Policy and Procedure Manual, Standards & Duties, Sec. I,C.: *"It's not the Department's intent to interfere with or constrain the freedoms, privacy, and liberties of employees."*

In the spirit of the government transparency political leaders such as President Barack Obama and Mayor Mike McGinn espouse, I have a story to tell my SPD brothers and sisters, of all ranks, concerning a Seattle police officer's constitutional free speech rights. I don't know about you, but when I swore my oath to uphold the laws of the State of Washington and the City of Seattle, including the U.S. Constitution, I don't remember saying "except for police officers."

The Department allowed its Internal Investigations Section/ Office of Professional Accountability (IIS/OPA) 180-day investigation into my speaking off duty to the media to expire. And after an additional 38 days beyond that contractual limit, and having ignored IIS investigators' recommendation of "Exonerated," OPA issued a mushy finding of "Supervisory Intervention."

What I'd done was supposedly so flagrant I was called in to work from home, verbally ordered not to give any more media interviews, and then the Department initiated a 7-month internal investigation into my "violations." All so OPA could suggest *training and counseling*? Or could it be something else?

Could it be the City and Department contrived the entire thing just to shut me up because they felt I was embarrassing them? Read on and you be the judge.

To refresh you, in my article, "Just Shut Up and Be a Good Little Socialist" (The *Guardian*, Dec. 2010), I expressed opposition to the City's Race and Social Justice Initiative (RSJI) generally, and specifically its Driving While License Suspended 3rd Degree (DWLS-3) enforcement policy.

I oppose Seattle government's RSJI because I support equal justice, not social justice, which is a political euphemism for a socialistic agenda. And I oppose Seattle's DWLS-3 policy because it doesn't treat all people equally. It's as simple as that.

The City is still prosecuting the crime of DWLS-3, according to City Attorney Pete Holmes' office, by determining which cases "merited punishment" according to a driver's race, ethnicity, and/or socioeconomic status, in pursuit of social justice.

While the city attorney has prosecutorial discretion, we're not talking about deciding if there's enough evidence to prosecute. DWLS-3 is a DOL administrative status applied to a violator who's failed to pay a traffic fine. A driver's status either is or is not suspended. And when the city attorney declines on a DWLS-3, not only is the suspended license violation declined, but also any other infractions written in connection with the incident, many of which are indeed public safety related.

I didn't interpret the policy this way, they did. Check out the links below for yourselves. [http://www.seattlemet.com/articles/2010/7/1/the-law-disproportionately-targets-poor-people] and

"...city attorneys would decide which cases merited punishment." Asst. City Attorney Darby Ducomb to Publicola.net

"DWLS3 change in pursuit of social justice."

[http://www.seattlemet.com/articles/2010/7/7/publicola-tv-city-attorney-pete-holmes] with City Attorney Peter Holmes, Publicola.net

Some on the political left may wish to manipulate the justice system in pursuit of some amorphous restitution for past wrongs. Some of which were truly horrendous. But the great thing about our nation is that the American ideal is greater than any individual espousing it. And Americans will always strive to make it a more perfect union, since perfect is not possible—Utopia is a socialist fallacy.

But who's the grand arbiter who gets to determine when, or if, restitution, reparations, revenge, what have you, is accomplished—if ever? Does the political left get to be the sole determiner of race and justice issues in America? I hope not. The best thing we can do is to strive for equal justice, be vigilant for when it doesn't occur, and then deal with those situations that do happen aggressively.

The Department actually launched an OPA/IIS investigation into my speaking publicly about an article it conceded I had a right to write ("I'm not the thought police," said Chief Diaz [when asked about Pomper's article], Seattle Weekly, January 28, 2011). The Department acknowledges an officer's free speech right to write and publish an article, but interferes with that very same officer's very same free speech right to speak about that very same article?

On January 24, 2011, I was a guest on the Dave Bose Show on KTTH 770 AM. This was the last of several interviews I'd done at my wife's urging to defend myself against the nasty public attacks members of the media, political activists, City Council members, the City Attorney's Office, the OPA Director, and the Mayor himself (the Chief of Police would soon join the chorus) leveled against me, all because of an article I dared to write espousing an honest political disagreement.

Our city and department leaders got to have their say, ordered me to shut up when I tried to defend myself, and then once they forced me to be quiet they continued to disparage me in the media. Really?

MEDIA PUNCHING BAG

Mayor: No "Room in This City" for Cops [Pomper] Opposing Race and Justice Programs. Mayor McGinn (the *Stranger-Slog*, January 2011).

[The director of IIS/OPA] who runs the SPD's internal misconduct oversight program says the [Pomper's] articles don't represent "a widespread culture" but rather "reflect the values of the authors and very few others." Kathryn Olson (the Stranger-Slog, Jan. 2011).

"It's a stupid thing to do…" and "It reflects badly…it's another way it degrades trust in our department." Seattle Police Chief John Diaz (Seattle Weekly, January 2011).

"Police officer rails against city's anti-bias initiatives." Lynn Thompson (the Seattle Times, January 2011).

"Seattle police officer, it's time to turn in the badge." Jerry Large (the Seattle Times. January 2011).

"Making a tough job tougher." Sally Clark's blog, Seattle City Council.

[Pomper's] comments are "not consistent with the values of the police department or the rules of behavior the department sets for our officers." Tim Burgess, Seattle City Council.

"He [Pomper] doesn't understand that the playing field is not equal yet." Bruce Harrell, Seattle City Council.

"…if Seattle Police Officer Steve Pomper would just stop polishing his billy club for a moment…" Ken Schram, Komo TV [Awarded a Schrammie].

Consider carefully the Department's actions: Within one minute of the end of the Bose interview, I was called at my home, on a vacation day, and ordered to the precinct. In a five-minute meeting, I was ordered not to give any further media interviews and handed copies of the SPD Manual policies I'd allegedly violated. I was told I could review them myself or with a Guild rep to find my specific violations. I guess they couldn't find the violations either.

Despite the fact I'd immediately complied with the direct order (as advised by our Guild), the department launched an official investigation. Incidentally, I'd like to publicly thank Guild President Rich O'Neill and Guild Attorney Hillary McClure for their support during the early stages of this ordeal.

After studying the policy language very carefully, it was obvious I'd violated no policies. In compliance with the manual, I'd given my own opinions, while off duty, in this case from my home. I documented these facts in writing at my IIS interview. The subsequent lack of a finding within the 180+38-day OPA/IIS investigation serves as further evidence of the frivolous nature of the charges brought against me specifically to keep me from speaking to defend myself and support my political position—while off duty.

The Department alleged I'd violated the Media Relations policy because I was of insufficient rank to speak to the media, and the Standards & Duties policy because I'd spoken in a manner representing the SPD, or which could be construed as representing the SPD. How ludicrous is that? How could I be speaking on behalf of the department when I was defending myself against the disparaging public comments city and department officials were making about me and an article I wrote?

Why, because I'm a public officeholder? Well, so are the Mayor, Chief, City Attorney, City Council, and OPA Director. For that matter, we had an SPD officer who is a state representative, who ran for

Snohomish County Executive. I hoped he would win, but he lost. Wouldn't it be a bit tough to do that job if he's not allowed to speak his political thoughts, off duty? According to the Department's finding in my case, he would have to seek permission from SPD prior to every public media appearance, since he's not of proper rank to speak to the media.

SPD Manual, Media Relations indicates only a Public Information Officer (PIO) or an On Scene Commander, lieutenant or above, may represent the Department to the media. An on-scene commander indicates the policy applies to representing the department at police incidents. In fact, references to a police incident, scene, or activity occur over 80 times in this six-page policy, while there are 0 references to speaking as a private citizen while off duty.

SPD Manual, Standards & Duties pertains to officers speaking on behalf of the Department or Chief of Police. And it prohibits officers from publicly criticizing law enforcement agencies, policies, and personnel, or interpreting Department policy, while on duty or in uniform. Which I did not do. (Ironically, the Chief and the OPA Director did do this to me.)

The investigation added to my forced silence because an officer is under orders not to discuss ongoing OPA/IIS investigations. So, with the initial verbal order to shut up and the subsequent investigation, I was effectively muzzled.

Incidentally, I find the City and Department official's purported shock about the article disingenuous if not ridiculous. This article was the last in a four-article series regarding the RSJI issue I'd written, which appeared in the Guardian in 2010. While conducting research for those articles I was in contact with the City and Department personnel responsible for RSJI and DWLS-3 policy implementation.

By silencing me the City and Department accomplished their goal. For more than seven months I kept quiet against my will. Do they hope thuggish intimidation tactics will keep me quiet in perpetuity? Well, I don't know about you, but my First Amendment rights are pretty damned important to me. It's not that I won't let this go, it's how can I let this go. I'd be letting down not only myself, but also every cop on this department if I did that. The order that applied to me, also applied to all my brother and sister officers and sergeants.

Police officers have the same constitutional rights while off duty and speaking for themselves as any other American—period! And it seems we must guard our rights jealously and when necessary fight for them fiercely because there are those who obviously don't believe cops have these same rights and will trample them if they deem it politically expedient.

The RSJI-DWLS-3 issue as a news story died early this year, but it didn't die a natural death. The local and national media had great interest in it, but after the City silenced me, an opposing political view lost a vocal advocate. National and local media had begun investigating the issue and several outlets contacted me to provide an opposing view on air as a private citizen, but due to the Department's order, I was forced to decline these invitations.

This resulted in the City presenting its side of the issue unfettered by something as pesky as an opposing political viewpoint. (Political opposition can be such a nuisance. Just ask the Chinese, North Koreans, and Iranians.) While Fox News' Megyn Kelly was superb in questioning City Attorney Peter Holmes about his DWLS-3 policy, she simply didn't have the background someone intimately familiar with the local issue would have, because the Department's order prohibited me, and I suppose by extension any officer, from accepting her invitation.

I know there are people in this city who don't like what some officers write in the Guardian. Don't these thin-skinned crybabies know it's called an opposing political opinion for a reason? It seems to me shameful when the mayor of a major American city says an employee with an opposing political view, a view shared by millions of Americans, including a very high percentage of cops (despite what some City and Department officials purport to think), shouldn't be a police officer if he or she expresses disagreement with the current leadership's political ideology. Or when the police chief of that same major city publicly refers to an officer's writing a political opinion as "a stupid thing to do" (Chief Diaz, The Weekly, Jan. 2011).

I'd ask those who disagree with me politically to consider the tyranny of using official police department disciplinary proceedings to silence opposing thought. To launch an investigation, in order to keep a city employee from expressing a personal political point of view while off duty, is astounding. Especially, coming from a Department that allowed an employee to send out an official Department email containing a closing quote from Communist icon Che Guevera.

Take for example the Stranger, within whose pages this controversy initiated, and with whose political point of view I almost always disagree. I don't hold any personal animosity toward the publication for the negative things they've written about me. They have every right to their opinion, just as we police officers have a right to express our opinions as private citizens while off duty, whether Democrat, Socialist, Republican, Libertarian, or Independent. I support the Stranger's First Amendment rights, as well as the Seattle Times, King 5 TV, Publicola.net, etc., and I would hope they support ours.

If the City and Department get away with violating my constitutional rights in this instance, does anyone have any doubt that certain City and Department leaders would repeat this behavior in a heartbeat against any one of us if it became politically "necessary" again? I don't.

The City and Department's actions have also had a chilling effect on officers' free speech in general. I know of one officer who pulled an article he'd already submitted to the Guardian and a sergeant who decided not to submit one he'd written, both for fear of similar media derision and retaliation by City and Department officials. How reprehensible is that? I can only imagine how many other officers have not felt free to express their opinions. Is Seattle being run (or should I say ruined) by an intolerant thugocracy?

I have been writing Guardian articles for about 19 years under various City and Department administrations. And while these administrations were also admittedly politically left, no one ever acted in such a mean-spirited way.

It's sad that too many people in Seattle, including some City and Department officials, apparently fail to acknowledge just how fortunate they are to have such remarkable law enforcement professionals still willing to serve and protect. If they're not careful, they're in jeopardy of losing what I am a proud veteran of, and what I truly believe is, the best police force in America.

Seattle Police Department Policy and Procedure Manual, Standards & Duties, Sec.: IV.B.4: "This provision is not meant to restrain an individual's expression of free speech rights."

* * *

As government social justices seize the People's liberty, they will need police officers to enforce their repressive laws.

ACKNOWLEDGMENTS

First, I must thank my wife, a recently retired firefighter, for nudging me back on task every time something shiny distracts me. My kids, Bryan, Heather, and Bobby, who make me very proud. And our grandchildren who always make me smile, Declan, Fallon, and Braden (who isn't born yet, so Heather and Matt, I hope you've settled on that name).

A special thanks to all the folks at Post Hill Press, especially Anthony Ziccardi for his kindness and professionalism, Billie Brownell for her spot-on suggestions that made this a better book, and to Jon Ford for his thoughtful editing.

I also owe a tremendous debt of gratitude to a great American patriot, Taleeb Starkes, without whom I would not have met Anthony and would not be sitting here inscribing these words. Thank you, brother!

My thanks to Cynthia Whitlatch and Adley Shepherd, for allowing me to tell their stories. They are two of the best cops I've known, and they didn't deserve to be sacrificed on the altar of leftist political correctness. I hope living well will be their revenge.

Finally, I'd like to thank all of you, the dedicated police officers who, regardless of how unfairly you are treated, continue to respond to every 911 call no matter what. You do your duty, helping everyone, regardless of who they are, where they come from, or what they believe. You may not agree with all of the laws and policies your leaders enact, but you do not take a knee in protest while at work. Because of you, Americans are free to pursue their happiness.

ABOUT THE AUTHOR

S teve Pomper is a published author, retired police officer, OpsLens.com contributor, and avid motorcyclist. He earned a BA in English Language and Literature, graduating Summa Cum Laude. He has three grown children, two grandchildren, and lives with his wife, a retired firefighter, in the Pacific Northwest.